HORSES IN THE GARDEN

Sue Millard

Jackdaw E Books 2023

JACKDAW E BOOKS

Daw Bank

Greenholme

Tebay

Penrith

Cumbria

CA10 3TA

http://www.jackdawebooks.co.uk

E-book ISBN: 978-1-913106-263

Paperback ISBN: 978-1-913106-256

CONTENTS

Horses are an addiction. Be warned.
So are native ponies.

Probably better for you than weed, though.

HORSES IN THE GARDEN

My parents never understood why I became a horsey child. Their own childhood rides on seaside donkeys don't seem to have had the profound effect on them that a small black pony had on me.

We were holidaying in a great-aunt's caravan at Rhuddlan in North Wales. I can only remember little details of the summer week: hot sunshine, sand between the toes, ice cream on the beach, crocheted blankets on my bed, the smell of matches and of the gas-ring that popped softly into life under the magical whistling kettle. I remember the dark underside of the caravan table, grown-up elbows that I mustn't jog for fear of having hot tea spilled on me, and ancient relatives appearing and disappearing from the foreign world that engulfed us. I must have been two and a half.

I had, so the family story goes, been induced to "be good" all day by the promise that I could have what I asked for at bedtime. My mother fondly imagined this would be a "blow-blow" – my term for a toy windmill on a stick, which I'd longed for on a previous holiday. I can only guess at the parental dismay when I asked to "stand up close to a horse". A promise was a promise, and I held my mother to it.

I don't really remember the animal in question, though my adult knowledge tells me that it was small, and black, and probably a Shetland. I do remember children stroking it or ripping up tufts of grass and dandelion flowers to feed it. Mum attempted to hold me at a safe distance from this creature that was so big and with unknown numbers of teeth, but to me it was simply a gentle furry creature and therefore loveable. I can still see its pad-saddle, the too-long stirrup leathers coiled round and round the irons to fit children's short legs, and the bare feet and summer sandals of the fortunate ones who were led sedately up and down the grassy lanes between the caravans. Perhaps I might ultimately sit up there too? I had no concept of this desire involving money.

My mother bravely asked the young lady – who was ready to pack up for the day – what the cost of a pony ride might be. "Half a crown," was the reply. That was five times the cost of the gaudy plastic windmill Mum had expected to buy, so she hooted and shook her head, which I well knew meant, "No chance!" Even more crushingly, if you were not five years old or older, it seemed you wouldn't be allowed to ride the pony anyway. I hid my disappointment by pulling some heads of "creepygrass" – the wild barley whose whiskery heads, if inserted between your wrist and your jumper sleeve, would travel from hand to armpit in a few minutes of play. Meanwhile Mum haggled nobly on my behalf and eventually brought the news that I could sit on the pony for a few minutes "before it went to bed."

Triumph? Modified rapture? Well, truthfully, I can't remember a thing about it.

Further holidays are marked in my memory by visits to the Rhyl funfair. Its main attraction for me was the pony ride. The ride premises were curiously constructed of inclined and intertwined wooden walkways, so that you were always riding up or down, or over or under other walkways, enabling a journey of perhaps four hundred yards in a space not much bigger than a small allotment. There were no safety precautions, no helmets, back protectors, jodhpurs or boots. You rode bareheaded, in your sandals and gingham frock, and the stirrup leathers squeaked and nipped your bare calves. For my first ride, Mum bravely accompanied me on foot, and I remember her walking along while trying to explain that I mustn't hold on to the railings because when the pony walked on I would fall off. "Sit up as though you're riding a bike," she said. As I didn't have a bike this wasn't very helpful, but somehow we got round without anyone galloping over the top of us. We ended up at the hitching rail and wooden mounting bench where I'd got on, and where Dad and brother were waiting for us.

Mum, having scraped her shoes clean against the ironwork, was impatient to whisk us all away from the pungency of sawdust, horse manure and urine to more sophisticated delights. Unfortunately it turned out that the Waltzer, the Dodgems, the Tunnel of Love and the Helter Skelter all made me feel dizzy or sick, so every time we went to the fair I pestered to return to the ponies. Only the miniature railway ride round the Marine Lake was any substitute for my four legged friends.

It wasn't until our last holiday there that I began to realise what a boring and weary life those animals must have led, and wonder if there wasn't something better for them than pounding along tortuous wooden walkways with all stages of youthful ambition on board.

I have no explanation for my equine obsession, except perhaps that I was born under the sign of Sagittarius, the centaur-archer, and that my great-grandfather Davenport was recorded in 1878 as being a "coachman (domestic)". Yet both are equally true of my brother, and he never showed any interest at all in horses; he took a degree in pathology and worked most of his life in pharmaceuticals. All our other ancestors had solidly industrial occupations such as "Pressman in a candle factory," "Ship owner" or "Iron-founder" – apart from Charles, who was at various times a coaling supplier in the Canary Islands, a "Foreign correspondent" and a "Detective Sub-inspector". With a German diplomat father and a French mother, Charles was a sport who struck an exotic note of which the English sector of our antecedents would probably have been rather suspicious.

God only knows why I took after the horseman as well as the sport, but I did; when I wasn't investigating things in the garden or countryside, singing, writing, or painting, I made my suburban family's lives a misery with the repeated question: "Can I have a pony?"

They appeased my hunger with equine books each birthday and Christmas. One of these, the newly published "Prize Pony" by Kathleen McKenzie, was being promoted with a competition for children. The best essay about what you would do if you won a pony would win you – erm – a pony. At seven years of age I already fancied my chances, and promptly wrote my piece and copied it out in my best handwriting for my parents to send in, along with the required clipping from the book jacket to prove we'd bought a copy.

I tried hard to be patient during the weeks leading up to the competition deadline, but I'm sure my parents got fed up of fielding questions such as, "If the postman brings me a pony can I keep it? Can it live in the back garden? Can it sleep in the shed?" And, most importantly, to my literal mind: "How will he get it through the letterbox?"

The postman didn't bring me anything of the sort, of course, the reason being that some time after I'd gone to bed, my parents had added a careful note to the organisers saying, in effect, "If she wins, for God's sake don't give her the pony because we have nowhere to keep it."

It wasn't until I was nearly thirty years old that I became the owner of a real live pony. Still, I must have got perilously close at seven, because I eventually received one of six runner-up prizes, which was another pony book. But today when I watch my equine friends munching the lawn, I still think I won.

A STUDENT IN THE 70S

A friend recently put me in touch with an alumna of the Anglican teaching college from which we graduated. The college were asking for reminiscences of student life. As I still have four large hard-backed journals dating from 1 January 1972 to October 1973, I've been sitting here leafing through them, plumbing the depths of late adolescence, and wondering whether I could publish any of it without risk of lawsuits.

In the early 1970s I was still working out the dynamics of living cheek by jowl with other people, and particularly with BOYS. The sexual revolution of the 1960s may well have been fresh in everyone's minds, but I'd spent the previous 8 years at an all girls' school and I really didn't know how to deal with flirtation, dating or any of that jazz. Of course I learned rapidly, but the diary reveals that there were a lot of inward cries of pain. The diary's cast of thousands probably spent a good deal of time rolling their eyes and throwing their hands heavenward and muttering, "What is this girl DOING?" and at least one of them said frankly, "I have pity for you, but no sympathy!"

In my journals I mentioned a few rumours about which of the lecturers (A.K.A lecherers) were said to be having affairs with other lecturers' wives, or with students. Many of the rumours may have been true. Some of those involved were, I know, teetering just on the edge of unfaithfulness but not quite succumbing.

For some reason, although both female and male friends said that male lecturers had made passes at them, I don't recall any scandal being publicised, nor any homophobia, nor any disciplinary action being taken – maybe if action was taken, it was taken discreetly and the student body didn't get to know about it. There was far more fuss when the Students' Guild proposed that there should be a vending machine on campus to sell condoms. That didn't go down at all well with the Anglican authorities!

One of the delights of student life was talking – unravelling the world and rebuilding it to our own preferences. Students, including me, commonly used to drop in on lecturers in their studies or in their lodgings on campus; on occasion I even became a confidante, being told far too much by lecturers about their home lives and extra-marital carryings-on. I remember one of these asserting that "all really passionate music is a series of climaxes" and - not having a clue what he was on about - I blithely said, "Of course!"

More innocently, my diary records the giggles when seven people who had been sitting on the edge of one bed in an attic room discovered that the iron frame had not been equal to our weight, and to try to straighten it we inverted it and jumped on it; or when a group rehearsing stage dance moves on the upper floor of a student hostel had to placate the blokes on the floor below whose ceiling lights were dancing along with us. I remember us sweeping down into Chester (and back), laughing and talking, singing in chorus and dancing in step, line-abreast with linked arms, to the dismay of other pedestrians.

The nearest I personally got to diary scandal was this: "I sat with the Opera Group secretary watching other principals and chorus rehearsing act 1 of "The Sorcerer", with Emlyn Roberts playing the piano and Alan Bownas directing. In one of the pauses for stage direction Emlyn came over and, looking very worried, touched my arm and said, "You haven't got a safety pin, have you? It's not for me, it's for a friend." I said, "I can go back to the hostel and get one if you're desperate." He put a hand on his jacket above his trouser waistband and admitted, "Yes, I am!" So I got him a pin, and saved, if not his life, at least his reputation."

On far more occasions I wrote in the diary about the long gossipy rehearsals of dramatic productions, and appreciations of vintage recordings of same. We all had LP record-players

6

and tape recorders to play performances by famous singers or actors, about which we argued endlessly.

We weren't all that rebellious. We sang along to the music of Tim Rice and Andrew Lloyd-Webber, the Beatles, Joni Mitchell, the Bee Gees, the Carpenters, the (Liverpool) Spinners, Martin Carthy, and Stealers Wheel. We performed operetta, from Gilbert & Sullivan and Offenbach to Rodgers & Hammerstein, and learned performances by Flanders and Swann or The Goons by heart, but Monty Python's Flying Circus bemused us, and we hadn't quite realised what a great solo performer Billy Connolly was going to be; he was still a bit too edgy, a bit too Glaswegian, even for us Scousers.

Whether we met in hostel rooms or in lecturers' lodgings, the discussions of music, literature, history and philosophy went on into the small hours. Officially, of course, there was a lock-up time at which females were supposed to depart from male accommodation, and vice versa, but in practice so long as you didn't annoy the neighbours, and you let the "offenders" out quietly, nobody really made any fuss. Those of us in off-campus accommodation often missed the last bus and faced a long walk "home", and my diary reminds me how my male friends gallantly offered to walk girls back to their lodgings when these late nights broke up; it also records my disappointment that the offers were all platonic.

I sat up late into the night with coffee and sympathy when friends, male or female, were suffering from rejected love; I learned that one of my mates was panicking because his girlfriend's period was late; I heard that the girl in the next room to mine had gone away quietly to have an abortion. But none of it seemed to happen to me. Not till I started my summer job up here in the Lake District.

And that's a whole other story!

HAIR CUT

I was twenty-three and almost broke. It was the end of my last university year, hot high summer, and the streets of Chester were congealed with tourists and dust. I had one suitcase of clothes, two big bags of papers and files and books, and a job waiting in the Lake District, over a hundred miles away.

My education had been completed under increasing financial strain, because my father had retired through ill health. I had just enough money to take me ten miles home, and while I knew I could borrow the Lake District coach fare from Mum, I was reluctant to ask for yet more help. It seems silly now to have been so worried over the lack of those few pounds. But back then in the 1970s I knew all about money being tight.

It was while packing up and throwing out the last of my college paperwork that I saw the advert: *Hair wanted.*

My hair was thick and strongly waved and it reached nearly to my waist. It also took twice as much shampoo as anyone else's and had a mind of its own. Did I need *all that* when the wig company would buy it? No contest. I looked at my bank balance and I booked an appointment with the hairdresser. I explained how I wanted the hair taken off and preserved. I pretended I was going to have a wig made for myself, so they wouldn't know how poor I was feeling. They happily styled me with the short, tomboy cut I've kept to ever since, the sort you can simply run a hand through and know it will look okay.

I parcelled up my shorn mane and posted it, using my future Lake District address for further correspondence. I went home and startled my parents with my new look. Then I borrowed the coach fare from my mother with a promise to repay her when the hair remuneration arrived, and off I went to work in Cumbria for bed and board, £4 a week "pocket money", and tips.

I sweated a fair bit in the following month, worrying that the hair parcel might go astray, or that the firm might not bother to pay when the goods were already theirs. But, pay they did, eventually. However, even long, thick hair doesn't weigh very heavy, and its value by weight was not quite twice the cost of cutting the hair and posting it. My profit was less than one week's bar tips.

Two good things came out of the episode, though.

My mother never asked me to repay the bus fare. I probably should have known that would be the case. And a young man who'd ignored my long-haired persona for the previous three summers suddenly began to come up to the bar and offer to buy me drinks. He's now been my husband for over forty-five years, and I think he's forgotten that I ever had long hair.

END OF TERRACE

Today, twenty years into the new millennium, the price of houses in Cumbria could scarcely be higher. Despite a fall in values during 2008-09, a family sized house on the edge of the Lake District is now close to half a million pounds, and even one-bedroomed flats will make six figures. The removal of "stamp duty" on property sales, and the pressure of Covid-19 lockdown restrictions, made moving to a big, rural house seem very attractive to a lot of people, and throughout 2021 the prices continued to soar.

The high price range isn't a new phenomenon in the Lakes, by any means. When Graham and I were looking for a home in which to settle down and produce offspring in the late 1970s, house prices in the National Park were already impossible for us. We did sniff around one or two of those, but if they were within our price range they were usually so run-down that you'd have thought twice about keeping pigs in them let alone small children.

We abandoned the idea of nesting anywhere in the holiday areas and began to look at the industrial ones. Tebay and Shap were associated with the railway system, while Knock, Kirkby Thore and Shap (again) were quarry villages. Although Brough and Kirkby Stephen were also possibilities, for us they were too far from the north-south motorway corridor on which Graham's haulage business relied heavily. Also, "somewhere to park the wagon" was a requirement that rather cut down our options.

The concept of "buying to holiday-let" was already around in the 1970s, and when we spotted a suitably-sized house in Shap and made an offer for it, this element appeared in the bidding almost immediately. We'd hoped to buy the two-up, two-down property for around £5,000 but a retired lady from the village had a business plan for it and we didn't shake her off until the price reached the £7,000 mark. This was high, in 1976, for an end-of-terrace quarryman's house, but by cashing in various small investments Graham managed to buy it for us mortgage-free – a condition for first-time house owners that's almost unheard-of today.

It was a sweet little stone-built house at the north end of the street, snugly protected by the rest of the terrace from the worst of the southerly gales. The garage tacked on the end became home to Graham's accumulating tools and equipment; we never kept a car inside it and towards the end of our ownership you'd have been hard pressed to get more than one human being in there either.

The kitchen was equipped with an ancient solid fuel stove, whose firebricks were so decayed that I could never coax it to do more than warm one kettle in a long afternoon. Of the alternatives, I wasn't keen on an electric cooker, and Shap's access to mains gas was still 20 years in the future; so a propane gas cooker was a priority if we were to eat anything other than salads. The installation turned out more of a job than we expected, since the three-foot thick kitchen wall stubbornly resisted the creation of a channel for the feed pipe to the gas-bottles in the garage. A boulder of Shap granite lay in the way and it defeated a powerful drill and the toughest bits that Graham could find. The only answer was to crowbar it out, so the hole for the one-inch pipe ended up two feet across.

Kitting out the house was an unexpected entertainment. House clearance sales-by-auction were a new experience for me, and it was deeply satisfying to our squirrelly souls to drive out on a Saturday morning to some rural location, and wander through the household jetsam, seeking the goods that we would need. We owned curtains before we owned curtain rails. Two Parker Knoll chairs – a static and a rocking chair – fell to our modest bidding as a pair because everybody wanted just the rocker but the owner wouldn't sell them separately. At another sale we bought a box of crockery and cutlery in which our main interest was the knives and forks, and it wasn't until we unpacked it that we realised the dealers bidding against us had wanted the three plain, white Wedgwood plates at the bottom of the box.

We got a three-piece suite for £3, and a double bed for 50 pence, and at Penrith Auction Mart we decided to bid on some black iron frying pans and saucepans; whereupon a tipsy gentleman standing nearby informed me solemnly that "you'll never burn the dinner in them." He also warned Graham that if I threw one at him he'd better duck because "if her aim's any good it'll kill ye." And I'll always remember the endless trails of small tools, "use-wood," tins of bent nails and rusty, cobwebbed objects described by one exasperated auctioneer as "real QUALITY tatt."

Once Graham and I were married and installed, the terraced house was easy to keep. We replaced the old stove with a redundant Rayburn belonging to friends who were moving from their ancient farmhouse into a newly built one, and the house became warm twenty-four hours a day.

The kids arrived – one in the black pre-dawn of snowy February, and one in the morning sunshine of August – and our nest was full.

We laid a lawn, and rented hard standing for the wagon (a space we later bought). Graham cultivated a vegetable plot and I started to acquire alpine plants, partly because they took up little space in the borders and could survive year to year under the rigours of the Cumbrian climate, but also to satisfy some urge to have wild and hardy things at hand.

The discovery of a hop bine on the gate of the next-door empty plot made me try brewing beer, though as I based it on a spare jar of honey it turned out closer to mead. A cupboard at head level under the stairs, above the Rayburn, soon became our brewery. Clearing this space brought to light a 1908 newspaper – *Harper's Weekly* – which reported a proposal from Norway that ladies should title themselves neither Miss nor Mrs but something unrelated to their marital status, like the modern "Ms". It takes a long time for ideas to trickle through stone… unlike the power of fermenting rhubarb wine, which projected clots of pink foam through its airlock and onto the ceiling.

Before long, like the wine, we and the kids were starting to burst out of the sweet little house. I was getting restless, so when my father died and we received some money from his will, we decided to look for somewhere larger; perhaps with room for a wild and hardy Fell pony … and that's when we found Daw Bank.

12

DAW BANK

When we came to look at the farm, one of the things that attracted me was the extension of the house into the adjoining barn. It created a long, split-level dining room with a split-level bedroom above it. We admired the beamed ceilings. The one in the bedroom was particularly attractive because it rose up into the gable of the roof and it provided an airy talking point for weeks before we moved in.

"You'll keep that room for the bed and breakfast guests," declared my mother-in-law when she saw it.

In the midst of moving house, with two small children, a haulage business and a Siamese cat, bed and breakfast work was a particularly revolting thought. I rebelled.

"We shall be sleeping there ourselves," I said firmly. "Bed and breakfast guests, if we need them, will go in the first bedroom off the landing."

"It's such a lovely room," she protested.

"How would they get to it? through the room next door. Either the children or Graham and I would be sleeping in there. Not very lovely."

She subsided, being a woman of sense.

There were some odd coincidences around the sale. I'd first noticed the ad for the farm because its telephone number was the same as ours, differing only by the area exchange code. The two solicitors, ours and the vendors', had almost identical names, and both properties were checked for sale by the same surveyor. The milkman's welcome-note about delivery days was spotted by our friend who provided muscle for the move; it showed the same 3-digit number as his own home phone. It was all weirdly familiar.

After we moved in we discovered more about the house than we expected. For a start, the ceiling beams in the dining room were so recent that one projected clear through the wall and into the kitchen chimney. When putting our Rayburn stovepipe in place we had to dislodge an accumulation of jackdaw nests from above it, and when we tried to test the draught some nests we hadn't been able to reach caught fire. Smouldering charcoal rained from above and the projecting beam began gently smoking. We had some anxious moments with watering cans and knapsack sprayers. My husband sawed out the beam with much scraping of knuckles and subdued swearing, and capped it with mortar. On our second attempt to test the draught, the smoke pouring back down and out through gaps in the stonework alerted us that the chimney had been capped too, with half a hundredweight of concrete. More hammering and swearing, this time outdoors. I don't think he killed anyone with the lumps he hurled down to ground level, but it must have been a near thing.

But we achieved success with the Rayburn at last, and we backed it up with the Calor gas cooker that had done sterling work in Shap. The system has served us well in both houses for nearly 50 years and has thumbed its nose on many wintry occasions when the mains electricity failed.

The "lovely" bedroom was less accommodating. Parts of the floor had a permanent loud creak. "Plywood," we had been told during viewing. "It makes that noise when it's new. The edges rub together when you walk on them. It'll settle down." We put our belongings into place and wondered how long it might take.

The roof over that bedroom was sealed by lead flashing to the wall of the house. It was, to all appearances, perfectly normal. However, when the house was under assault by nocturnal rainstorms, I would be awakened by drips of water on my forehead, which was decidedly *not* normal.

The flashing sometimes pretended *not* to leak, but I can't remember whether those "dry spells" coincided with a visit from the builder or whether, as many things seem to be here, it was spontaneous. Our hopes would rise that the problem had been solved, until the next rainstorm proved that it hadn't. I was grateful that Nanna's mahogany bedstead had castors under each opulently turned leg, because we had to move it southwards at least once every October.

The leak was not solved permanently until we had the roof replaced on the barn next door, which extended over our bedroom. The night after the old slates were taken off and the polythene sheeting was tacked on, we had a huge thunderstorm with high winds – yet the bedroom, unbelievably, remained weatherproof even under this temporary covering, and it's been dry as a bone from that day on.

But its floor still tells me, downstairs and three rooms away, when my husband is on his way to bed.

THE GARDEN

It was late afternoon on our viewing day when we came out to look round the garden. Up in the top corner was the old privy, stone-built, pent-roofed, and with its single-hole wooden bench seat still in place.

The kitchen garden had been well cultivated in its time and although the soil was stony, it was strong and looked fertile – possibly due to the proximity of the privy. A stout drystone wall and a hedge protected three sides of the garden, and we were given to understand that the wire net fence and gate would keep out the hens on the fourth. Growing between a cranky-looking gooseberry bush and some handsome ferns there was a blush-pink rambling rose of considerable beauty, and a honeysuckle.

The sellers, understandably, had not sown any vegetable crops that spring, but we could see that the weeds which had colonised the space were only easily-pulled annuals. The rhubarb, by local repute, been there since at least 1940 and to judge from its size it was probably drawing its resources from Australia.

As we walked round, I noted there were no flower beds in the rest of the garden, the main features being a beech hedge, a rhododendron, a forsythia, roughish grass and a couple of mature trees. A splendid weeping ash was the centrepiece of the lawn, while to one side there was a garth edged with spruce and Scots pines. Under these was a rather leggy shrub, halfway to being a small tree.

"Pear tree," observed the lady of the house, following the direction of my glance. "Lovely pears we've had off it too."

"That's odd," I remarked to my mother-in-law in an undertone, "seeing it's a damson."

We've since discovered that these hedgerow plums will fruit, sparsely, *if* they are pollinated by two other different varieties, but I'd like to put on record that even after Graham took down half the sycamore to allow a bit more light into the garden we've never seen *any* fruit off the "pear" tree.

On the other hand, over the years a series of daffodils has emerged from the lawn. At first there were only a few leaves, but as Graham carefully mowed round them, gradually they gained strength and began to flower; and now I can see a Wordsworthian sweep of varieties from the end of February to the middle of April, everything from Dorothy's native "host" "fluttering and dancing in the breeze" to doubles, whites, and oranges, some of which have recently flowered for the first time in our 40-year tenure. As they revived we've identified them as varieties that were old even when the house was built: the 17th century double Telamonius plenus, Princeps, Butter-and-Eggs and sweet-scented Pheasant-eyes, and Victorian and Edwardian varieties like King Alfred (Dutch Master) and Mrs Langtry; some score of types in all. They, at any rate, have appreciated our stewardship.

THE DEEDS

The language of the deeds is historic and difficult to read; I have kept it for its quaintness. You can easily skip this chapter, though, without losing your grip on the rest of the book.

Daw Bank has been a working farm for centuries, with the main emphasis on stock rearing – sheep and cattle. At some time, though, the land was ploughed in the old style, leaving "rig and furrow" patterns slanting across the fields to the south, which you can see when the sun is low.

The old deeds of the house are magnificent. As wide as a broadsheet newspaper, they are handwritten in copperplate with coloured embellishments, and record that on 4 April 1812 William Birkett conveyed the property Daw Bank to John Wilson "subject nevertheless and charge and chargeable with the payment yearly and every year unto William Earl of Lonsdale his heirs and assigns the yearly rents thereinafter mentioned and doing paying and performing all or rents dues and debts services therefore use and right accustomed." The property was still tenanted and belonged to Lowther, with a "yearly and customary rent" of 5s 8d and the "yearly free rent" of 6d.

8 February 1815 "between Rt Hon William the Earl of Lonsdale and Viscount Lowther... and John Wilson for the consideration therein mentioned the said Wm Earl of Lonsdale did grant bargain and sell enfranchise release and confirm unto the said John Wilson his heirs and assigns forever the hereditaments and premises thereinafter described and the freehold and inheritance of the said premises freed and discharged...." The tenancy ceased and land became freehold.

A directory of 1829 gives the owner of Daw Bank as Isabella Wilson, Yeoman... possibly the wife or daughter of John Wilson.

A date and initials were scratched into the south side of the byre doorway: JH 1858. We haven't been able to match an owner to the initials. The doorway is now the main bedroom window of the holiday cottage.

12 April 1865 saw a Conveyance "between Rev John Wilson of Upper Broughton in the county of Nottingham Clerk and George Atkinson of Bridge End in the Parish of Orton in the County of Westmorland Farmer ... John Wilson did thereby grant bargain sell alien release and convey unto the said George Atkinson his heirs inter alia

"ALL THAT messuage or tenement called or known by the name of Dawbank consisting of a dwellinghouse barn byer stable and peat house with the garden and garth thereunto belonging together with all rights liberties easements profits privileges advantages hereditaments appurtenances whatsoever....

"SAVE AND EXCEPT – Lord or lords lady or ladies reserve hunting, shooting and fishing rights and rights to mine or mincrals..."

Thus, if we should strike oil or find a seam of gold nuggets, they would belong to Lord Lonsdale!

I have never found out why "The said George Atkinson did thereby declare that no wife or widow of him the said George Atkinson should be entitled to dower in or out of the said hereditaments and premises or any part thereof..."

On 2 February 1885 the Will of George Atkinson of Bridge End was signed... whereby he appointed "his son George Dixon Atkinson and his friend John Howson of Cracalt near Kendal Timber Merchant (trustees) ... he devised 'all his estate called "Daw Bank" unto his son Thomas Atkinson absolutely subject to... the payment of the sum of £360 to the executors within 12 months after the decease of the said George Atkinson...' " I have sometimes wondered how George Dixon Atkinson felt about his brother getting Daw Bank, and about his mother not being allowed any say in the matter. But perhaps he already had his own farm elsewhere, and at least he got £180 in recompense.

George Atkinson's other son John Atkinson was to occupy Bridge End [the adjoining farm] but if John died childless the property was to be sold to pay funeral expenses, and the remainder be divided into three parts to pay various legacies. George died 14th November 1889 and John did indeed die childless eleven years later, so on 10 November 1903 George junior and John Howson sold Bridge End (including Daw Bank) to Thomas Atkinson who was living at Bridge End.

Around then, Daw Bank farm house was rebuilt. Joyce Postlethwaite, our neighbour who lived at Low Greenholme all her life, said that her aunt could remember when Daw Bank was rebuilt, the date being "the early 1900s". The obvious date for the rebuild would be after the death of John Atkinson, and before Thomas moved in, so probably around 1903.

Probably Daw Bank was originally a Cumbrian "long house" built into the bank, with one straight roofline through to the barn; which would help the house itself to sit just below the brow of the hill, snuggled in away from the westerly gales. This pattern can also be seen in White House, in Greenholme village itself. During the rebuild of Daw Bank a passageway was cut between the bank and the house to prevent damp tracking through the back wall. The new Daw Bank house, however, was two feet higher than the barn, hence the problems we had with the leaks in the roof where the two adjoined.

At some time in the years 1910 to 1920 the wood against Bretherdale Beck was planted; an elderly gentleman passing by in 1985 informed us that he could remember it being planted "70 years ago."

On 30th October 1930 Thomas Atkinson died at Daw Bank.

On 14 July 1947 "Thomas Atkinson of Brooklyn Gleaston Ulverston Electrical Engineer and Joseph Capstick of Ivy House Tebay retired railway guard … personal representatives of T Atkinson deceased assent to the vesting in Thomas

Atkinson of all the property : all that messuage or tenement called or known by the name of Daw Bank consisting of a dwellinghouse barn byer stable and peat house with the garden and garth thereunto belonging and all those three closes or inclosures of land formerly called and known by the respective names of High Dawbank, Low Dawbank and Cross Green all adjoining each other but now known as Great Dawbank the Home Close and Little Dawbank ... Formerly holden under the Rt Hon William the Earl of Lonsdale as parcel of his Manor of Crosby Ravensworth by payment of the yearly and customary rent of 5s 8d and the yearly free rent of 6d ... "

On 31 Oct 1956 the Land Charges Search noted that "the property lies within an area of great landscape, historic or scientific value". This statement was repeated in a 1964 Land Charges Search. It was this quality of landscape that defeated a speculative plan in 2006 for a huge wind-farm on Whinash, two miles to the south. The whole area now joins the sister National Parks of the Lakes and the Dales, just north of the Lune Gorge where their boundaries are closest to each other. It has been titled the Westmorland Dales, although that seems to annoy certain people as the name signs on the roadside verges are sometimes knocked down or defaced.

On 3 July 1957 Thomas Atkinson and The Agricultural Mortgage Corporation conveyed Daw Bank to Joseph Edward Cox and Eliza Jane Cox of Bridge End, including an agreement to install a septic tank in the field across the road, thus ending the long reign of the privy at the top of the garden.

A date and initials, JC 1959, were scratched into the north side of the byre doorway to match that cut on the south side in 1858. The initials and date match those of Joseph Cox's ownership.

On 8 August 1968 Joseph Edward Cox died, and on 21 April 1971 a "Parcel of land" to the west of the road and on the northern bank of Bretherdale Beck, was sold to Westmorland County Council, to straighten the road over Dorothy Bridge.

On 5 April 1975 Eliza Jane Cox died, and on 21 October a Conveyance records the sale of Daw Bank to David Walter Rogers, quantity surveyor, and Helen Margaret Rogers, of Low House, Docker.

On 25 May 1978 their plans were approved for a part-conversion of the barn into a bedroom and dining room/kitchen extension.

The last transaction to date was the Conveyance of Daw Bank to Maurice Graham Millard and Christine Susan Millard, on 31 August 1983. In 2005, when we stopped dealing in hay and straw, we converted the barn and its cow byre into a 2 bedroomed cottage.

The known Occupants of Daw Bank:

William Birkett pre 1812 (tenant)
John Wilson 1812 (tenant)
John Wilson 1815 (tenant purchaser) (Family ownership 53 years total)
George Atkinson 1865 (38 years)
Thomas Atkinson 1903 (44 years)
Thomas Atkinson jnr 1947 (10 years) (Family ownership 92 years total)
Joseph Edward Cox & Eliza Jane Cox 1957 (18 years)
David Walter Rogers & Helen Margaret Rogers 1975 (8 years)
Maurice Graham Millard & Christine Susan Millard 1983 (40 years in 2023 and still counting)

Longest ownership: Atkinson family, 92 years.

POULTRY ARE A NUISANCE

At Shap I had had a fine collection of alpine plants, most of which I wanted to take with me to the big new garden. "You're a real plantswoman," said elderly Mrs Hall approvingly, on learning that I was spending more time digging out, potting or bagging the alpines than I did packing clothes and furniture. The solicitors handling the exchange of contracts agreed I could take anything I liked provided I listed what was going with me so the new owner understood the situation. I gleefully hand wrote a list of my alpine travellers, all in scientific binomials, for them to type up and append to our contract. Linguistic cowards, they only photocopied it.

I moved all my precious plants into a temporary plot in Daw Bank's kitchen garden. The garden was huge – the whole ground floor of our house in Shap would have fitted in, along with its lawn and rockery – and although it was gated and fenced so no sheep could get in, in my innocence I overlooked the free range hens which the vendor had offered to us. At that time I subscribed to the classic idea that for a farm to be A Proper Farm it needs brown hens scratching about; free range chickens are therefore A Good Idea.

Big mistake.

As the weeks progressed towards our moving in date, I noticed that some of my alpine plants had vanished. When I paid more attention I saw that other remaining specimens had odd, arrowhead marks pointing into them, as though a comic artist wished to indicate they were exploding. Later they too vanished.

It wasn't until a week before we moved that I saw the culprit at work: a small game-bred black hen whom we had observed to be fit, active and a tremendous layer, sometimes producing two eggs a day. Peck, scratch, scuffle, pause (hunker down, pop out an egg) scratch, peck.

I possessed a lovely alpine plant called Primula williamsii. It was a downy-leaved primrose from the high forests of Asia, white flowered, scented, not invasive, a plant of sweetly perfect character and one of which I was immensely proud. It had cost me quite a lot of money as a small seedling but it had grown to perfection at Shap and moved very happily.

Black Hen approached it with stealthy determination. First the arrowhead marks of her scratching round it to find any insect life under its handsome leaves; then the relentless pecking at its juicy central buds. Chicken wire on the gate was no deterrent; she went through the hedge, whose length had been fenced against four-legged livestock but not, as yet, against hens. Over that week, when we were massively busy with moving in, she ate the whole plant.

I forget, now, what else she and her cousins consumed; I know it was a lot. They certainly cost me a lot of money. On the value of what she ate, Black Hen alone ought to have given me half a dozen eggs a day.

And then – eggs are all very well, but what do you do with the glut in spring and summer when all your hens are laying? I ran out of egg boxes and trays. I made sponge cakes; I whisked useful sized groups of eggs into plastic tubs and bags and froze them; I even sold a few, though passing trade was small. There was also the social dilemma that friends and relatives thought our eggs should be free, while I – looking at what the hens were eating – knew they shouldn't.

The hens officially lived in a couple of huts at the foot of what we still call the Hen Field. The children had the job of rounding them up at night and shutting them in, while I let them out and fed them in a morning. Night was the only time the hens spent under control; the rest of the day they were raiding the hedges, the fields, the garden and the roadsides, leaving destruction, footprints, feathers and hen shit wherever they went. I was upset when I saw one hit by a passing car; but as I adjusted to siege by poultry, I began to feel it would be more honest to rejoice.

For a couple of years we reared table chickens. We bought a hundred tiny yellow fluffballs in the autumn, which were due to grow into big white Ross crosses. We raised and fattened them in an empty cow-byre, and sold some for the Christmas trade while freezing the remainder for ourselves. By that time they were superbly big, some over twelve pounds, and because we hung them for a wintry week between killing and freezing, they were wonderful eating. They themselves ate as though they were designed for nothing else, and they put on weight at an incredible speed. I suspect they were bred to be killed at six weeks old when they would have weighed three or four pounds. As they grew on past that age, some developed breathing problems and weak legs. In a morning we would find one dead although unmarked, and when I plucked, cleaned and dressed it I would discover that the overworked heart was surrounded by a sac full of fluid - sometimes filling the whole body cavity. Often the livers of the birds were enlarged, soft and pulpy, like Foie Gras, as a result of their endless eating. They had no social problems, though, and seldom pecked each other; they were too big and idle.

Plucking at Christmas, out in the barn, was miserably cold work; we still had our other stock to tend, and the drawing and dressing operations proved that our little kitchen was not designed to process a hundred birds. We had to do them in batches and the job took several nights because Graham was driving the wagon during the day and we both needed to be there to work efficiently with the birds. Besides, I never really liked doing the killing. We were in the midst of this chore in 1988 when we heard the news about the Lockerbie air disaster, 50 miles to the north. The transatlantic airways pass right over

25

us here. If the bomb had gone off a few minutes earlier … it didn't bear thinking about.

When we bought more cattle we didn't have a building to spare, so the chicken job stopped. I missed the product but not the chores.

One summer we invested in some ducks; Aylesbury crosses they were supposed to be. We bought six which we brought home in canvas bags. There was a lot of Mallard blood in this first lot and they were not very big. Released outside the wooden "duck hull" they stayed roughly half an hour and then took flight, disappearing north-eastwards over the cowsheds.

The children and I tracked them feverishly, envisaging their total loss down the Lune valley along with our cash investment. After a long hot slog, we found that they had gone in a reconnoitring circle and returned to the hull where, no doubt, they were anticipating a scoopful of grain as a refresher after their journey.

I can't recall what happened to these ducks; maybe we ate them. The next year we bought fertile duck-eggs, from someone in the village, and incubated them in a circular polystyrene incubator. Later we bought six big Aylesburies, two drakes and four ducks, and hatched their eggs too. It was nice to see the ducklings breaking out of the shell, but the little incubator's thermostat was unpredictable and sometimes excessive warmth resulted in "July Sprawlers", ducklings that had no control over their legs and couldn't stand upright. Sometimes they got better; more often they didn't.

The Aylesbury females never sat on any eggs themselves. They were too busy avoiding the drakes, who harried them endlessly. The morning release from the hull was like a Viking invasion: the drakes came out into the open and stretched their wings a few times, then with furious quacking, waddling and flapping the rape and pillage began. All the ducks became bald-headed from the grip of the balancing drakes. In a mad way it was entertaining. The males' selfish behaviour was a complete

26

contrast to that of the cockerel. Yes, he would come running the moment a hen cackled that she'd laid and was ready for her next egg to be fertilised, but he was also protective and community-minded and called the hens to him if he found anything good to eat.

I was glad that the ducks couldn't negotiate the gate out of the field, because inside there was duck-muck everywhere. Through the constant activities of the foraging few, the field developed a series of interconnected mud holes where the rain ran through hollows to the beck, which in turn became empty of fish, empty of snails, empty of plants, and so dirty that the other animals wouldn't drink from it and would only use the trough. The lack of snails may have severely annoyed the liver fluke, but for the sheep it was a benefit that left them thirsty.

One night our evening round of farm jobs was interrupted, I forget by what, and we omitted to shut the poultry in. The fox, who also made his rounds every night in the hope that this might happen, took away one drake, whole, and two ducks' heads. We found the hens next morning perched in strange places, on roofs and in bushes, with even more worried expressions than usual.

They were right to worry. Not long afterwards we forgot again and the fox killed the other drake and ducks, plus several hens. Only two remained, of which one died later of shock.

We stopped buying hen food. I bought eggs in winter from Joyce. She too had given up keeping her own hens and now bought in trays of eggs to sell. Graham talked of getting some more hens but "not until that old one dies, she'll teach them all to come ratching in the garden." As she had been several years old when we got her he didn't expect her to live long. He reckoned without hybrid vigour. She just went on. And on.

Chucklebuddy, as she became known, was clearly a sharp bird. Hens in a group appear daft as brushes, but one on its own is noticeably intelligent. Having cheated the fox twice, she developed strategies that were endearing. She decided the safest roost was among the farm buildings; she never again used the hen huts. Her preferred sleeping-places were in the hayracks above the sheep pens where she enjoyed the convected warmth from woolly bodies during the night. She became tame enough to stroke and allowed the children to carry her about. She laid energetically each summer. Occasionally she moulted, usually choosing midwinter – in severe frost she'd be half naked. This was her only aberration, and despite it, she survived. She ate almost anything and would pounce on and kill mice, from which she most enjoyed the brain. Her method of stealing dog food was to tempt Shep and her chain to follow her round a tree, then to return to the food bowl, to which the chain would not now reach. By the time Shep had unwound herself (or, since she tended to be unidirectional, wound herself up even tighter) Chucklebuddy had had her pick of the goodies.

Before long the dogs were resigned to her thefts. Shep occasionally pounced at her if she thought no-one was watching but since she had been smacked for doing it and knew that it wasn't allowed, most of the time Chucklebuddy was safely in charge. Unfortunately, one summer day the old hen pushed her luck too far and Shep caught her and plucked all the feathers off her back.

We found her crouched in a corner of the shed. We carried her tenderly her into the byre with food and water. She was no more naked than she had been in her midwinter moults, but evidently she was in deep shock. She did not eat or drink and two days later she died.

She was one casualty chicken which I wasn't in the least tempted to eat.

TUPPING TIME

The ram is elemental in his strength,
stalking about the autumn's work, his lip
lecherously curled as he tracks the ewes.
Who would suspect a beast of courtesy?
Yet watch his manners from the first approach
and delicacy is the ruling code –
soft his advances, till consent is given.

The world is full of knowing little minds
that twist and poison but that never speak.
The ram and his magnificence deride
their taint of shame, cut off from the deep well
of adult tenderness. Such secrecy
makes sex a monster, spoken of only
in whispers. How can whispers say,
because she does not lie or blush
my child of ten cannot be innocent?

Hold me, my love, my strength, and let us make
our one safe haven with our children here
tending the sane, unknowing animals.

BUMBLEBEE'S NECK TIE

It was three twenty in the morning, pitch black, and I could hear scraping noises. Irregular, repetitive, rather loud scraping noises.

I held my breath in order to listen, though I didn't really need to. Downstairs, and just one wall further south, was the cow byre, the "front" byre which faced the gates onto the road. We had five young cows stalled in there, held by toggled ropes round their necks which were fastened to hooped "cow irons" shaped rather like an omega or astrological Leo symbol, designed to allow the rope neck-tie to run freely up and down the iron stanchion when a cow wanted to lie or stand (or scratch). We were familiar with the noises that our livestock made, and quite enjoyed being able to interpret what they were up to through the wall, although it sometimes caused round eyed consternation among dining visitors, who would pause in mid chew to enquire about the eerie sawing and clanking of chains next door. "Just So-and-So having a scratch," we would say airily. "I wonder if we ought to delouse her?" Reactions to such comments were stored away with glee and our dining table saw rather fewer guests than before.

On this occasion So-and-So's scratch seemed to be unnecessarily persistent. It was now twenty to four and her grating noises seemed to renew themselves every minute and a half, following a pattern of jerk, wobble, scrape and stop. My husband – not a snorer, but a deep sleeper nonetheless – slept on.

I'd have to investigate. I wasn't going to get any sleep anyway, for wondering. I put the light on, I dressed sketchily (the cows never seemed to care – shocking pink leggings or scarlet sweatshirts were all one to them) and I fumbled my way downstairs to the kitchen. I bumped into walls and banisters, and made clumsy noises with the kitchen door latch. My brain was awake but my body seemed still in the twilight zone.

I put on my disreputable Farm Hat, wellies and dirty waxed jacket, and ventured out.

It was a pleasant night, although November; no frost, just a light breeze and a grey blanket of cloud hiding the stars. The lights of Kendal, fifteen miles away to the south-west, outlined Shap Fell with a dull orange glow. A ewe in the caravan field coughed consumptively, *ahough, ahough,* and the cows lying in the six-byre stirred a little at the familiar sound of my boots going by, but their internal clocks told them it was not yet close enough to breakfast time to make it worth getting to their feet.

In the front byre I offered my routine greeting before I put on the light. I always spoke to the beasts, who, dazzled by the suddenness of the electricity, would otherwise not know who was there. "Hello girls, how are you?" Two of them, lying tied in a shared stall, blinked sleepily at me over their shoulders and went on chewing.

The third, Bumblebee, was a brindled Hereford/Jersey cross whom I had bought as a calf at auction the previous Christmas, for a maiden bid of two pounds. She was penned in a stall by herself so she wasn't neck-tied, and she should also have been lying quietly, but she was standing up. All I could see at first was her rump. Her tail had a strange, tense quality and her hind legs were spread as if she needed to keep her balance against some unseen force. I walked forward to bring her fully into view.

She had pierced her lower eyelid with the loop of a cow-iron.

"How the hell did you manage to do that?" I said. She blinked at me, painfully, and didn't move.

Our cow irons – shaped like Omega Ω – were mostly blunt ended. This one, however, which we had not previously observed, had been blacksmith made and its curled ends were tapered to fine points. Somehow, while lying down, Bumblebee

31

had rubbed her face on the stanchion and hooked the point of the iron through her eyelid.

She was a quiet little heifer, but she was still too big for me to push her into the place where I knew she needed to be. I couldn't see how I was going to persuade her to give sufficient slack to disengage the curl of the iron. When I pushed her forward from behind, I couldn't reach the iron at all. When I approached from the front, she backed away with the rope taut, to the furthest distance she could bear.

"Come on old dear, don't be so silly."

She wouldn't co-operate, and I couldn't blame her. Eventually I went back indoors and woke Graham.

"Bumblebee's got herself caught on a cow tie."

"Mh?"

"It's through her eyelid and she won't let me get it out."

He groaned. "How the hell did she manage to do that?"

"I don't know. I need you to hold her, to give me some slack while I wiggle it out."

He fumbled his way into trousers and jumper. On our way out I collected antibiotic, a syringe, and some dusting powder; he went to the wagon shed for pliers and a small hacksaw. Thus armed we returned to the fray.

The other two heifers had reluctantly got up by now, and had cocked their tails and left heaps of dung in the muck channel. Bumblebee still stood skewered, not scraping any more, tensely convinced that she was doomed.

"Silly old dear," said my husband, exasperated.

We couldn't get anywhere near the metal with the tools. I had a dread of puncturing Bumblebee's eyeball. Graham tried pushing her forward for me but she twisted her head and I still couldn't manipulate the curled iron out of her eyelid, so we swapped places, but I couldn't push her hard enough.

Tempers were beginning to fray.

"Let me get in by her head," said my husband grimly, picking up the pliers.

At which point Bumblebee shook herself and simply walked away.

She winked the freed eye coquettishly at us and nibbled at an overlooked bit of hay. Her eyelid was slightly puffed, with a small bead of blood where the end of the tie had been.

We stood and looked at her and at each other.

"How the hell did she manage to do that?"

THE ACRYLIC CAT

It is very tempting to write about all the endearing things that kids say and do, but I must admit that with the passing of years the majority of my "Little Johnny" stories have faded into insignificance. The ones that stick with me mostly originated with our son David, though there were one or two episodes where he shared the limelight (or, more often, the blame) with Jen.

The most public incident happened at Ravenstonedale Show, which used to have a carriage driving class, to which Rosie-the-Fell-pony and I had managed to get a lift. Graham brought the kids along later in the car, but after the show class was over and we'd all been concentrating on reloading the carriage up the ramp of the friend's horsebox, we couldn't find David. Until, that is, someone asked, "Whose kid is that, peeing up that post on the ring-side?"

One day, before he started school, David accompanied my mother and stepfather and me to the Barnaby Rudge Tavern in Tebay for lunch. The landlady gave us all menus, and jokingly included David. Sitting there on the bench seat with his legs stuck out in front of him and the menu upside down in his hand, the four-year-old announced gravely that, "Whenever I go into a pub I always like to see the menu."

In another summer, both he and Jen were grounded following a phone call from the local motorway services shop where the supervisor, a neighbour, had recognised them nicking pocketfuls of sweeties. (Well, it was *serve yourself*, wasn't it?) I told the supervisor I would send them back with the swag to apologise, which they did, and they didn't repeat the trick – as far as I know. The disadvantages of being a kid living in a small village…

However, local knowledge also worked in their favour, such as when a police sergeant came knocking one summer day and asked if the children were about. We'd only been home half an hour, and the kids were playing in the garden, so I called them in and he asked if they'd been down into the village that day. They said No (well you would, wouldn't you?), and though I had to admit they'd had time, just, to go there and come back since we arrived home, I was pretty sure they hadn't. It turned out the Fire Brigade had received several hoax calls from our village phone-box and that day someone had seen a girl and a boy in the red kiosk during the relevant period. Jen innocently grassed up two other kids who'd been talking on the school minibus about making emergency calls, and we never heard any more about it.

Thinking of the minibus – and policemen – reminds me of David's collection of china birds.

Joe Davies, a retired police motorcycle instructor, owned a fine china shop in Penrith, and because he and I shared a common interest in Fell ponies and carriage driving I often dropped in to share a cup of coffee in the back office. Joe used to give David a bit of discount on delightful Beswick models, for which he saved his pocket money. David's bedroom soon sported a large kestrel and a kingfisher, and several smaller birds such as wrens, robins and blue-tits, bizarrely interspersed with his model cars.

Fridays were "show and tell" day at school, and when it came to David's turn he decided to talk about his china birds. He was very proud and excited, so we carefully wrapped the models in paper and packed them into a box nearly as big as himself, and in the morning I handed him and the box onto the school minibus.

I think the show and tell session earned him a lot of praise, but when the minibus brought him home, just as he climbed out of the back with his precious box, his foot caught on the step. He pitched out head first and he and the box hit gravel

from a height of five feet. Very little survived. Oh the howls…
It took him a long time to forgive Friday the Thirteenth.

Then there was the cat. For many years our cats were of the Siamese persuasion, and since they were gentle, vocal and characterful the kids were fond of them, although the first of them loved to lie across David's hot little knees, holding him captive in spite of his plaintive cries of, "Get OFF, Moglington!"

After Moglington came Tristan, with whom David sat on the kitchen floor while they each contemplated the wonders of a new front-loading washing machine; their heads circled in unison with the sudsy sheets.

One day David enquired, "What's Tristan's coat made of?"

"Fur," I replied.

"Yes, but what's it made of?"

"Well, cat fur, I suppose."

"Yes, but is it nylon or acrylic?"

After the acrylic cat, his question about why Australians didn't fall off the world was a mere bagatelle.

FELL PONIES AND CARRIAGE DRIVING

You may have gathered that I like horses. I enjoy their lack of complication, I admire their kindness, and I am humbled by their constant willingness to please humans. Enjoying them, though, doesn't mean that I fool myself about them. They are scruffy beasts by nature, enjoying nothing better than a roll in a communal mud patch or a serious bout of scratching, whether via the teeth of a reciprocating herd member or via an algae-green branch. They enforce good manners amongst themselves with a summary display of flattened ears, threatening squeals or raised hind hooves, and those who still step out of line are tooth-punched or kicked into behaving in a way that benefits the herd.

I'm fully aware that so long as horses have grass to eat they would not care one bit if they never saw me again, so it's perverse that much of my motivation for moving to Daw Bank was the thought of space, and time, to do things with horses.

I've mostly had Fells over the 40 years we've been here. I love Fells and their natural ability to look after themselves and not need to have anything to do with humans. Their independence, close to wildness, adds a strange and humbling value to their friendship with us.

When I first holidayed in the Lake District, in 1968, I was determined not to like my mother's choice of venue. Until then, our holidays had always been in North Wales. She persuaded me by promising that if I accompanied her planned "little toddles" round Keswick, she would come pony trekking with me. As you may have guessed, I found I enjoyed plodging in the rain over Catbells and round Stonethwaite and Watendlath – but the highlight was always going to be the pony trek.

My mount was a Fell pony, brown, rounded and muscular, with a long black tail and a massive curtain of mane that entirely hid his face. Nonetheless, the eyes underneath were friendly and I fell instantly in love. He also carted me up Latrigg with an eagerness I hadn't met before in ponies of his size. His name was Wimpsey. It was only many years later that I learned the origin of his name: when I was judging a Fell pony class, my steward turned out to have owned him as a yearling, and told me that, running unhandled in the fields, he had "looked just like one of them Wimpseys" (ie, *Whimsies* – a line of pottery animal figures made by Wade in the 1960s).

The trekking business belonged to Peter and Edith Robinson. I didn't know, on that first ride, that the woman in charge of us all was Betty Walker, a leading light of the Fell Pony Society. She rode another brown Fell pony, Angus, and fed me snippets of Fell pony lore at every opportunity. Did I know that Fell ponies had been in the Lakes as long as the Herdwick sheep? No; I was much more impressed by the ponies' strength and willingness and the fact that they were capable of living free, all year round, on the fells where I'd been walking. I was 15, and independence was a magnet.

I wheedled to go trekking again, and I've been hooked on Fells ever since.

It was because of the Fell ponies that I spent every university vacation in the Lake District, working for Peter and Edith at their new location at the Troutbeck Hotel, helping Betty, riding Angus, putting good riders on Wimpsey because I knew how much they would enjoy him.

Over the years since then I've done a lot of background research about Fell ponies, and their spell over me has only grown stronger. They are a distinctive part of our farming and industrial history. Until the 20th century they were the mainstay of local transport: hardy and hard-working, they took the shepherd up the fell, carried hay to the stock in winter, pulled the trap to market, or walked hundreds of miles as pack-

38

horses with wool destined for Europe. For thousands of years we'd have gone literally nowhere without them.

Rosie was the first pony I owned, a dark bay Sleddale bred Fell, a mere three and a half years old. Rather than the traditional horse reaction to traffic of "Oh my God, a big growly thing, let's all run away NOW!" Rosie's attitude was, "Get that wagon out of my way!" which in spite of her youth made her a pretty safe driving pony. Clive Richardson kindly lent me equipment, recommended books, and offered advice. As Rosie had been trained to drive by our blacksmith, Bob Atkinson, she knew more about it than I did and we got through the early stages without any accidents. Well, nothing more serious than me being tipped out in the hayfield and having to retrieve the beast and the carriage from the next farm... but she and I both learnt from it. The next time she and the carriage departed without me, she stopped and waited, while one upturned wheel gently rotated, horizontal to the ground. "Oops – got it wrong, Ma, sorry!" Bless those Fell brains.

I had bought a cheap harness, and, being used to making things when I couldn't afford to buy them, I used it as a pattern to make something better. Bob Atkinson put me in touch with someone who wanted several sets of harness and was therefore prepared to buy me a heavy duty sewing machine, from K Shoes' works store outside Kendal. That gave me scope to trial different designs and construction techniques. I realised very quickly that if I made webbing harness commercially I might keep Rosie in hay and bedding and perhaps afford to enter a few competitions, where I would be able to demonstrate my harness in action and sell some more. It was an arrangement that made sense business-wise, though it didn't always go down well with Graham. When I attempted National qualifiers he got a bit impatient at my disappearance every other weekend to events around Cumbria, (and even as far away as, ooh, Lancashire and Dumfries).

However, it wasn't Graham but Kestrel, the handsome Fell x Arab I bought as a foal, who ended my competitive ambitions. Athletic, tough, intelligent and handsome, he nevertheless inherited issues from his dam about strangers, and eventually we had an accident at a club drive, entirely due to his paranoia. Then we had another at a competition on the Holker Hall estate, in which we had to cut him free of the carriage; he escaped us and galloped unhindered until someone diverted him into the enclosed yard of the doctor's surgery in Cark. Chastened, I went back to the pure Fell breed, and bought Mr T.

Dear Mr T. He was small and stout, with a droll way of flapping his lower lip when relaxed. He just wanted to please, and he adored young animals, whether human or equine; "Foals," he would say, nuzzling Shetland or toddler with equal kindness. I did try pushing him into competition, but his heart wasn't in it; we compromised by allowing him to trot the marathon at his own best pace, which let him, and me, enjoy driving the hazards at the end. We didn't win anything but we had much more fun.

Ruby the Magnificent has sneaked her way into the family with fluttering eyelashes, her nose and neck insinuating themselves into everyone's bosom whether man, woman or child, but particularly man. If Old Rosie hadn't been still alive, I'd have sworn Ruby was a reincarnation. They came of the same Sleddale breeding and Ruby almost was Rosie, with all the boldness Rosie had had, but with added stamina and class. She flew round her first marathon with such gusto that when we reached the finish line she wanted to go round again. Once she had worked out what hazards were about, the faster you turned her the faster she wanted to go.

She is retired now, and arthritic like me, only there is no orthopaedic service for ageing equine joints. Her understudy, Eric-the-Dales, with his flash trot and flowing white mane, has revealed only too clearly that, these days, I'm the partner who lacks courage.

DON'T FEED THE HORSES

Visitors staying in the converted barn are mostly delightful, but…I have to say I worry about the common sense of some of them. We stipulate that the holiday accommodation is non smoking, and most of our visitors don't smoke, but if they do, they obediently smoke outside. I put out a bucket they can use for their cigarette ends. Given our rainy climate the bucket usually has water in it. The trouble is, the presence of the water seems to suggest to some that they can also use the dog's drinking bucket and the horses' drinking trough as extinguishing places. I can't believe that liquid nicotine and ash can be good for either of them. Today I found plastic picnic cutlery in the dog's bucket, too.

I have put up two notices on the stable doors that say "Please do not feed the horses." There are various good reasons for this. One is that I've got greedy Fell ponies who are curious and will take something offered by hand which they would refuse if they met it in a bucket. They could very quickly learn that strangers offer food, and strangers' hands then become a target. I hate pushy horses who are constantly bullying for treats. Another and stronger reason is that when we have small children staying - and we frequently do – then a greedy horse who's been encouraged by the ignorant "feeders" to nip, would be dangerous to innocent stroking hands. Yet another reason is that we had a group of serious smokers last year (rafts of ciggy butts in every bucket and trough) and I think they must have given one of the ponies tobacco to eat. At any rate, that weekend Mr T had "the runs" something horrible for 24 hours, despite no change of diet. Some people seem to have no idea what is sensible to feed to a horse. And no consciousness of the dangers, to either party, of their own ignorance.

This morning on mucking out I've found a paper plate in the stable. What part of "Do not feed the horses" don't they understand?

CARRIAGE DRIVERS

An interest in horses, particularly carriage driving, brings you into contact with other like-minded people, and one of the most generous and knowledgeable I've ever met was Fred Todd.

At our Dalemain "fun" event in early May, Fred brought his grey Fell x Dales pony, La'al Sod, for a jolly round the hazards. I watched him gear up and listened to him talking to her.

"Now then La'al Sod, stand still till I put this on.

"Now then La'al Sod, stand still till I tighten this up.

"Now then La'al Sod, stand still till I put trap on.

"Now then La'al Sod, stand still till I get up.

"Now then La'al Sod - go like hell, but in a controlled manner."

He advertised her for sale in the Farmers' Guardian; possibly because he more often drove his big grey Irish-cross mare, Katie, so La'al Sod didn't get enough work. He said, afterwards, that the ad was a big mistake: "I was a bloody fool." He did his best, in fact, *not* to sell La'al Sod, but the ad was in circulation so eventually someone challenged him to name a price. He set a huge figure, and was appalled when the man agreed.

He put off delivering La'al Sod for some time, but eventually he was persuaded to drive half the journey up to the Scottish buyer's farm. They would meet at an agreed time on the auction mart car park at Carlisle and transfer the mare to the buyer's trailer. "If he'd been a minute late, I was going to turn around and bring her straight back," he said. "But he wasn't, and I kicked myself all the way home."

I now drive a younger, male version of La'al Sod, called Eric.

One of the hazards, though, of driving a horse and carriage on the road is that you and the horse are *outside*, whereas car drivers are on the *inside* of their boxes and travelling much faster. It makes you very vulnerable. I try hard to minimise the risks by wearing a fluorescent, reflective waistcoat, and displaying flashing cycle lights on the carriage. Most of the time this works well, and even the boy racers see us far enough in advance for a smile and a wave to slow them down. Farming neighbours always pass quietly, or sometimes stop and wind down the window for a brief chat.

Just occasionally, in spite of the hi-viz and flashing lights, we're carved up by a car full of youngsters. It's not always boy racers – a boy racer's girlfriend perhaps. I admit to having flicked the driving whip-thong defensively between my horsepower and cars that passed too close, but Fred used to take self-defence a step further; he tied a metal nut on the end of his whip-thong to whack the roofs of reckless overtakers. "They shouldn't be close enough for me to hit them." A friend once went out driving with him at that period. A car passed with the approved amount of circumspection, and Fred saluted it with a gentle wave of his whip.

The friend said, "Did you see that?"

"What?" asked Fred, replacing his whip-hand on the rein.

"When you waved, all the passengers ducked."

THE LAST HORSEMAN

In a box at last; Fred Todd. I never thought
that death could catch such a wise old devil.
He was a man whose age you could not guess,
a hewn-oak character, wicked as life.

Fred and his horses drove in step together,
in work or sport, to sow or reap. A steady
champion of all between the two poles
of the farming year, he winked at death,
told tales of graveyards, mocked his own gallantry –
"Here's some dahlias, I stole 'em for you – "

So at this funeral, a stout Dales cob
pulled a flat cart up the hill, and brought him
coffined to church with us walking behind.
Sad? Yes; but there's never been a passing
at which so much laughter was heard, and rich
life-memories of the man we came to mourn.

His daughter spoke of lessons that he taught
to her and to her brothers in their youth;
they hunted and they fished. They learned respect
for every creature. Fred had brought them up
alone, quite happily; and all his days
he used his skill with horses in the fields;
dined under the hedge and, with content, watched
the wildlife of the land pass calmly by.
"I am not wealthy, as things go," he said,
"But with my horses, and the birds and beasts,
I am the richest of all men alive."

BOY RACER'S WOMAN

Behold my neighbour, Mrs Rush,
who lives a life of dash-and-push.
She goes at such a furious pace
I've never met her face to face.
She flies past in her Subaru
ignoring such as me and you;
expects the narrow lanes to clear
whenever they are blessed to hear
the music of her two-tone horn,
whether at evening or at morn.
She'll never pause to say Good-Day
while ponies jump out from her way,
nor worry, if a straying sheep
should knock a wall down in its leap
to safety as she rushes by –
"Let others trouble, why should I?"

I heard though that the other day
a wagon loaded high with hay,
delivering it to a farm,
caused Mrs Rush substantial harm.
She, flying home with her well-worn
fantasia upon the horn,
found the leviathan astride
the farm-road, and her way denied.
Her neighbours, sweating high in air,
pretended that she wasn't there,
but prompted by the klaxon wails
they accurately dropped two bales –
fifty pounds each from ten feet up –
and, wonderful, the horn shut up.
White faced and shaking, Mrs Rush

reversed amid the mirth-filled hush
and with her dented roof and boot
turned tail, and found another route.

This morning, Mrs Rush went by
rather more slowly, to my eye.
The neighbours hope they soon may quell
her husband, Mr Rush, as well.

LAMBING 1

We kept between 60 and 90 sheep as a "flying flock". We bought them in the Autumn, tupped and over wintered them; we lambed them and sold them in Spring. The lambs and ewes went together, as family units. However, we always had a few left over. Perhaps a lamb had been fostered onto a ewe whose own had died, and still needed occasional supervision; or there were late twins, who wouldn't make up a level pen for the auction among their older cousins. In our early days on the farm we lambed outdoors and chanced the weather, but later we brought the ewes in to a shed built of corrugated iron and metal stanchions (mainly cannibalised structures from my husband's various scrapped wagon chassis). Inside, we fed them on silage and meadow hay, supplemented either with "sheep nuts" or with "pot ale syrup" which was a brewing by-product, sweet, rich and sticky, that the ewes adored. We poured the syrup onto their fodder and all through winter they wore brown circles round their muzzles from burrowing through the sticky hay into the bottom of the racks to lick up the dribbles. It took a storm or two of rain to remove the evidence of their greed after they were turned out. Even in a field of spring grass there were still several who would lick it up endlessly from the supplementary feeders, which Graham made by fitting a rotating spherical float into the side of a plastic jerry-can.

Our lambs, on the whole, were sturdy and rewarding. Suffolk tups on Herdwick ewes produced grand lambs – often black – but usually singles, which were hard work on the ewe at lambing because of their size. Later we used Texel or Charollais x Texel tups on Swaledale or Rough ewes. We averaged "a lamb and a half" – about equal numbers of ewes with twins and singles. I didn't like triplets. Our hill sheep seldom had milk for three and the smallest one was not often strong or determined enough to leave with its dam, nor to make a good candidate for "setting on" to another ewe, so it had to be hand reared. We were lucky that we didn't have many of those.

A horsey acquaintance used to chide me for spending so much time on lambing - "they'll lamb theirsel's, ye know" - but it isn't the birth that takes the time (though lambing jumbled up twins is an art!). It's keeping things going right after the lambs are born that takes doing. And this includes:

- feeding the families who have been turned out in the fields - where the nursing ewes, with every justification, are HUNGRY;

- making sure the new families have not become mixed up with lambs trying to feed wrongly from someone else's irritable, conservative mother;

- walking round the fields twice a day in case some lamb is lying in a hollow with pneumonia, unseen from the main buildings;

- and then there's the ewe who achieves her lifetime's ambition immediately she has lambed – she leaves you with a pair of small whickering offspring to foster-on, if you're lucky, to another ewe who's managed to smother her own.

Every season there's a couple of "pets" to whom no ewe will give suck. They develop a remarkable attachment to your knees, because those are next to the milk bottle when you feed them.

You daren't get too fond of lambs, because they are after all destined for the freezer, but there are few finer sights than a little flock of a fortnight old, racing each other on a warm Spring evening, their sharp little hooves drumming the drying earth with the promise of Summer to come.

SPRING

hazel catkins hang
shimmering in a cold breeze
sprinkling spring on me

COOKING IN MY WELLIES

We have lived at Daw Bank for 40 years now, and we farmed it ourselves for 15 of those. Most of the time, our main income was from Graham's haulage business that served the needs of neighbours, bringing in fertilisers, hay and straw, and taking wool from their farms to the Wool Board mills at Bradford. However, since the wagon-driving took Graham away from the farm for most of the week and from first light until dark, the day to day running of the place devolved first on me and later on the children.

This is probably why I am not a very good cook.

Let me explain: most of the time our farming was not demanding. We had 15 acres (5 hectares), and our farm stocking rates were not high. We had, at most, 90 sheep and their lambs, a couple of tups, 10 cows and their calves and a Hereford bull.

The kids would board the minibus for school by 8.30am, when I'd feed-round, muck out the ponies, and be ready for another challenge by 10. Except at lambing or calving, this left me a lot of spare time in the middle of the day to do other things, such as training ponies, writing for magazines, and making driving harness. I managed everything fine during the early part of the day, including running the local carriage driving club, but by "school home-time" in winter there were always several things that needed doing at once.

It didn't help that the passageway between house and yard was not waterproof, so Wellington boots tended to sneak into the warm dry kitchen – even more so after my daughter put on an outdoor-stored welly without checking it first: "WAAAAA! There's a slug in it!" There was also no option but to keep the coats hanging in the kitchen, because they never dried in the passageway. Four sets of wet coats and boots take up quite a lot of space. There were also the spares, stealthily dripping behind the larder door.

The evening's outdoor jobs always coincided with a stab of panic – "What are we going to have for supper? Well, we could have such and such, if I got it started now and put it on the Rayburn." I'd be preparing potatoes and carrots, persuading the children into their farm clothes, frying-off onions and meat for a stew and putting my wellies on. Looking back, I can't really have been too disorganised because we never starved, but sometimes it felt a close-run thing between competence and panic. Yes, I should have prepared stuff beforehand – and in my own defence, often I did – I just remember an awful lot of kitchen activity taking place to the accompaniment of rain running off my coat.

We'd sally forth into the weather to do our bit, then halfway through supplying the animals with food and water, mucking-out and re-bedding, I'd take a breather and dive down the steps to the back door, do a few additional things in the kitchen, then plunge back out again once I was sure tea was progressing safely.

Taking off the wellington boots seemed like a waste of time.

"DRIVING CLUB" 2002 STYLE

It's one of the well-known facts of the Millard household that if Father goes to buy a new car, we all know what colour it will be.

This would be less surprising if he ever actually bought a genuinely new one with all the options of specifying preferences, but none of the family – me included – has ever thought it a good deal to lose several thousand pounds simply by driving a completely new car out of a show room. The newest car our household has ever claimed was six years old; many have reached their teens and the much loved and sworn-at Morris Paralanian motor caravan celebrated a 21st birthday.

Looking back over four decades, we have had an assortment of high mileage, low cost cars. They included the aforementioned "caravanette", all two-and-a-quarter tons of it, in which we took our summer and weekend breaks and did the shopping, until it quietly succumbed to old age some time in its twenty-seventh year. It then served another six years as a children's play house. We had a Triumph Dolomite (or its nearest relative whose model name I can't now recall; a 1300 perhaps?), and a long, long series of Vauxhalls: Cavaliers, Belmonts and Astras. Finally, too, I have to reveal my husband's liking for MG-Rover Metros, all dubbed "monkey trucks" by me and "pogo sticks" by our daughter who learnt to drive in the first one. Graham himself referred to them as "rust buckets" but nevertheless bought three in succession until, with MG and Rover having both gone out of business, the second-hand supply finally ran dry.

Out of forty years' worth of vehicles, I can only think of four we owned that weren't the same colour; we had, briefly, one blue, one red and one silver Metro, and one blue Cavalier. Ah, and also the retired, up-on-ramps Lotus (Lots Of Trouble

Usually Serious) Elite that hasn't turned a wheel in many years and is, somewhere under the dust and swallow droppings, fibreglass red. But as that doesn't go anywhere, it doesn't count. And neither does the Rover 400 that I borrowed for ooh, all of six weeks, till I bought my present car which is gunmetal grey. The Rover's colour was probably described by the paint-shop as "British Racing Green", but it became known as Tarnhelm because when you were in it you were, apparently, invisible.

You are working out by elimination what colour I'm talking about, aren't you?

The last of the Metros (the silver one) failed its Ministry of Transport road-worthiness test, so the hunt was on for a replacement to get my husband to work. There being no Metros still knocking around, the field was wide open; would it be another trusty Vauxhall? A Ford? Or even something Japanese, like mine? He spent hours poring over Auto Trader, finding suitably aged and priced beasties that were also within a reasonable distance of us. As we are a long way from any cities this last requirement narrowed the field considerably. Then he'd sit there trying to relocate the adverts because he hadn't marked them or turned over the page corners or even written down the page numbers.

By last weekend he still hadn't phoned anyone about any of these cars and his copy of Auto Trader had been superseded by the latest issue. We were back to the local newspaper.

Saturday morning: would I cash a cheque for him with the greengrocer? Noting that the sum was conservative, I did.

Sunday morning: he announced that we (I loved the "we") were going to go and look at an 11-year-old Peugeot, 13 miles away. Compared to the Auto Trader ads, this was nearly on the doorstep. I brought out my car and we set off.

My husband doesn't talk much when driving or being driven. I used to think this might be due to a) concentration on the job in hand or b) terror at being driven by me, but now I know he's just ticking off the farms we pass and tallying all the things he remembers from when he used to collect their annual wool clip, or deliver fertilisers, feeds, hay or straw. It makes for absent-mindedness about such mundanities as where we are actually going; besides, there is a sort of belief in spousal telepathy that assumes if he has thought about something, I automatically know what that thing is and should not need spoken instruction.

However, having enquired about our destination before setting off, I got us there quietly and safely. The last time I'd been to this village, it had been with my daughter, and we had brought home in triumph a very pretty lightweight carriage for our Fell pony; a vehicle of the one horse-power kind which I'd known about for years and coveted from the moment I saw it. When the original owner had asked if I knew anyone who might like to buy it, there was only one possible answer. It had the very strange characteristic of being attractive even to people who knew nothing about carriage driving; they walked up to it on a show field, when it was just sitting there waiting to be put to the pony, and they stroked it, which was quite bizarre to watch. It didn't get used much, but I still adored it and I was sad when I rationalised that it really ought to be sold. Anyhow, that's another reason why I knew where I was going, on this car hunt.

"Where do we want to be, exactly?" I asked as we entered the village.

"We're looking for an elderly Peugeot parked on the roadside. And I would say," he added, "that that's it there."

So I pulled into a small parking space just opposite, and he got out to start poking round the potential purchase.

I didn't need to ask its price tag; I knew how big the cheque was that I'd cashed. I didn't need, either, to follow Graham round the car and peer at the tyre treads, or under the bonnet at the engine, full radiator, and oil; but I did, out of pure curiosity. We had been warned that the car hadn't been used in the last few months, so I was charmed to find proof of that in a mouse nest on top of the air filter. We didn't disturb the contents of the car itself, which included two folding walking sticks, a large golf umbrella, a portable television and enough scrap paper to build a small house.

My husband went along to knock on the door of the converted barn where the owner lived; he eventually appeared in shorts and sandals, his bare legs and feet apparently impervious to the biting wind. Producing the keys, he started up the beastie and offered to let my husband take it for a spin round the block. I made small talk while Graham disappeared down the road and when, in a few minutes, he came back, we moved indoors to discuss price.

It was a foregone conclusion that he'd buy it. The owner made one proposal, Graham offered a smaller amount and pointed out that we had brought cash with us, and the deal was done. I sat through the ensuing search for the registration document, and his daughter's emptying of the car, while I did my bit by trying to entertain two of the three small grandchildren. However, as the boys were very young, and preferred dummy-sucking to speech, I think the sheepdog actually had more to tell me.

How did I know my husband would buy the car? Well, quite apart from having the initials of the carriage driving club as its number plate, the Peugeot was, you guessed it, white.

SHEPHERDING

Basic shepherding is observation and counting. How many legs per sheep are touching the ground in a normal manner? (note to self: this should be 4) and does the number of live bodies present equal the number you put into the field yesterday? If more, then you have gained trespassers from a neighbour; if fewer, something has escaped or died. In either case, investigation must follow.

Shepherding in winter often involves feeding – a race between self with heavy sack or bucket, and many sheep with large, aggressive horns. Hence trousers most of the time to hide the bruised legs.

Shepherding also involves maintenance of digging equipment prior to:

Lambing

A seasonal and near terminal disease of shepherds. Symptoms include shortness of temper and congestion of the face. Involves repeated, often blasphemous requests to the Almighty to rid the world of bereaved ewes and orphaned lambs. Occasionally, a source of quiet pride.

Gathering

Gathering is an attempt to collect and pen a predetermined quantity of sheep from a fell or a field which has grown larger overnight. Involves many feeble whistles (although you can whistle *perfectly* when the skill is not urgently needed), oaths hurled at disobedient dogs, and subsequent visits to neighbours to agree a time for a) removal of their unwanted stock, b) help to mend walls.

Clipping

Yearly backache and cramp for shepherds (especially tall ones). It involves hiring a neighbour to bring a clipping machine, or else sharpening your hand shears. It starts with Gathering (see above) and then catching the ewes in the pens one by one for the shearer; followed by rolling up and sorting different coloured fleeces for the Wool Board; marking the newly naked-looking sheep with suitable colour to distinguish them from your neighbours'; then turning them back into the field. Where, before long, they need:

Dosing

A sheep's worst enemy is another sheep – worms, and worse, lurk. Hence Gathering (see above) in order to treat present or future infestation. Involves: dosing "gun", backpack of custard-yellow worming mixture, minor swearing.

Foot trimming

Chiropody for sheep – to prevent or cure athlete's foot between the cleats, foot rot and other nasties. Another cause of Gathering, and an extremely frequent cause of backache for shepherds.

Showing

Not be confused with showing off. Various breeds of sheep, like cattle and ponies, have their own classes at agricultural shows. Basically they are intended to make sure the she-herd doesn't get bored with her bit of time off during the break between clipping and turning out the tups in the autumn for the work to begin again...

ROGER'S COURTIN' ANGIE

Roger's courtin' Angie. He's a townee but a' right.
He'll chop mi kindlin' for me, then tek 'er out at night.

She'll 'ave what money I can leave, my farm an' Mother's too.
He's a worker is that Roger, what she gets he's welcome to.

She's not bad lookin', sees-ta, though she's forty now, or more;
But our Angela's an odd one, an' her temper's kind of raw.

So don't look for t'engagement in "Hatched, Matched an'
Dispatched";
It'll tek a damn good Roger to keep our Angie catch't.

BLACK DE CHAR

or: How Willy and Chris invented a new breed of sheep.

It was a hot day during clipping-time, and down at Bridge End Willy and his son Chris were easing off from their morning's work and looking forward to lunch. Our neighbour Jennie, who keeps rare breeds, stopped at the gate to chat. Among the newly clipped sheep was one that took her eye: its fleece was pearly grey – a delightful, soft smoky colour. Other than that it looked rather like a Swaledale.

Jennie took a long look, admiring its colour. Then she asked Chris what it was.

"It's a foreign 'un, a Black de Char," he said.

"It looks good," said Jennie, seduced by the French name – something similar to a Bleu du Maine or Rouge de l'Ouest perhaps? "How many have you got?"

58

"We just have the one, at the moment like," said Chris.

Willy added, "Mind you she's got twins and they're a tup and a gimmer, so we might breed a few more."

"What's the wool like?" Jennie asked, thinking of showing her discovery to the wool growers' co-operative she had just joined.

The men looked sideways at one another, and puffed at their cigarettes thoughtfully, waiting to see how Chris would respond.

"Come and feel it," said Chris, leading her down the dark and greasy shed to the heap of newly rolled fleeces.

"Lovely shade," said Jennie enthusiastically as she approached, envisaging sweaters, perhaps even a fine jacket, of that delicious pearly grey. She plunged her hand into the fleece he showed her.

"EURGH!" she said loudly. Her fingers came out smeared with black. "It's horrible! It's all gritty!"

Outside there were smothered noises – whether of merriment or of coughing, it was hard to tell.

The old Swaledale and her twins had been sleeping in the nice dry ashes of a bonfire.

STATION SNAPSHOTS

I live near a motorway service station, one that has – contrary to expectation – an excellent reputation and the framed certificates to prove it, plus a recent four part TV series.

We local yokels take it for granted that it will be open 24/7 apart from Christmas and New Year, and apart from its famous Farm Shop it offers occasional bizarre sights that add interest to our peaceful, cheery (insert platitudinous adjectives here) rural lives.

A trip across the petrol forecourt, specially on summer evenings, crosses the path of scantily clad personages (I really can't call them Ladies) wearing pink bunny rabbit ears, fishnet tights and cottonpuff tails. They stagger from coach to loos and back. My daughter tells me they are probably en route to Blackpool or Morecambe for a hen party. I feel sorry for poor Morecambe, but at least they won't be staying here to scream their drunken remarks – and that's just on the outward journey.

Another time, when I was driving peacefully homeward past the service exit, I encountered a kilted bag-piper heel-and-toeing along the grass verge with his pipe and drones in full voice.

Once I'd shaken myself and decided it wasn't an apparition, I approved his choice of rehearsal room – the open air. Mind, it was possible that his fellow passengers (or his employers) had forced him to remove himself there: confinement indoors with a set crying come-to-battle is a form of torture that even the deafened disco generation might find it hard to tolerate. Bagpipes are an outdoor instrument.

The arrival of winter was marked again this year by the lady and gent who walk a team of huskies. They always appear to be northbound. However, as I've never yet seen them wearing anything red or furry, I'm not sure whether they are Santa substitutes or merely heading for a UK version of the Iditarod.

RESERVE

Such friendly calves; their silky bodies breathed
black-and-white pedigree. A gentle, calm
and innocent pair. How could I sell
such charm?
Our dairy neighbour called on auction day
and looked them over with approving eye:
"If they don't make your set reserve,
I'll buy."
They dodged about the ring with lowered head,
confused as I.

The bidding stopped. And when
I should have said, "No,"
only one word, "No,"
I stood there dumb. And with the word unsaid
the auction hammer cracked on my reserve.

Our neighbour, and my husband, didn't salt
the wound. Accepting I had lost my nerve,
they both shrugged. But I knew it was my fault.

2001: UNDER THE SHADOW

A letter to friends in America during "Foot and Mouth" year 2001

It's raining as I look out of the window. Ponywise, 2001 hasn't been the most exciting year. Spring came late and in Cumbria we are still under the shadow of Foot and Mouth Disease. The "men in white suits" are a dread signal that the old "Cattle Murrain" has been found at work and the UK slaughter policy will have to be applied yet again.

I am lucky; I have no susceptible livestock of my own any more, just a dog, a cat and of course, a Fell pony; but we still have grassland being used by our neighbour for his sheep. We have to be careful about disinfection as we go about our business. A straw mat at the farm gate is doused daily with weak citric acid to disinfect wheels and hooves and boots. We don't go near cattle or sheep. The College where I work lost every animal on its home farm in March, has pressure washed every building it can and will demolish several more, has taken 4 inches of contaminated soil off some livestock areas for disposal elsewhere, and still does not know when it dare restock. Roads and lanes everywhere around here have dip baths and disinfectant mats for people's feet and vehicle wheels.

Our wagon's business is to deliver hay and straw to farms locally, and it's rusting away from its three-or-four-times-daily spraying-off with disinfectant under the chassis and wheel arches. My husband collects loads from Yorkshire or Durham, from "clean" farms without livestock or disease, and brings the hay or straw onto those farms in Cumbria which still have cattle but dare not turn them out from their winter housing. The fear is that they will graze grass which has been infected with the virus from nearby farms whose stock were either diagnosed and slaughtered, or were culled-out as possible contacts. People are right to be worried, because there are new cases appearing although there are now no sheep, when as the cattle are put out to graze, they develop the fever, foul hooves and ulcerated mouths and tongues of the disease, and the horrible cycle of diagnosis, slaughter, isolation and disinfection begins again.

Even in areas that are still free of disease, you need a Ministry licence to move livestock to fresh grass, or to the bull or the stallion. Farms with roads through them (and there are a lot) cannot move stock across the tarmac without a licence; the terms of granting such licences change week to week. A farm that needed to move stock across 15 feet of tarmac received a faxed set of instructions 17 feet long.

I quote the Fell Pony Society website: "We have many members who are livestock farmers in the infected areas. Several of them have already lost stock and others are likely to do so before the disease is halted. The sense of isolation, helplessness and despair can only be imagined. Often a lifetime's work is destroyed or, at the very least, a whole way of life is disrupted and put on hold." It isn't just the loss of stock. It's the loss of something to do with the day. Farmers say they have no reason to get up in the morning. Maybe it's a little easier for the Fell pony breeder who has at least his herd to tend.

Ponies out on the fell have to stay there, unless you can get a licence to move them. Yearling and two year old fillies are still out in allotments with colts who would normally have been brought in and gelded. Licences have to be obtained even to bring feeding stuffs from one "D notice area" to another, even though there may be a lot of silage lying unused because there are no animals there to eat it, and even though other animals are about to starve if the farm doesn't have something delivered in the next 24 hours.

There are questions to ask of the Ministry. Can you get them to answer? Will you have to contact another office because your animals or feeds are in a different county? Will that office answer the phone? Can you get a licence to take a mare to the stallion? How long will the paperwork take? What precautions must be taken? On culled-out farms there's still disinfection to handle, which is very rigorous; there is the question of what can be done with the land that would normally feed sheep or cattle - can hay be made? Or will it have to be silage, whose acidity is said to kill off the F&M virus if it's present on the grass? Who will buy grass off a farm that's been infected? Who will move it for you? Who will need to be present to ensure it is done correctly? How do you arrange for it all to be done? There are new and vital organisations developing to help farmers deal with not only this paperwork but the planning of what they can do to minimise their financial problems while they cannot sell stock, and what direction their farms should take in the next few years.

We've just had a General Election and the same political party is back in power for another 5 year term. Rumours and accusations flew around here during the run-up to the polls, mainly about oddities concerning Foot and Mouth. I won't repeat them here because they sound very stupid when lumped together, but I have a file of over a dozen that I have heard, the last of them being that the Ministry of Agriculture is planning to slaughter all the animals in Cumbria's infected areas as soon as the new Government is elected. This one has been very strongly refuted both in the newspapers and on the Ministry website so it must have been spoken pretty loudly. A more plausible suggestion is that all cattle within areas where sheep had been culled as possible infectious contacts were to be blood tested and if found to be positive for the disease, then slaughtered; but even this one hasn't been confirmed.

You can see from this how uncertain life is. One day you can walk a footpath; the next it's closed. Many of the fell areas are out of bounds; this weekend (9th June) some were reopened; some were announced as open then closed hurriedly because of a fresh outbreak of disease. A local farmers' market is announced as restarting; but today it's cancelled because farms within a few miles of the village have been confirmed with Foot and Mouth just two days ago. Movement licences that have been issued for stock one week are rescinded the next, if F&M appears to be reviving.

We no longer have the immense funeral pyres that were such a dreadful feature of the landscape in March and April, but the huge burials of animals continue at the airfield outside Carlisle. We sniff the air suspiciously in Penrith in a morning - is that sickly stink the protein reprocessing plant missing its clean-air target again, or is it from the burials in that quarry four miles upwind?

Tourist visitor numbers are, not surprisingly, heavily affected, and with them the takings from tourism. Cumbria is a walking and climbing area for many people but they are reluctant to come when their recreation areas are out of bounds. Day trippers in coaches may still pass through but if they don't stop they don't eat, stay the night or leave any money behind!

Of course – and almost as an afterthought – there are very few equestrian events. Every summer show I would normally attend as spectator, judge or driving competitor has been cancelled. In March our North West Driving Club cancelled all its events up to September; when disease outbreaks seemed well on the way to zero again it optimistically announced a resumption of some events including one for today (9th June) but it says a lot about the continuing caution of our membership that only one competitor out of 13 actually turned up.

People have said that living in Cumbria this spring is like living in a war zone. You just don't know where the enemy will turn up next, and you can't see him coming. Your neighbour may bring him on his breath, his boots, the muck under the Land Rover wheel arches. Some farmers are, shall we say, "less than careful". Some don't seem to put two and two together.

One farm only a few miles from here, that had been diagnosed with F&M an hour and a half previously, allowed a milk tanker in to collect its milk. That went on to another three clean local farms before an official realised what had happened and got a message through to stop the driver going any further on his daily round. Luckily milk tankers have a virus filter on their air system, so no harm was done; but bulk feed "blower" wagons, for example, have no virus traps and have been implicated in spreading the disease from infected farms to previously clean ones. Now, vets are being sent to ride-in with milk and feed wagons and with the rural postmen to assess whether they could be a source of the disease spreading.

There is a very strong feeling that the Ministry of Agriculture, and even the vets, are becoming the enemy as well. A newly qualified woman vet diagnosed the disease in a farm's cattle and is reported to have exclaimed to the stricken farmer: "This is so exciting for me! It's the first time I've seen Foot and Mouth!" Stories abound of official high-handedness: animals culled although they were perfectly healthy because of wrong map references being given to the slaughter team; cattle being rounded up by motorbike and shot with rifles; cows attacking slaughter teams in berserk fury because their calves were being killed in front of their eyes. I am just surprised that I've only heard of one incident of a farmer resisting the slaughter teams with a shotgun.

Yet farmers have spoken also of the care and discipline of other teams. Slaughtermen wait while a farmer's wife defiantly feeds the pet lambs before they go onto the wagon to the mass burial site; they pat the farmer's shoulder consolingly when he breaks down and cannot bring in the last field of his sheep to be taken – then they have to go to complete the task themselves. Farmers' wives give flowers to the tired vets who have pronounced the death sentence on their family's livestock. The Brigadier in charge of the Army slaughter teams at Carlisle tells a young squaddie that he need not be ashamed of finding the relentless death-dealing "very upsetting, Sir".

What makes us angry where Foot and Mouth has hit hardest, is that there are people in other areas of the country, in cities and businesses, who simply have no awareness of what it has meant to us. Have you seen the advertisement on TV where Hewlett Packard show us a young lady working to bring TV programs to your mobile phone, so that two actor "climbers" in alpine conditions can weep over a soap opera? I saw it in May when it directly followed a very moving advertisement for the availability of the counselling and support charity, the Samaritans. That showed farmers whom I know, weeping over the loss of their livestock, over the fact that they no longer had any reason to get out of bed in a morning. I cannot begin to explain how angry I was that these anguished people had been so insulted by the TV company's utterly thoughtless advert scheduling.

Foot and Mouth seems to have been here forever. I almost feel guilty when I look around and see the healthy sheep and cattle in our local fields: I know how vulnerable they are. Every night as I drive home from Penrith where there are virtually none left, I give thanks when I come over the fell and see that our valley is still untouched and normal. People perhaps talk a little less about it than they did in March and April, but it's still like a dark cloud on our shoulder when we should be welcoming sunshine and new life to the farms.

But my daughter has just phoned to say that a farm two miles away has been confirmed with Foot and Mouth. They have stock all around us and their people drive through our side of the valley every day and past our farm…

Cumbria and Devon will not forget this year, not in a lifetime.

NORA FORTHRIGHT: A MONOLOGUE

Enter Nora: dressed in ragged waxed jacket, gent's trilby hat, wellies and waterproof leggings. She addresses an audience of agricultural college lecturers; herding them throughout with an (invisible) dog.

(Shep! Ga by! Git away bye yer daft dog. Oh well, mebbes yer right. It'd tek more than a daft dog like thee to pull this bunch into shape. Cum 'ere then, good dog. I said cum here!)

BY, what a flock ye've got 'ere Mr Scott. A right rough bunch o' tups. Evenin. I 'ope yer not enjoying yerselves - that's nut what I've called ye here for. Now ye may not know me. My name's Nora Forthright, an' I've cum 'ere fra Tebay 'cos I've heerd some vicious rumours, not to mention allegations, and I want some answers.

What I've heerd is that you clever buggers at Newton Rigg are planning to run courses in Droving. A National Vocational Qualification, a level 2 no less. In Droving? Is that reet? An NVQ in Drovin'? Whativver are things comin' to? Ah can hit cows wid a bit of alkathene and I can oppen gates fer sheep and I reckon up on't fell I need nowt in the way o' bits o' paper to say so. If't sheep land up in't reet spot, that's aw' t' qualification I need. An' if they dun't, it's me own daft fault.

(Cum here t'me Shep! Sit.... an' leave me leg alone. Good dog now. Settle thissel.)

Well, if ye reckon ye should be teachin' an NVQ in Drovin', aw you lecherers in smart ties and shirts, I'll tell ye summat even more useful that yer SHOULD be doin'. You should be running a degree course fer farmers' wives. Hast ivver thowt aboot that? A grand long course it'd be too. Ah can give yer a start right here. Ah hed ter mek a few notes like - an' here they are.

Now I's heerd that t'most important thing aboot a fancy coorse is gettin' t'name reet. So I reckon what ye'd caw this coorse wad be:

AGRICULTURAL ESPOUSAL SYSTEMS

Dun't that sound grand and smart? Frighten yon University lot to death, will that. Mind, I's nut clivver. Ah can't plan coorses, 'cept ter yell SUPPER when t'tractor stops at neet. So I'll hev ter gi' ye a job description and I reckon ye can work forrad fra theer. Awreet? Pin back yer lugs.

Farmer's Wife Required:

Wanted, for a small fell farm - one general fac-to-tum, dogsbody or slave.

Minimum physical requirements: She'll have to be fit - at least Gladiators standard,

she'll hev ter put up wid rain, wind, snow, frost and sun widout a change of clothes. (Mind, in't it hot in here? There's a gey queer smell too ....)

she has ter be able ter carry a standard bag of fert - or two bags of tatties. That's the minimum, remember.

CharACter: She'll have to be telepathic. That will mean she can predict what the boss wants so he dun't ha' to bother wi' formulating it into words. She'll hev to be prepared to work all hours, wi'out instruction, praise or reward.

She mustn't criticise what he does - although whativver she does, she'll have got it wrang.

This job involves putting up wi' ignorant behaviour, so all you college folk would manage just fine 'cos tha'd be used to the students. Tha'll get no information, no recognition, no affection, but there won't be a formal contract either, so t' boss wain't be responsible if tha cracks up.

Appearance: A farmer's wife must hev long legs, but she shouldn't show 'em off. They're on'y needed for climbing over gates or sheep, or running up't fell. She must 've no disabilities whatsoever, and not mind wearin' holey, dirty, smelly clothes and muddy boots most of the time, except when sellin' stock at auction. O' coorse if she tarts hersel up too much then, she'll be accused of carryin' on wid auctioneer.

Mental capacities: This could be yer stumblin' block fer a degree course, 'cos eddication of any sort is pointless, or so t'boss says. But maybe ye'd like to count how many things a farmer's wife has to know about:

> the Ministry of Agriculture, Fisheries and Foods, also known as DEFRA – Department for Excise,
> Frustrating and Ravaging of Agriculture that is;
> IACS forms,
> Sheep Annual Premium Scheme,
> Beef Special Premium Scheme,
> Suckler Cow Premium Scheme,
> Hill Livestock Compensatory Allowance Scheme and Environmentally Sensitive Area Scheme,
> auction companies,
> insurance claims,
> the vet,
> the NFU,
> VAT and
> Income Tax,
> the bank manager,
> reps,
> bad debtors,
> and dosing rates for every animal the boss happens to fancy keepin'.

I made that seventeen specialised subjects. (I've started and I'm finished.)

If a farmer's wife fails in any o' these areas she'll be criticised over mugs of tea between t' boss and his cronies; if she succeeds, it'll just be accepted by t' boss as his own achievement.

(Wheer's that daft dog? Shep! Shep! Cum here to me. Ugh, what have yer been rollin' in... geddown. Sit.)

Job specification. Naow then.

Sheep management: A farmer's wife has ter have the ability to raise sheep from the dead, and cure the blind, the halt and the lame. Her feeding speed wi' horned ewes has ter be pretty quick, else her legs must be made of stainless steel. Hes ter untie knotted string while wearin' gloves - essential for access to building's and aw fields. She needs double jointed hands and arms for bottle-feedin' pet lambs, and a double jointed back for clippin', dippin', trimmin' feet, etc. If she can turn watter into wine it'd be appreciAted, but the boss wad rather she could create lambin' pens from nowt.

Cattle management: She has to be able to calve cows widout assistance - or a cattle crush - worm 'em, dose 'em, inject 'em, or dodge 'em in inadequate pens, muck out every building that the boss can't get into wi't slurry scraper and then throw wet cow muck uphill in a Force nine gale. Oh and she mustn't complain when she's heavily kicked or trodden on and unable to walk widdoot a stick.

Forage handling: She must be able to push a round-bale by hersel, and lift little bales in any situation whether in blazin' sun or drownin' rain. She mustn't get altitude sickness on top of a wagonload of crop. T'boss wants her to throw OFF, not throw up.

Technical expertise: She'll be expected to learn in one sketchy session how to drive any tractor. Howivver, when there's a job to be done, t' boss'll be the one using the tractor and she'll be the one using t' wheelbarrow and gripe.

Domestic duties: She's expected to do all the cookin', firelightin' and coal carryin' (gas? What's gas?), pet feedin' (GET OFF ME LEG SHEP), tidyin' up (muckin' out), washin', ironin', cleanin', oh aye and decoratin'. There'll be a la'al bit o cash put away to provide aw this - but not a lot. (For God's sake siddown, dog.)

There'll be a car available, but it'll always be full o' hayseeds. Time that she spends shoppin' for groceries will be counted as time off. Any household and buildin' maintenance will be her

71

responsibility, but there'll be no cash at all for it if the boss considers HE could do the job himself, but he hasn't got the time.

If there ever should be enuff spare time in HER day, she'll be expected to take on self employed work such as envelope fillin' or bed and breakfast, so that she'll still be available at a moment's notice, and her income'll support the farm business, only t'boss won't notice.

Hours of work: wakin' to sleepin'. Half an hour allowed after doin' up in the morning, so she can prepare the mid-day meal. Half an hour allowed after bullockin' at night, to prepare the supper. Followed by washin' up, and then paperwork until bedtime.

At bedtime... well. I suppose Ah hev ter mention it. Advances IN bed, if she ivver gets theer before t'boss has fallen asleep, will be regarded as unwarrantable demands on HIS energy.

Wages: neether love nor money.

Sickness benefits: if she breaks a leg, she can have half-day off.

Holidays: t' boss dun't know what these are, so she won't be offered 'em.

An' the reason Ah know aw this, is that I's spent fifteen winters up on Tebay Fell learnin' it. A bit ower lang even fer a degree coourse, I wad think. Anyway, now that I's graduated, I's retiring to a less demanding position. I's away t' join t' SAS.

(Wad any of ye like a sheepdog? Shep? Shep! Put that lamb down! Shep... Shep...)

Exit

THE GRUMPY OLD WOMAN AND: THE WEIRDEST GREAT BUILDING COMPETITION

I've managed around fifty years of hiding my nasty streak, but gradually as the grey hairs have taken over I find they give me licence to be a battle-axe, to march in where Charlie's Angels fear to tread. So let me introduce my new Grumping campaign.

I thought at first, perhaps I should grump about odd-smelling Cumbrian towns. Penrith smells of chicken guts, Carlisle smells of biscuits. But I couldn't decide what Kendal smelt of (it's not mint cake) and I couldn't be bothered to trek over to Wukkinton to remind myself of its particular pong. Grumpy, yes; energetic, no. So, gravelled for lack of matter.

One thing I'm sort-of qualified to grump about, however, is public architecture, which I studied for A level Art. It's irrelevant that said A level was back in 1970; architecture goes back a lot further than that and it's public, all around us. It's just begging to be criticised.

The ideal Grumping target has to be large. I wouldn't want to bother with some feeble Legoland housing estate. I want a target that once thought itself imposing and arrogantly wonderful, and the impact will be greater if the object is reverently singled out for admiration in tourist brochures and web-sites.

So, for this one I'm going to the very top. My candidate is Carlisle Cathedral. "What," I hear you gasp, "you can't Grump about the House of God. Everybody knows that a Medieval Master Mason is now practically a saint." Well, I think if God exists he already knows how nasty I am so it won't come as a shock to him. For three years I worked next to the seat of his

Bishop and, sacrilege or no, I can tell you, an awful lot of that seat was built by cowboys, five hundred years and more of them, building in a hurry with one eye over the shoulder at the Scots side of the Border.

The Norman part of it was second-hand from the start, being composed of nicked bits of Roman fort. That's now represented only by a tiny, grey West end, because Cromwell – not being noted for his reverence towards Catholic foundations – put most of the Roman stone back into military use by nicking it a second time for army barracks.

As a result Carlisle Cathedral feels extremely weird. You enter the main church through the choir stalls, instead of a door into the nave – mainly because there isn't one. Then you pass under the rood screen, which normally separates the body of a church from its choir. The chancel should properly accommodate only the singers and clergy, but it's much bigger in all three dimensions than the nave, so the choir is where the congregation sits as well.

> Choir, Length 134 feet
> Choir, Breadth   72   feet
> Choir, Height 72   feet
> Nave, Length   39   feet
> Nave, Breadth 60   feet
> Nave, Height   65   feet
> Transepts, Length   124 feet
> Transepts, Breadth 28   feet
> Tower, Height 112 feet

Any well-brought-up Christian's internal compass will go haywire in here. It's an uncomfortable place altogether. It has an unfinished feeling. The 15th C choir stalls underneath the canopy are missing their lower finials, and hang there chopped-off at head height. Most of the niches stand empty of the wooden saints who should have populated them. Mind, you can't see the choir stalls when you attend a service, because when you face the altar they are behind you. Of course. Silly me.

Sitting there, other weird things begin to creep into your attention. For instance, what is the surreal arithmetic of the arches underpinning the sandstone clerestory? As a foundation for the upper storey the arcade must have been built before the clerestory above it. Why, for Heaven's sake, does it consist of three *and a half* arches with seven above? Why not four complete arches with eight windows above? Did they cut back the length just to meet that marvellous window in the end wall? The real weirdness is that these things are not altered, worn out or damaged, but incomplete – visually wrong – by design.

I can forgive any idiosyncrasies due to the activities of Scots or Puritans; after all, it was fire and war that reduced Carlisle to the smallest Cathedral in Europe (until the building of the Cathedral of the Isles in the 1850s). I can forgive changes of fashion, because most English cathedrals have lived through several styles, the changes occurring later the further north you travel. I can forgive rebuilding that was needed due to dilapidation: the action of wind and rain has had a disastrous impact on the soft red sandstone, and the rich, delicate, hollow carvings, so the saints whom Cromwell didn't knock about have to stare at visitors through safety netting. But this interior is mad.

Stagger out with me to look at the exterior, which if anything is even more dizzy.

Between the buttresses that support the walls, you find there are windows – of a sort – charmingly Early English in style but Viking in their unpredictability. Sometimes there are three, and sometimes two; and sometimes two huddle aside apologetically in a space meant for three. Sometimes they are defined by pretty mini-pillars and sometimes by a remnant of mini-pillars which, again, you can't make up your mind about: was there ever a lower part to them, that perhaps has eroded to nothing, or were they always just tops, unsupported? And we have further peculiar half-arches, where, although complete sets of mouldings outline some of the lancets, elsewhere blank halves disappear into the adjoining buttresses. "I'd like some arches please, Master Mason, but don't make them too ordinary." "Right-o, I'll build you something that looks half-arched."

Whatever Carlisle Cathedral is, it isn't ordinary.

Some of it is genuinely beautiful. Honest, reverent devotion was combined with an extreme skill and understanding of geometric harmony to create the curving tracery of that East window and the dazzling azure vault studded with golden stars. But war, bigotry, and erosion have made the rest into a space that doesn't know which way to direct you, while schizophrenia appears to have built the rest. No matter how kind you were feeling before you went in, you come out feeling ruffled and disturbed – possibly even as grumpy as me.

As an exercise in forcing you to define normality by showing you the bizarre, perhaps it succeeds. I don't think that was its intention, but it's undoubtedly the weirdest building in Cumbria. Get out of that one, God.

THE GRUMPY OLD WOMAN AND: TALL FOOD

We are not great eaters-out, the pub at Shap being the height of our ambition, and at the time of writing it doesn't stoop to any of the mean tricks I'm about to describe. Our unadventurousness means that the esoteric specialities offered at shockingly high prices to the London gastronome had, until recently, escaped my notice.

But during my daughter's seven-month stay with us, with our new grand-daughter, our mealtime habits have changed. Where we used to listen thoughtfully to Radio Four, we have had to compromise with the chewing-gum-for-the-eyes that is presented on TV over the supper-time period. This isn't because daughter is particularly lowbrow or we particularly highbrow. The fact is that the needs of the baby at that time of day tend to make her rather vocal, which means that the thread of a radio story, or a nuance of comic timing, will come off a very bad second to her demands. So we have perforce become visual rather than aural consumers of the broadcast media at mealtimes.

However, as a newcomer to the early evening TV time slot I've been very surprised by how many foodie programs are put out. Despite being fully occupied in my own kitchen around that time, I'm constantly made aware of how fashionable food is, and how vital is its presentation. Inconvenient plates of vast acreage are placed lovingly before the foodie, bearing an array of edibles garnered from all corners of the globe. Sorry, I know globes don't have corners, but the plates often do.

I admit that many of these arrays look delightful, and as tastyvision and smellyvision have yet to reach us, their colours are everything. So colours we are given, along with facial and vocal expressions of delight from the people who actually get to touch-smell-taste the products of the many celebrity cooks. What piques me, though – and piques me even more when I am just occasionally out there, dressed up and paying for it – is the excess of presentation that food seems to need, as evidenced by the catering profession.

I did applaud one well known foodie person on TV disparaging a wannabe chef for producing "tall food". Not only is it so 1990, but a plate a foot wide with a tower of tiny edibles tottering in the middle is a waste of effort on everyone's part – chef and customer alike. Chef spends time assembling the edifice, waiter has to move like a ballet dancer from pass to table, while customer has to calculate how he can safely eat without the whole thing collapsing into his neighbour's lap. I have to say that the critic, for once, got my applause. I don't want to puzzle out how to deconstruct *le gros bonnet*'s presentation. Stick it all on a plate – prettily if you must – and just let me eat it.

Then there are drizzles. Irritating, dreary and wet. I don't want anyone to drizzle on my grub for me, thanks; whether with olive oil, mayonnaise, tomato purée, green-pea purée or greasy-spoon brown sauce. Give me the choice of doing it for myself.

"Coulis" are snob's blobs, smudged artistically into a plate with the back of a spoon. Squiggles or stripes of sauce look like punctuation marks around a central noun of food. If you really are offering me a nice sauce to complement your dish, give me enough of it to let me pick it up and eat it. I suspect this drizzle-smudge-squiggle-dot school of presentation is no more than a cheap cheat. It offers me "food" in such a stingy way that I couldn't even slide a palette knife under it. If I want *not* to eat food, I won't put it on my plate in the first place. Don't ask me to pay for it just because it has been pretentiously painted onto a bit of porcelain.

And puddings (as opposed to desserts). A proper pudding needs a pudding dish. Pudding dishes are designed bowl-shaped so you can get your spoon into the duff and eat it, sumptuously, down to the last puddle. They are meant to cradle juices or sauces in their sensous curves, to be scooped up and savoured at the end of a delicious experience. Serving a pudding on a flat plate defeats that satisfaction. Again, you're giving the waiter no chance; how's he supposed to control custard when it wants to flood over the edge every time he changes direction?

Finally, there's a pointless tendency in fashionable eateries to present you with a miserable little spot of pud surrounded by, not even drizzles, but dustings of cocoa powder or icing sugar. If the drizzle-smudge-squiggle-dot is mean, this miserly dusting is just plain pointless. You can't *eat* such culinary daftness because it is impossible to pick any of it up, not unless you lick your finger, wipe the plate with it and suck it.

Join me in exorcising this ghostly pretence at food. When your pudding is eaten and coffee is imminent, the proprietor, chef and/or waiter will be unctuously hovering, all-but prompting you to say that everything you ate was simply lovely. Don't be swayed by their desire to be praised as well as paid. This is your cue to sigh ostentatiously – if necessary, several times – and then say loudly and with deep regret, "I do wish you had washed the plates."

THE GRUMPY OLD WOMAN AND: VEGETARIANISM

Lingering over breakfast this morning I noticed that the butter packet I had just opened carried the words "Suitable for Vegetarians".

This puzzled me. Since when has butter, a product made from the milk of cows, been a vegetarian option? By no stretch of the imagination can you call a cow a vegetable. So how can butter be vegetarian? (Go away with your silly definitions and versions, lacto-vegetarian, ovo-vegetarian and the like.) To call yourself a vegetarian, strictly you should be eating only PLANT material. This particular stance has become known as "vegan". But the other, longer names are really an excuse to put a fancy label on a personal appetite.

I understand that some people do not like the taste of meat. I know that people's opinions on what is acceptable as human food can vary wildly, and principle can make people feel they should not eat anything sentient. Our own farm-reared children, though they have sometimes asked "who" they were eating, have then happily carried on with their stew or chops. At work I have taken part in a lunchtime discussion that ranged from one person's dislike of the texture and flavour of meat, to whether a second person would really eat witchetty grubs, to a third's question about whether, if stranded in an air crash with no food, one should eat the babies first while they are still nice and fat.

I do understand that to the people for whom the idea of eating meat provokes the same reaction as eating babies, being vegetarian is the only option.

What I don't understand is how the logic of the philosophy gets applied so differently by different individuals. As an example: I will often take the "veggie option" in a canteen. That choice only makes me a person who prefers not to eat re-heated sliced meat; it doesn't make me a vegetarian. But I have met self-styled vegetarians who say, "they don't eat meat" but when you watch them, do eat fish; and others who say, "they don't eat meat" but who do eat cheese and milk and butter and eggs; I even knew one who ate chicken. That is not being vegetarian – that's just being picky. Super-picky was the bloke who was veggie but got cross because the canteen offered him dishes made of cheese or tomatoes.

Fortunately, most humans instinctively behave as they are designed, as omnivores – albeit greedy ones who are inclined to eat too many things they shouldn't.

Often, vegetarians will cite humanity's cruelty and exploitation in keeping animals to kill for meat, as the reason for their own dietary choices. There is sometimes an implication, because of that accusation of cruelty, that if one is not vegetarian one is barbaric. But it may be more honest to admit that here in the West, vegetarianism is a personal indulgence.

I suspect most of the people who tell me they are vegetarians have never worked on a farm or met a live cow or indeed any animal larger than a pet dog. I would put money on them never having been nearer to an abattoir than their television screen.

Leaving aside the urban perceptions of a farm as either a totally inhuman meat-or-grain factory or an incompetent muck-and-smell factory, the lack of logic in vegetarianism confounds me.

Here we are in a small island supporting more than 60 million people. Arable land, what there is left of it, has its limitations for food production, while large orchards and high volume fruit, cereal and vegetable production need kind climates. Due to climate change and careful plant-breeding we are seeing maize being grown successfully on a large scale in Britain (ironically for the vegetarian argument, in strains designed mainly for cattle consumption), but in the higher northern and western regions fruits, cereals and vegetables will regularly get flattened by our cold rain and wind. The only edible thing that these hilly and wet areas can do superbly well is to grow that ultimate survivor: grass.

Now, as humans can't eat grass, we need to process it. We do this through the animals that thrive on grass. Cattle eat grass; we eat cattle. This is a simple food chain that schoolchildren at Key Stages two and three are expected to understand.

So. Let's imagine a Great Britain populated entirely by vegetarians, who have been persuaded en masse to adopt it as a national ethos, while all the recidivist meat-eating villains have either been eliminated or have been reduced to living in scraps of relict woodland, competing with the foxes for a rabbit or two.

As GB will have legislated that animals should not be eaten, there is no point in anyone keeping cows, sheep, deer or pigs; neither will they farm salmon or any other fish, nor ducks or hens (to say nothing of the ostriches). The lacto-vegetarians might perhaps have argued to keep the dairy herd for butter, cheese and milk, but the trouble is that these foods are only obtainable as by-products of the cows having calves; the financial burden of keeping bull calves only to look at soon shot the dairy herd option down in flames. Therefore the veggie Briton would not be able to buy milk, butter, cheese, or eggs, and in fact has no access to protein of any kind other than that found in vegetables or fungi. I seriously doubt if there is enough land available in these islands to grow protein for 60 million vegetarians, even though all farms not growing hazel nuts would have had to go under the plough for cereals, peas and beans, because it isn't warm enough for soya. Yet.

So the only domestic animals would be those kept as curiosities in zoos. Where the rest of the population of dairy and beef cows would have gone I leave to your imagination; you can decide, too, where the hens and the sheep flock of over 35 million would have had to go. I have no idea what the tens of millions of obligate carnivore pets would live on. Black-market beef, chicken, ham, eggs and cheese? For a while anyway! Wholesale vegetarianism doesn't seem likely to do a lot for the animals, after all, does it?

Leather artifacts such as shoes, and woollen clothes of any kind, and duck- or goose-down duvets, would become museum pieces. Everyone would wear cotton, linen or synthetics, and be cold in winter. Greenhouse gas levels would be – er – inflated – by the methane production from 60 million sprouts-and-beans consumers, though perhaps the extinction of the dairy herds would balance that. Gardens and the remaining farms would have to be fertilised solely by inorganics from the bag, or the sludge from sewage farms, because the natural cycle of manuring the crops with animal muck would have been broken. Firms might make millions selling artificial fertilisers, but the Soil Association would soon have to give up; they simply haven't a chance of maintaining organic food production without animal inputs.

And I bet you that, almost all the time, vegetarian Britons would actually choose to live off the greater variety of imported foodstuffs that could not be grown here, the produce of warmer climates: soy beans, tomatoes, peppers, squashes, avocados, pineapples, and rice, rather than cabbages, swedes, turnips and potatoes.

Are we happy to wait for climate change to bring drought-loving species into British cultivation?

In the meantime, have a nice plate of grass.

THE GRUMPY OLD WOMAN AND: GOODBYE MR NICE GUY

I used to feel that I knew a lot of nice young men. Most of those with whom I trained at college were lovely blokes. I met one of them again recently and the encounter supported my guess that most of them got married shortly after they found their feet in the workplace and are still married to the lass they chose or were chosen by. But the older I get the more I wonder: where have all the nice young men gone?

That isn't a yearning plea for lost youth and missed opportunities. I still consider my husband to be amongst those who are nice, and am glad that he manages to remain so despite much provocation on my part. He regularly updates his mocking-stock of self-adulatory phrases from ads on TV; while his basic mantra of "Loveliness is Me-shaped" continues to be trotted out just as regularly as it has been ever since we wed, he has recently decided to be both a L'Oreal male ("because I'm worth it"), and a human Jaguar ("gorgeous is effortless"). Age, he tells me, has only added to his personal distinction. By contrast he disparages my figure in robust terms, except under certain conditions that I'm not silly enough to discuss in public. When I tell him firmly to shut up and get on with peeling those parsnips he just grins. And I hide a smile.

I can leave him to his DIY work while I sit at the computer typing for hours on end, or I can read, and steal fruit and nuts from his weekly selection, while he watches football, and with a liberal use of the phrase, "Yes, dear," he and I seem to rub along just fine. We have done so for over 40 years – give or take a year off for bad behaviour.

However, during that give or take period, Graham and I actually got divorced before deciding that we really were better suited to each other than to anyone else. In the interim I did quite a lot of personal research into the state of the middle-aged, self-styled Nice Guy. There were reasonable numbers of them about if you knew which stones to turn over. Mainly they were recovering from divorce, though I also discovered one or two still-married shits who were deservedly on the way to that condition. Some were ordinary and nice looking, most were ordinary and nothing to write home about. One or two were downright ugly, and perhaps because of that they were lovely men who were kind and helpful, funny and self-deprecating and genuinely good to be with. Their tactful disappearance on my remarriage still makes me vaguely sad, but I would not embarrass them now by trying to get back in touch nor by putting their names in print here. I hope that each has found someone good to share that funniness and kindness: whoever she is, they certainly deserve her and she doesn't need to know anything about me. But consider yourselves thanked, boys, for being friends; for being nice.

I hear you asking, gentle reader, "Why are you fretting about the state of the gender Male, if you have been happily married (albeit with a hiccup) for so long?" Well, Graham and I have a daughter, and all the men she has told me about during her courting years seem to have suffered a personality arrest somewhere in late adolescence. The thirty-something males of her acquaintance are, she says, feckless, selfish, possessive, immature, self-pitying, controlling, violent, or criminal. The only adolescent self-indulgences they don't seem to display are alcohol or drugs. And perhaps I don't see that because I don't spend much time in their company.

It might seem reasonable to put Jen's attraction of dead-heads down to some failure on our part. (It's always a parent's fault. Motherhood has "guilt" written on the reverse.) Had I omitted to point out her father's sterling qualities to her? or had she perhaps became deaf, from an overdose of his mocking self-praise? But there's plenty of evidence that Jen's girl friends have also been coupled to dreadful men, who seem to crave a woman barely out of her teens, preferably without ideas of her own. They treat their children as trophy possessions, and the responsibilities of partner and parent appear to be entirely foreign to them. When I listen to the tales the girls tell and through them see the posturings of the young males, I am irresistibly reminded of Attenborough's nature programmes, recording the behaviour of a tribe of macaques or chimpanzees. Maybe it's something in the water round here. It's just a shame they weren't born with a prehensile tail or two heads, as a visible statement of their peculiarities.

Yet, among the twenty-somethings whom I taught at the University, the nice did outnumber the awful by about four to one. Jen did finally manage to meet someone who is both grown-up AND intelligent, and they've been married for ages now and have two sons. But why are her friends having such a hard time, when this should be the best part of their lives, enjoying relationships and raising a family? The mothers of my own age, like centuries of Cumbrian women before them, have done a reasonable job in educating our daughters to be strong and independent women, but somewhere along the line we must have forgotten to pass on responsibility and self-assurance to our sons.

Perhaps my husband, in his retirement, should open a charm school for them.

CONTROL

He doesn't meet my eye.
She says, "He's shy."
He stays aloof from talk:
"He needs to work."

Her face is sore:
"I walked into the door."
She wears long sleeves.
She never did before.

*

I visit them at work.
He's dull and curt.
"Is that your bloody mother?"
"It's OK, Mum; don't bother."

"Where did you go today?
Did you shop alone?
Who've you been talking to?
Who's on the phone?"

*

She says, "I'm pregnant, Mum."
"You'd best come home."
She says she can't:
"He hates to sleep alone."

She's heavy, milky-mild.
"He wants this child.
Though early on he said
87

He wished it dead."

*

In hospital she fears
his angry arm;
under her pillow
the attack-alarm.

He punches the wall.
"Scared, that's all.
Illness makes him upset;
he sees a threat."

*

Penned with his parents
In their crowded home
she with the infant
loves it alone.

THE BABY AND THE BATH

I can hear you right now thinking that this is going to be one of two things: either a paedophile's prurient peep through a bathroom window or a grandmother's gooey cooings.

It isn't either really.

I am indeed a grandmother but, contrary to received wisdom, grandmotherhood is actually none of my doing so I don't require congratulations. My grand-daughter Naomi is fun, but her lively curiosity gets us too often into situations that remind me of all the things my body doesn't like doing any more. Small doses are as much as I can cheerfully take.

The central character in this piece is actually a horse; specifically my Fell mare, Ruby. In my experience Fells are very maternal. Even the males seem to like small children, and I'm not going to make the joke about them not being able to eat a whole one.

Ruby went to a show yesterday, and as per usual, my daughter Jen came to give her a bath a couple of days before. When the weather is dull and chilly, this is not usually an experience that horses enjoy. However, Jen set to and, since Naomi seemed determined to take part, she gave her a tiny brush and a mini bucket of soapy water, and let her get on with it.

Ruby's nostrils were crinkled with her disgust at being washed in cold water. She was just dying to swing about and squash Jen against the wall to get rid of her annoying attentions, just as she would whisk off a bloodsucking fly. Instead, she was rooted to the spot, only moving her eyes and ears. The reason? Out of the corner of her eye she could see Naomi, crouching fearlessly by her feet and rubbing them with her little brush. No matter how much Ruby hated being bathed, she would not move in case she hurt the little one.

You might assume that next time Ruby saw Naomi she'd snort with anxiety that the child's presence heralded a repeat. Not a bit of it. At the show yesterday, Naomi prattled and chuckled and played round Ruby's feet and the mare just followed her progress with soft, gentle eyes. In the ring Ruby was all snorting fire, all spirit, power and presence. But when we came back to the horsebox with our prize rosettes, Naomi demanded to be held up by Jen so she could give Ruby a proper cuddle. And damn it if that fiery mare didn't wrap her head and neck around the baby and cuddle her right back.

If you want to bathe a Fell, use a baby.

SELLING UP

In 1996 I hoped that we could cut down our responsibilities as livestock farmers. However, Graham was quite definite that as far as cutting down went, it was all or nothing. There was no room for any half measure. I had to admit that while there isn't quite as much time involved in feeding one cow as there is in feeding ten, you do still have to be on hand, dressed against cold, wet and cow muck, twice a day at suitable intervals. I knew I didn't want to talk myself back into a job that I was finding more and more physically difficult.

Once the decision was made, life seemed to become easier. Each task I undertook seemed simpler because no matter how demanding it was, I was now able to say, "No need to fret. This is for the last time. I will not have to do this again unless I choose to do so." As I struggled with a bereaved ewe who refused to take an orphan, patiently pushed a bewildered lamb into place under her, or refilled - for the third time that morning - the bucket of water which the fractious mother had knocked over in her trampling retreat from the adoptee, it was amazing how cheering this thought became.

We had hardly come to our decision to sell before BSE and CJD became the bogey letters of the year. Bovine Spongiform Encephalopathy or Mad Cow Disease, which had been a source of minor worry to the British farmer since the late 1980s, suddenly became of prime importance. On 22 March the Secretary of State for Health announced that a new strain of Creutzfeldt-Jakob Disease in humans had been identified. It was apparently so similar to BSE that the cattle disease could not be ruled out as responsible for CJD. Unhappily, though it is common for British Government Ministries to be cautious when making scientific statements, there was little other news that day and the subject received wide media attention.

Supermarkets, those fickle market watchers, instantly put up notices stating that all their beef was foreign. With dealer-butchers unable to sell UK beef to the supermarkets, prices at the marts crashed. Farmers then decided it wasn't worthwhile to take cattle to market. There were photographs of rows of empty mart pens with a total of two beasts entered for sale. Yet nobody really knew what to make of the "panic". Every person to whom I spoke, male or female, young or old, farmer or non-farmer, seemed to be far from panic and to believe firmly that it was all political, but, depending on the person to whom you spoke, the sources of this policy were either British incompetents or Euro Machiavellis - sometimes both.

I listened to people talk as I did my shopping, and never heard anyone say he or she was going to stop eating British beef, mainly because the one thing that had been publicised was that you were only (possibly) going to die from CJD if you had eaten half a tonne of poor quality beefburgers before 1989. The Great British Public's feeling about beef itself was definitely, defiantly, positive. When that feeling percolated through to the supermarkets, the initial rash of counter-side disclaimers disappeared, to be replaced by labels saying that the beef was from under 30 month old animals, these having been declared to be safe from BSE.

Posters and car stickers blossomed, some more telling than others: *British Beef not Euro Bull. Eat British Beef with confidence* (not one of the snappier efforts, probably cooked up in a Government kitchen). *They've been giving British Beef a roasting - now it's your turn* (in butchers' shops). *Europe Buries BSE with a JCB* (slogan at the Conservative Party Conference in autumn - a reference to the suspicion of farmers in the UK that our apparently higher incidence of BSE was due more to under-reporting in other EU countries than to higher numbers of infected cattle in Britain – a suspicion later confirmed by an investigative committee of British and European vets).

A slaughter scheme took shape and at one point the papers horrified us by saying that up to 4 million cows could be culled. The figure of 42,000 that eventually emerged seemed paltry, yet even this small selective cull program caused backlogs of designated cattle intended to be disposed of through the marts. Abattoirs were accused of exploiting the disruption for their own profit. The German EU Farm Commissioner Franz Fischler, welcoming the cull, also admitted that the European ban on beef imports from Britain was partly a political move designed to boost the failing German beef industry.

May turned to June. Although our grass did not seem to be growing under the busy teeth of the sheep and their offspring, the summer grazing at Raisbeck was apparently greening up at speed. John Burra pressed us to bring some cows before his own sheep flock was overwhelmed by sprouting herbage.

First we turned the cows out at home. Petal, Petal's Child, Bluebell, Hooky, Crooky, Curly and Lea and Perrins all went out in a procession of joyous hop-skip-and-jump antics. They rubbed their faces in the spring grass with sharp exclamations of delight. Petal had to boss her juniors all over again just to keep them in their place.

Hooky's bull calf, however, was a fixture in the calf pen. He was familiar with the fact that Mother had always gone out to drink, but as he had never ventured to follow her, he didn't believe outdoors existed, and the byre was where he was going to stay! Hooky rushed back from the field to find him, with a great deal of anxious mooing, but we still had to corner him and propel him bodily through the door after her. I thought the exposure to sunshine would instantly blow his brain – I remembered that Willy Kipling's newly-turned-out young beasts had galloped through a wall the previous spring - but surprisingly the calf didn't hurt himself in any way.

A week later we gathered the cows in the cool damp of dawn and set off to walk them to Raisbeck. Graham started the job off without giving anyone any instructions and was annoyed when no-one understood exactly what he had in mind. Jen and her then boyfriend came along to help and at one point we all got told off for being in their car following the herd while Graham was driving our own car in front. Quite what difference it made having us trudging along on foot behind them, we didn't make out then and still haven't. It was a shame having a grand morning spoiled but I reminded myself that each midsummer and autumn in future years I wouldn't need to walk five and a half miles in simmering frustration.

Once the cows were away at summer pasture, the demands on time and physical stamina dropped sharply. The weather improved, the days were longer. College work finished for the summer. I began cleaning the good harness to take the driving pony to shows on Saturdays. The weekends were usually followed by weighing lambs, to go to sales on Mondays, Tuesday evenings, and Wednesdays, and gradually the sheep dwindled from a blaring mob to a few peacefully grazing late lambers.

A wide horned Blackface, whose own lamb had died and whom I had had a struggle to persuade into adopting an orphan, was distraught when the orphan died also. She accepted a third in record time, which was a relief after the fights we'd had earlier. Fortunately number three seemed to thrive, and she went around cheerfully getting fat again after her ordeals.

On the other hand, we had to wait to see what would happen about BSE in cattle. Our cows and calves would not be for sale until October, and surely prices would have settled down by then? But the BSE debate rumbled on through the summer. Was it true that BSE had been transferred to cattle by greedy feed compounders mixing scrapie-infected sheep offal into cattle feed? Could BSE really be linked to CJD in humans? Would you catch it by eating beef? If so, why had long-term vegetarians died of the disease? Was BSE really the same as scrapie? If so, why had it only been found in cattle in the past two decades and not the preceding two centuries? Was it linked to organophosphates in warble-fly insecticides and in sheep dips, precipitating manganese poisoning? There were far too many questions and not enough believable answers.

Whatever the answers, the new regulations said that cattle over 30 months old could no longer be slaughtered for food. They had to be destroyed under a compensation scheme, which took a long time to begin, since the slaughterers and the auction marts had to be co-ordinated and payments arranged before any stock could be "processed". Farmers with animals over the permitted age found winter looming very bleakly. Just before the BSE scare broke a neighbour had speculated by buying up worn-out dairy cows to sell as fat beasts. Now they still had to be fed but could only be sold, at a fixed price, when the system allowed. With prices still low even for younger cattle there was going to be no profit for him this year - and in many cases farmers saw only loss.

Summer went by. Some of the cows at Raisbeck developed New Forest disease, a fungal infection of the cornea of the eye. Between Bill Potter and ourselves we had a joint herd of thirty-odd cattle on as many acres, and so a Greenholme veterinary posse (comprised of myself, Graham, David, Jen and current boyfriend, and Bill and his wife Isobel) took several hours to catch and treat them.

I was hobbling about on a badly sprained ankle, and Jen's boyfriend Chris, as a farmer, made an excellent forester. Still, the posse cornered the beasts and drove them into the cattleyard, and Perrins, "the biggest black bastard of them all", was eventually coerced into the crush. Her usual technique for preventing veterinary attention was to throw us off by thrashing her huge hindquarters about. This was foiled by the stout planking of the crush, so her treatment was punctuated instead by attempts to fling her head free of Graham's grip on her nostrils and lower jaw, followed by ferocious snorts of anger when she found this too was impossible. We squeezed ointment into her half-closed eye, and let her go, to meditate on the indignities she had suffered.

Another "black bastard", Crooky, had a lightning kicking ability, again foiled by the cattle crush. She had an ingrowing horn, which gave her the nickname. We needed to cut the tip of the horn off, and salve the sore it had made on her face, to keep off flies. With an ordinary rigid saw this would have been a nasty, dangerous and unpredictable job, but luckily Bill's brother had lent us a flexible wire saw. It had handles either end, on which you pulled alternately, and it made itself a groove and sank through the horn in no time. Crooky's cheek healed so well that within a week or two it was impossible to tell that it had ever been injured.

Perrins' eye had not been seriously infected, so she and Crooky could stay with the herd at Raisbeck. Curly and Petal's Child, however, had a more severe eye infection so each had to come home for a short time so that their eyes could be treated regularly.

In October we were given to understand that the UK beef industry was still being held down by the political fears of EEC member states. Yet it seemed that the cattle dealers had decided to ignore them, and at the early autumn sales the bidding was firm for healthy suckler cows and calves. Graham entered ours for a catalogued sale at Carlisle. That was it. They were going.

First of all they had to be walked home from Raisbeck. It was a dark overcast morning. We got up well before dawn and drove over to Tebay to rouse one of David's friends, Andrew, who had said he would help us to collect and move the cattle. He got into the car creaking and yawning and we drove to the field.

It looked at first as though all would go well. Our cows and calves were as usual lying in a small sub-group, a dark blob in the gloom, and well separated from the other beasts. We got them to their feet with care and walked them gently towards

96

the gate, but just as Andrew opened it, one of the calves broke back at a run, mooing. The cattle stopped, then turned to follow him, and we realised with sinking hearts that the calf was one of the other herd, who'd just realised that he was being abducted.

Things rapidly disintegrated from that point. The whole group by now was moving at a canter and we discovered as we panted up and down hill in their wake that the six-acre field in which we had assumed our cattle were shut was in fact open at the top into a further twelve-acre field – and that field was open into another twelve-acre – and that came down into the other six-acre in which we had caught the cows for veterinary treatment in August. We had to run just to keep them in sight, skirting bogs, jumping becks, shutting gates, feeling the long wet grass soak our socks, and unanimously swearing – when we had enough breath to do so.

We eventually managed to pen them in the cattle yard and, one and a half hours after our planned dawn departure, we sorted out the last calf, released the unwanted cattle back into the pasture, and persuaded our own bunch out onto the road to walk home. There was now a mountain bike rally trickling into Orton, and despite our fluorescent waistcoats and signalling the car-borne spectators behaved in an astonishingly foolish fashion. The best I can say about the whole exercise was that it didn't start to rain until we were nearly home, and at least I was the one driving the car. Andrew tried to keep things cheerful as far as Graham was concerned but David, reluctant from the start and constantly chivvied by Graham, sulked over the whole job and lagged so far behind us that we had all got home, put the cows into the field, and eaten breakfast before he arrived.

I tried not to be maudlin next day when I walked round the herd to check calf eartag numbers. The cows had munched their way through most of the available grass and were looking hopefully at me for hay. The late Henrietta's daughter Curly amiably pushed her white head at me to have her neck scratched. I felt a traitor. I was the one who had agitated for the cattle numbers to be reduced, but I didn't want Curly to go. Yet hard logic told me that she and all the others would find a good home, in fact probably better than ours. They had fine strong calves with them to prove their breeding ability. No-one was going to pay hard cash for cattle and then neglect them – were they? I concentrated on the eartags and reminded myself that it was going to be a long hard boring day waiting to go through the auction ring.

Chris Swift, one of the vets from Penrith, came to pregnancy diagnose the cows a couple of days before the sale. He made the usual cheerful comments but was taken aback to learn that we had, as he put it, "had enough" and that the herd was being dispersed. I felt guilty again. Perhaps I should reassure him that there would still be occasions when we would need his services, what with dogs, cat and pony.

On the sale day George Winder, our usual farmer-haulier, had arranged for a neighbour's articulated wagon to carry the entire herd as one to Rosehill. The artic wouldn't fit in our yard, so Martin, the driver, had to reverse up the public lane from Greenholme and let down his ramp two hundred yards from the farm gates. The postman, who delivered once a day, and the binmen, who collected once a fortnight, immediately materialised and required access. Martin just grinned at them and held his ground.

George and I meanwhile were walking across the fields to round up the cows, and with his son Timmy helping we drove them down the road to the waiting wagon. Chris Kipling had assisted Martin to block a gap alongside the ramp with a big metal gate.

Curly, never one to fear betrayal, placidly led the way up into the box. Once inside she turned round and, seeing that the Black Brigade were not following, ambled down again. Eventually we persuaded her, along with Petal, Petal's Child

98

and Bluebell, into the front partition. With rather more force and swearing we hustled the deeply suspicious Black Brigade into the second partition and slammed-up the ramp. The postman and binmen were by then nowhere to be seen.

The wagon set off and I hurried home to pick up purse and paperwork, then got into the car to follow.

As I drove up the motorway the radio news was full of scientific findings. Once again emphasis was placed on a probable link between BSE and the new strain of CJD. What a day to pick for the debate. I turned the radio off and started a cassette of classical music to calm my nerves.

Martin must have made good time, because I didn't catch him on the motorway and when I reached Rosehill he had already backed up to a dock and unloaded the cattle into their outdoor pens, 317 to 319 in Alley S. We spent a brisk half an hour pushing calves from one pen to another to join their mothers, but then it was a case of sitting and waiting for their turn to come.

The cows and calves didn't look nearly as good as they had before they were loaded. Their end-of-summer shine had vanished in a smear of grass-green muck. Some of the other vendors were washing their cows with dandy brushes and pails of water, but I couldn't see the Black Brigade allowing me to do that. I simply hoped that it would rain. Martin went off to clean out the wagon, and then to lunch in the cafe.

My next job was to deal with the paperwork. I had made arrangements earlier in the week to collect a new Cattle Identification Document for a calf which had lost an ear tag. I took the car into Carlisle, parking as close to the centre as I could and then walking to the Ministry, but the promised envelope was not waiting for me at the reception desk. A delay ensued while it was hunted out. When I opened it, a standard letter enclosed with the CID admonished me to make sure, next time, that I gave them sufficient notice to get the documentation through in time for a sale. As there wasn't going to be a Next Time, I rather enjoyed tearing this letter into two irresponsible halves.

I returned to the auction and put in the complete set of cattle documentation. In the quadrangle between the sale rings, I could hear the amplified voice of the auctioneer which confirmed that bidding was going fast and strong.

Lunch time approached. I bought a cheese bun and a piece of gingerbread from the cafe, and went in to sit on one of the wooden benches above the ring where I watched for a while to gauge trade. Selling had reached Pen 120. A man from south-west Scotland was selling cows with calves, followed by in-calf heifers. I reckoned from the catalogue that he sold a total of 75 females at a rough average of £800 apiece - £60,000 less commission. I wondered whether our eight beasts would average-out as well, 200 pens later.

I wandered outside after another half hour and went to the bank for some cash. Was it only coincidence which brought into my path the bank manager who had sanctioned our initial purchase of Daw Bank, thirteen years before? I suppose so, although I hadn't seen him in ten years. We smiled and exchanged brief platitudes. We were both too concerned with our day's purposes to talk properly. I gathered my cash and looked at my watch. By then it was half past two.

I crossed over the road to the WCF store and bought Graham some new jeans. The store was quiet and the female staff were talking by phone to a young manager in one of the other branches, giving him mild insults and "a bit of grief" to cheer the day along. I fell into conversation and then wished I hadn't, as the assistant recalled for me the sale of her favourite young bull and how heartbroken she had been when he went. I hurried through the purchasing with my head held high, dangerously close to tears, cross with myself for being foolish. Maudlin. Sentimental. Outside it was raining, big heavy concealing drops.

I sat in the car for an hour or more, reading a novel, listening with half an ear to the classical tape, watching the day clear to extremely warm sunshine, break again to thunderous rain, then compromise on a muggy greyness which matched my mood perfectly. Bored and nervous by turns, I constantly imagined that the cows had been sent through the ring without me knowing, so I kept going round restlessly and checking, although I knew from experience that there was no likelihood of Pen 317 passing through until gone six in the evening. I wished I had brought some hay for them. It was small consolation to see that only one other farmer had given his beasts anything.

I rang home and David answered. I told him I wouldn't be home for tea, and to make something for himself and Graham. I didn't feel at all hungry myself; I'd done nothing.

I returned to the sale ring and sat again, alone, quietly watching. The auctioneers wore white coats over their shirtsleeves and ties, like some kind of bizarre medical staff. Among the crowd I saw only one or two people whom I knew, and the rest were anonymous men, not the friends they might have been at more local auctions, only a parade of mud coloured clothing, unkempt hair, dirty hats, and expressionless faces intent on the cattle passing through. One couple, a thirtyish man and a twentyish woman, sat on the top row of the seats, with their hands and legs touching, more brightly dressed, cheerful and relaxed than the rest, but still focused on the action in the ring.

I tried keeping records of prices to pass the time. Cattle of similar type to the Black Brigade were selling well. Big black Hereford crosses were also in demand. I wondered how little red Curly and Friesian-type Bluebell would be looked upon.

There was a lad slouching after the cattle round the ring, left right, left right, smacking the unprotected bones of their pelvises in unrelenting rhythm with a length of alkathene pipe. He hit them so hard that I got annoyed after a while, and made

101

up my mind that I would threaten him with my own stick if he was still working like this when our cattle went through.

After an hour another boy took over who was a better stockman, not needing to hit to keep the cows moving, so I relaxed. An hour later, the first lad was back on duty and I prickled once more, until I observed that when a woman came into the ring to sell stock, the alkathene pipe was less in evidence. Something must have been said about female sensitivities. Maybe I would not need to get my dander up after all.

Now the auctioneers had a changeover too. The new man was sharp and set optimistic starting points for the bidding so that prices began to rise a little.

I saw that outside, it had gone dark. The mart lights shone on wet concrete and stippled puddles.

A bunch of Herefords was catalogued and I waited for them to appear. However, when the next lot came into the ring, I suddenly realised that the vendor's pen number was ten further on from the one I had been expecting. Clearly, many farmers had looked at the late ballot numbers their stock had been given and had decided not to come, so the tail end of the sale was going on much faster than the beginning and middle.

I grabbed a few pound coins from my purse and went out quickly to shove my bag, catalogue and paper into the car. It was dark and still raining. The quickest route to the pens was always to run through the patches of light and shadow round the outside of the mart, but by the time I had found alley S, and pen 317, my worst fears had been realised. There were no cattle to be seen, no Curly with her kind white face, no piebald Petal, no Black Brigade. I ran down the alleys, my long waterproof coat flying out behind me like Dracula's cape. To have waited seven hours and missed my cattle being sold! What a fool!

The stock men hailed me, still easy tempered, despite nearing the end of a long day. "Millard, is it? Here y'are." A white slip of paper with our name and pen numbers which they had been going to pass to the auctioneer for me. An experienced bunch, wryly amused, not condemning.

They let me into the system, and gave me a hand to sort out the calves in each group as it reached the ring. I barely had time to think - handing in my entry form, giving the auctioneer assurance that the cows were PD'ed in calf, then popping back from the ring to the holding pen, sorting, dodging, calling out, "Yes, this calf - this one!" and back again into the ring. I didn't have a chance to confront the lad with the alkathene pipe.

I registered the prices, but I didn't think, at the time, about precisely how the herd was being split up.

Outside the ring once more, among the bidders and spectators, I was accosted by all the buyers. I had never been asked for luck money at Carlisle before, so my cluster of pound coins proved embarrassingly small. Two buyers were experienced dealers and one of them had bought five of the cows. When I could only offer him my remaining three coins I got a loud, only half amused telling-off. I promised him that I would draw some more cash from the mart office against the sale cheque, and went off to do so. The mart clerk was used to such requests. "You've got to keep the buggers happy," he said. I found the dealer and held out my handful of coins. "Here you are, something to keep the others company!" I said. He was placated. Why did I bother? I will probably never sell another cow.

The cheque, when its details came through to the office computer ten minutes later, was satisfactory. I held it in a death grip all the way round to the car, where I put it in the paying-in book ready for the following day. Then I drank the remainder of my flask of coffee, tidied up the car, and set off home.

The traffic was light. I slipped into the shimmering convoys of the motorway, settled more comfortably in my seat, and reached for the radio switch. 24 October 1996, 7.08 pm, just into the first few minutes of The Archers.

Well, it hadn't been so bad. A long day, rather like a war - mostly very boring, with tactical skirmishes and bursts of sudden excitement. It seemed that most of the cows were going together, although to dealers, while Crooky had found a home with a farmer moving into a new farm. I had matched the ear tag numbers on the CIDs all right. I had sold the right cattle with the right calves. The prices had been good enough - averaging £660 a head. Now Petal and her Child, Bluebell, Lea, Perrins, Hooky, Crooky and Curly were gone. It was all over. I should forget them and listen to The Archers.

I had controlled myself throughout the day, in the face of the paperwork, the boredom, the coincidences, the worries, the pipe-wielding boy, the luck-hunting dealers and all the hectic activity of the sale. It was also the night the Grange Farm fire episode was broadcast, when the Grundy family lost their herd of cattle, and this single, totally fictional disaster broke down my hard-won composure. I wept all the way home.

The "beef ban" was finally lifted on 23rd November 1996.

DRUNKEN MICE

The mice had been out drinking.
Their tails wove in and out.
They staggered up the piping,
and slid off down the spout.

They reached the airing-cupboard
and nested in the sheets,
they peed upon the bedspreads,
on towels wiped their feets.

Then leaving several pellets
of shit upon shelves (upper)
they hiccuped, belched and farted
and went to look for supper,

for as you know when drinking,
though lager fills your belly,
it also makes you feel as though
you'd eat a docker's welly!

So gnashing sharp incisors
and scraping needled paws,
they set about a drunken search
to find that bedtime course.

And when I rose at seven,
and flicked electric power
to heat the flowing water
and take a nice hot shower,

I found the mice had feasted
behind the cupboard door.

They'd shredded paper wrappings
and dropped them on the floor:

they'd punctured all the toothpaste
and then to top their tope
they'd guzzled anti-frizz shampoo
and eaten half the soap.

Then finally, hung over,
they'd made themselves at home
and sprawling bloated fast asleep
were snoring shaving foam.

DUCK

She steps clumsily from grass to tarmac,
intent on the riverbank and its spring-given bounty,
trusting that ten yellow-brown striped ducklings
cluster behind. Still innocents in the world,
they pause, black eyes assessing a step forward,
small bills reaching, webs patting on gravel.

She knows no other way than leading.

From the blind bend the screeching white monster
scrapes black tracks of rubber, but can do no more
than brake, cannot avoid the brood.
Under its metal, into cold shadow she goes,
no warming down, no spread coverts for her,
cut off from light by grinding power.

When the sun comes back, she and her family
still fill the road. Determined, though bemused,
she heads for water. Nine ducklings
are still enough to tend, the journey no longer
or shorter than before.

Seeing the scattered feathers in the mirror,
I am the monster.

THE GRUMPY OLD WOMAN AND: HALLOWE'EN

Well, I thought I'd got all my grumpyness out, but as
October fades gently into autumn here it is again. People who

live in the Land of the Free (A.K.A. Uncle Sam's Home for the Strange) are exhorting me via their Internet communications to "Have a Happy Hallowe'en". From being mildly puzzled I am developing a full-on peeve about this. It's just not British.

In Northern English and Scottish tradition the end of October is Mischief Night. For one gloriously silly evening, children and youths could play pranks that on other nights would earn them a swift clip over the ear and a complaint the following day to their parents. Door knockers were tied together with string, black cotton stretched across streets to knock off people's hats, one man's wheelbarrow was mysteriously appropriated and filled with the potatoes of another then run down the street until it tumbled over in the front garden of a third. Signpost arms were turned round, gates removed from their hinges and hung from tree limbs.

Groups of silly maidens (and I was one, once) sat by candlelight or by smelly turnip lanterns and told each other ghost stories. We bobbed for apples with fortunes slipped into them, then cast nutshells and apple-peel over our shoulders to discover the initials of future husbands. To forecast our futures we used Tarot layouts or played endless games of patience. Occasionally we even surrounded a polished table that bore an alphabet and an upturned glass, and each placed a finger upon the glass in the unlikely belief that it would travel to letter after letter because the spirit of a dead person had been called upon to answer our questions.

Here's where the practices of Hallowe'en start to reflect its origins, and where I begin to become uneasy.

It began as a pagan celebration: the feast of Samhain, the endpoint of the annual sun cycle, the "night between the years", the end of summer and beginning of winter. As such it was a portal to the world of the dead, and a mythologically important day for magical occurrences of all kinds. The Christian Church sanitised it into a celebration of past lives and named 1st November as All Saints or All Hallows and therefore 31st

October is "The night before the Feast of All Hallows" which gave us Hallowmas, All Hallows' Eve, Hallow Eve or Even(ing), or Hallowe'en (with an apostrophe indicating that missing V).

Hallowe'en is emphatically not something you should wish someone to have a "happy" one of, unless you know them to be of the pagan persuasion. Tradition has it that on the Eve of All Saints, evil spirits are abroad. The Hoarstones on Pendle Hill are "ridden by the Devil." It is a night when the honest and decent should wrap up tightly by their firesides and pray all good angels to defend them against the powers of darkness.

With that in mind, I am uncomfortable when I walk through a daytime supermarket and see witches' hats on sale, along with vampire masks, cloaks and plastic broomsticks. Why should anyone buy trays of chocolate witches, with which to placate those juvenile Al Capones, the "trick-or-treaters" who will blackmail you on your own doorstep?

Get thee hence, Commerce. Do not make mock of the oldest fear of all; the fear of the departed dead.

THE GRUMPY OLD WOMAN AND: HOME RULE FOR CUMBRIA!

Ah's cu' yam frae trainin' wi' t' SAS wi' a few new ideas.

Hast ivver thowt on yon political gadgies? Whit a wazzock ye hevta be tae tek that job on! How diz a normal, red-blooded feller git t'idea he wants ter be a politician aw 'is life? Tellin' other folk how ter live their lives, when he knaws nowt?

Some on 'em in Parliament hevn't ivver done a stroke in their life. They cemm oot o' school and went intull a University an' learnt aboot Politics. Dista knaw, tha can pass University examin-ations wi forty per cent? That means tha didn't knaw sixty percent o' t'answers. Then tha went fer a job wi' a council or as a Parliamen-tary Ree-searcher. Or else tha read a few books on law an' went solicitin'.

Now sees-ta, ivverybody hates politicians. Ye'd think a feller wi' any brains wad tek yan leuk at a job as ivverybody hates, an' decide he isn' gonna dee it. He'd hev ter be a banana to try it. They cum green, they turn yeller, they hing aboot in bunches, an' they're nivver straight. But there's six hunderd an' fifty bananas hingin' aboot down at Westminster. We're payin' fer their second yam, an' poppies an' duck 'ulls an' sink plugs an' mucky videos, an' on top o' that we're lettin' 'em mek our laws!

Ah think it's high time we declared uni-lateral in-de-pendence.

Nora's Laws

1. Naebody as wants to be a politician will ivver be allowed to be yan.
2. Naebody will ivver be allowed t' mek policy if they ken nowt about farmin'.
3. Government busy-ness and legis-lation will be limited to that fine spell o' weather between t' end o' lambin' and start o' haytime.
4. T'Cumbrian Parliament will hevta move te a fresh spot ivvery year. Seascale, Cumwhitton, Ambleside, Barrow, Shap. SCABS. All proceedin's ter tek place standin' up, in't open air. Rain's warm enuff in May an' June, even MPs'll tek nae harm.

That way we can get at 'em an' tell 'em straight out what we think o' t' new ideas they're tryin' ter fetch in. If MPs on'y work six weeks in a year, then by, they'll hev ter crack on and tackle t'big stuff, as folk thowt mattered. Won't that keep a lot o' petty laws from ivver clutterin' up our lives?

An' we won't stand fer any nonsense about money nor second yams, eether. MPs can git a proper job for t'other forty-six weeks o't year an' then they won't need but the yan hoose.

5. Think on – t'whole o't country cud kick oot aa them windbags. An' then, Whitehall cud be turned into flats, Downin' Street into a Disney theme park, an' t'Houses o' Parliament, bein' handy for' t'river, cud be turned into a brewery.

THE GRUMPY OLD WOMAN AND: BLOODY DATABASES

I don't enjoy visiting medical establishments; I suspect few of us do. I am uncertain in the face of medical expertise; I am uncomfortable in the presence of the strangers in the waiting room; and despite replying to acquaintances' "How are ye doin'?" with "I'm fine, thanks" I am not physically on top form – after all, why else would I be there?

The nurse is calling a name from the other side of the central pillar. She doesn't raise her voice, she just repeats the name. By the time I realise she means me, she is thinking that "Christine Millard" is deaf, if not actually stupid. I put away my magazine and follow her into the little surgery to have my blood pressure checked. It's a six-monthly ritual that doesn't vary a lot, and the most annoying part of it is the response I get when I ask if my preferred first name could be noted on my records as "Susan", rather than "Christine".

For the first 4 years of my life I was Christine, until this turned out to be a very popular name at school enrolment and so to save confusion in class my parents changed to calling me by my second name, Susan. What my parents could not have foreseen was that the computer revolution of the late 20th century would compound my identity problems. Let me walk you through the usual exchanges in the surgery.

> Me: "Would you make a note that I'm called Susan, please?"
> Staff: "Yes, I see on the computer notes that you asked that last time."
> Me: "But you still called me Christine when you came for me."
> Staff: "When we open your record, the computer only shows Christine as your first name."

> Me: "I don't use my first name. My husband doesn't
> use his first name either. Nor do lots of my friends."
> Staff: "We do get a lot of people asking if we can
> change their records to show that they use their second
> name. But the database doesn't let us."

That's why, when I go to see a doctor or attend a clinic, I am always hailed by a name that is unfamiliar. Is it surprising that I don't respond and seem deaf or stupid? I arrive in the surgery feeling insulted and difficult, when we both ought to be doing our best to co-operate. However, it isn't the fault of medical staff that they don't customise their patients' records; they want to but they can't. They want simple interfaces: "I want to deal with people, not this ****** software!" is their cry. There is absolutely no reason why a database cannot be designed to store a patient's preferred form of address, no matter whether it's a first name, second name or nickname. Why didn't the NHS database designers think of adding such a field? or of the rewards in terms of efficiency, reassurance and goodwill between patients and staff?

It would even be refreshing to be addressed formally once again as "Mrs". But when I asked my doctor, she said the database doesn't even store patients' courtesy titles any more. Her colleague, to whom I am now allocated, said he'd tried to get the NHS database people to add the preferred-name feature, but they told him it couldn't be done. "And all that means," he said, making a note of my preferred name on his surgery PC, "is that they can't be arsed."

I've even had my legal signature queried on a surgical consent form because it didn't match my first name on the bloody database.

Eventually, one of the nursing staff dealt with it. She opened the database, replaced my first name with my middle name and vice versa, and the problem went away.

THE GRUMPY OLD WOMAN AND:
TRANSATLANTIC MARITAL
MEDITATION

I'd like to introduce you to four American women.

I have changed their names in case they should ever happen to read this piece. "Anna" and "Patti" are both in their sixties. These two are tall, straight, slender women of Irish descent, with reddish-blonde hair and freckled, faintly golden skin. Bespectacled "Dana" and "Vicky" are younger, in their fourth and fifth decades respectively; one has Italian antecedents, and the other German ones. By birth all four are Yankees, though they've actually lived all over the place, from Oregon to New York. Like me, they enjoy chatting via keyboard, on internet forums.

I often find it hard to separate Anna and Patti in my mind. Not only do they look alike but they are both horse breeders, carriage drivers and handywomen in wood, leather and other materials. Vicky, too, has bred horses and is heavily involved with equestrian charities. Dana is the odd one out, because although I met her via a common interest in horses, she no longer owns a horse, nor does she ride or breed them.

Since meeting them, I've discovered that all four were, as my mother would have said, "inoculated with a gramophone needle in childhood." I don't know if this is an American characteristic, but certainly all the Americans I have met can talk. They talk, and talk, and talk. And then they talk some more. You can't starve them or wear them down. The hungrier and tireder they are the more they babble. They only shut up when they are asleep, and even then they seem to have vivid dreams that they have to communicate as soon as they wake. I must be fond of them though – either that or I'm a masochist. I invite them to stay, and I accept their invitations to stay with them, though after 24 hours I find them terribly wearing. I wonder sometimes if they don't actually know what silence is.

They have a common addiction to coffee, from which they attempt to go cold turkey every now and again, by weaning themselves onto decaf for three weeks or so before going back to their drug. Maybe the emigrants from Britain and Europe were all inured to semi-starvation and that made them and their offspring over-sensitive to caffeine.

These women are helpful, keen to educate, friendly and knowledgeable. But their political opinions are powerful, even dogmatic. For three of them, Bush was their number-one target, the foolishness of the American voting public another, the war in Iraq a third, and a fourth was the worrying tendency of American Christian views to move toward fundamentalism. The fourth, Dana, until quite recently was a steadfast churchgoer, but she's wavering a bit, since she prefers to commune with people whom she respects, and her church doesn't command her respect right now. She shares the other three's disdain for politicians, but she questions, rather than making statements, so she prefers to start discussions rather than give instant answers. And although the other three are equally articulate, she is the one who gets paid for writing.

But Dana is also the odd one out because she's married. Anna, Patti and Vicky are now determinedly unmarried. Although they've all been married one or more times they have opted for remaining divorced. They are immensely energetic, apparently well capable of managing their lives and raising and educating children as well as horses, but by their own accounts the multiple husbands they chose were either control freaks or drunks. In all three cases, they gave their spouses ultimata: Reform or Get Out. And in all cases, these stern warnings strangely failed to produce any alteration in behaviour, so to the law courts they went, and divested themselves, serially, of their men. Someone once wrote that American women seek in their husbands the perfection that English women only expect in their butlers, so I sometimes wonder if the divorced American men sighed with relief.

Of the four I've listed, the one whose company is least wearing is Dana. We've shared some hysterical laughter at wacky activities like "photographing our Death scenarios" – Dana with her head in a cannon's mouth, me having mine pressed with an electric iron, or each throttling the other above a long drop at the summit of Kirkstone Pass. But what I appreciate about her is not the wackiness, but the ability she has to worry her way into the heart of things. She's done a lot of local journalism and can hit a deadline, in spite of which she is both a sensitive investigator and a truthful writer. Perhaps because she's younger, in the years I've known her I've seen her alter and grow up, from an airhead reformed pot-smoker to a thinking woman; and although she is as big a perfectionist in her way as the other three, she's a good deal less dogmatic. Agonising over The Right Thing to Do in family matters, she is the ultimate guilt-tripping Mother. She is the one who can most afford to have horses, but she has realised she doesn't actually want to build the life of her family around them, or to develop the force of character to manage them. And she no longer bothers with internet forums, preferring to negotiate the time zones via Google Talk to speak directly to just a few friends.

I don't have any authority to say whether Anna, Patti and Vicky are happier than Dana. I divorced my husband but I remarried him. I still have a horse, and I still write. I'm obviously sitting on whatever fence it is that divides their two positions. What I do know is that whenever I come across a husband and wife argument, it isn't Anna's or Patti's or Vicky's voice that I hear inside my head, insisting on what is Right; instead I hear Dana's single quiet question: "Which do you want to be: Right, or Married?"

116

GRANDMA'S CHIP

Second thoughts about food… Growing up in the 1950s.

I remember the face my mother pulled when she told one of her friends about the pan in Grandma's cupboard. Chin lifted, a line of distaste from mouth to jawline, she exclaimed, "Two pounds of solid lard. With a chip sticking out of it like a sinking ship. Ugh!"

Grandma and Grandad, my father's parents, lived next door, so once a week when my mother made the 90-minute trip to visit our Nanna my brother and I were shunted through the gate in the fence, from the garden of number 20, to number 22.

Grandma suffered from severe arthritis and really preferred us to stay out of the house, so on fine days we romped on rough grass under Grandad's relaxed eye while he earthed up potatoes, rubbed blackfly off the broad bean shoots, or used a brass push-action spray gun to treat the Dorothy Perkins rose for mildew.

We played Cowboys and Indians with "cap guns." Wikipedia tells me I must have lived through "the Golden Age of the cap gun." Whatever the mixture inside the caps was, it made a realistic crack and flash and a sharp smell. Sold as singles like miniature paper ravioli, or as rolls of individual charges, they came in a round penny-sized pressed-cardboard case. In contrast with the fiddly singles that had to be placed one by one between shots, rolls were satisfying because once installed, you could fire a fast sequence and get a really rich sniff of the smoke. The single caps very much curtailed both our gunsmoke and the amount of noise we made. I can guess, these days, which variety my mother preferred.

In between forays into the Indian country of the black-currant bushes, my brother and I practised the art of starting fires. We had read about the bow-drill method, but invariably the string broke before we had done more than wear the skin off our fingers. We discarded that technique for a magnifying glass and paper. Behold – a blinding point of light that scorched a trail and eventually produced a flame. Sometimes, if we'd gathered enough dry grass and prickly rose prunings, we managed to feed that flame and create a blaze. The smell of a garden bonfire still reminds me of those crouched and intensely focused afternoons. We fastened string round the neck of a jam jar and held it over the hot embers in the hope of stewing rose hips and water into something like jam. Inevitably the bottom cracked and we lost the lot.

On wet days, however, we had to play indoors. We were limited to the dining room, where a coal fire was rigidly confined by a wooden fender, a smoke-shield, and a dense black wire fire-guard. Out of our reach on the mantelpiece my Grandad kept his tobacco and a couple of straight, dark wooden pipes. "Foursquare" tobacco came as flat slices in round tins and had to be rubbed to be ready for the pipe. "St Bruno" came in oblong tins that my Dad used, once emptied, to store nails in his shed.

The tin and the pipes kept company with a box of Swan Vestas, a jar of white woolly, wire-cored worms for cleaning inside the stem of his pipe, a metal reamer to scrape out the ashes from its bowl, and a patterned, cylindrical "spill box". Spills were thin slips of wood, about six inches long, and they had two uses. In a morning Grandad arranged knotted paper, wood and coal in the fireplace and lit a spill from a match to kindle the fire. He would then blow out the spill to re-use in the afternoon, when he lit his pipe. Both fire-lighting and pipe-lighting could be lengthy operations, so the spill gave him a greater window of opportunity than a match. The mantel piece also sported, as an alternative, a Bakelite spill holder, bright red and smoothly volcano shaped, that housed a coiled length of twisted paper which poked out of the top like a thread of smoke. Of the two, Grandad seemed to prefer the wooden variety, perhaps because the paper refills were no longer available.

Grandma's idea of giving us children something to play with was limited to bringing out a gloss-white, slightly battered cardboard box of sewing threads and beads. The threads were remnants of real silk in Victorian dark green, rusty black, purple and maroon. Some were wound on cardboard, others around wooden reels that varied from tall and imposing to short and dumpy as Victoria herself. Most of the threads were so old that they snapped if you put tension on them, but one or two held enough sound length to thread beads - round, square, oval, diamond-cut; blue and green and black glass bugle beads; necklace beads, dress beads, sequins. We spiked the bigger ones on spent match-sticks and if we forced them they broke. The tiniest green glass tubes had a bore so fine that none of Grandma's needles would pass through. They were hardly bigger than the sugar crystals in her tea bowl and when we tipped the box they made the same sort of crunchy noise. Black glossy chips of jet must originally have been stitched onto the corsage of a dress. Sequins, small flat shiny discs with a hole in the middle, shimmered purple and green like dragon scales and slithered over each other with a faintly sinister hiss.

Sometimes Grandma would send us into the chilly front room to bang on the upright piano. The piano was a walnut-cased overstrung, much better quality than my Dad's, but in Grandma's front room it suffered from the cold and was supervised by an aspidistra that sulked on a home-made table. The piano keys were sticky to the touch and it was never quite in tune. However, a friend of mine bought it when Grandma died, and despite its 80-plus years it now lives a very happy life in Shap in a former coaching inn, where it's used every day to teach music.

119

After half an hour at the piano, where we sat on the prickly velour stool butchering "Chop-Sticks" and "Oh Will You Wash Your Father's Shirt", we would be summoned into the kitchen to wash our hands, and then told to sit up to the table in the dining room. Grandma spread a hand-crocheted tablecloth over the green plush bobble-edged cover. She would brush it afterwards with a semicircular "crumb brush" and tray.

At tea time we had bread with butter, Grandma's home-made and semi-crystallised jam, and "shop cake" bought off the travelling Co-op van. It was either a fine textured sponge with a skinny layer of white mock cream and a trace of something that could have been raspberry jam, or a pink-and-yellow chequered Battenberg wrapped in granular yellow marzipan. In summer, we sometimes got broad beans with white pepper and butter. More usually it was eggs, fresh peas, and Grandad's home-grown potatoes cut into big chunky chips and fried in that brown-spattered pan of boiling fat.

Nowadays I suppose most people would share my mother's horror of their cholesterol load, but I just remember the taste. They were delicious.

UNDER THE INFLUENCE

News in November 2007 of a tidal surge in the North Sea and its flood potential reminded me of the Great Flood of Carlisle in January 2005.

It also brought to mind a local furore about the alleged baleful influence of the Cursing Stone of Carlisle. Erected in a local subway to celebrate the Millennium, this is a massive 14 tonnes of polished granite, with an incised comprehensive curse which was proclaimed on the local "Border Reivers" in 1525 by Gavin Dunbar, the Archbishop of Glasgow. But more of this later, when I've told you about the storm.

Living as we do on a Northern rural hilltop, high winds and lashing rain are nothing unusual On the 8th of January 2005, my husband had gone to work well before dawn, to deliver fertiliser with his 24-tonne wagon, and he says, looking back, that the weather when he left home was calm. I was snoozing in bed when I began to be disturbed by the sound of the wind. It grew from occasional gusty shouts to a howl that throbbed and hammered at the windows, rain clattering on the glass like gravel. I huddled under the bedclothes while the howl rose to a soprano scream. Something heavy hit the wall just below the bedroom window, so hard that the old house shuddered. The scream developed an accompaniment of crashing and clanging. I had absolutely no intention of of going out into the pitch black to find out what was happening, so I stayed in bed trying to analyse the noises until night paled into dull, uneasy daylight. By then, although it was still raining heavily, the scream had slackened back to a howl.

The electricity had failed. I dressed and went downstairs, and put on coat, hat, gloves and boots, ready to go out and feed the ponies who were in the adjoining stone stable block.

When I opened the back door, it was clear I couldn't actually get out. Broken branches and a sheet of roofing tin blocked the steps up from the back door to the yard. A twenty-foot pine branch had crashed through the perspex roof of the passageway and was curtaining the outside loo. If that branch was the heavy "something" that had hit the house, it had flown over the top of my Transit-van sized horsebox from the other side of the yard.

I shut the back door against the wind, and went out through the front, on the sheltered side of the house. At the bottom of the field, the beck was running at twice its normal width, its fences swallowed by the flood and all the riverside trees standing waist-deep in churning brown water.

I braced myself to go round the end of the barn into the battering wind and rain. For a long moment I hung on the gale like a kestrel, gasping, before I covered my mouth and nose with my hand and forced myself round to the stable. Lots of the roof-slates were askew, but the door was still shut and the rafters and battens had held. Inside, the ponies, though nervous, were unharmed. I picked my way through the debris on the yard to the feed store and back, and gave up any thoughts of shovel and muck-barrow. Later, perhaps, if the wind died down.

Once I had fed the dog and the ponies, I started to take stock. The clanging noises of the dawn explained themselves when I saw that the haystore roof had gone. Its twelve-foot-long corrugated iron sheets were scattered across the farm as twisted wreckage. They had gone north into the trees, west into the paddock, and east over the roadside fence into the field a hundred yards away.

The fallen pine branches in the yard were impressive but they paled into insignificance when I looked across the pastures down to the wood. Despite the driving rain I could see that several of the magnificent spruce trees had been snapped off, as though a giant hand had wrenched them up like a tuft of grass and cast them away. Two-foot-thick trunks had been split and twisted at ten feet from the ground and the crowns spilled through the treetops to make a crazy alphabet. A dark mass of foliage, wood and broken stone blocked the river bridge. Between flying metal and falling timber, the pre-dawn hours had been lethal. Thank God our little road is a quiet one.

I dragged away the branches blocking the back door steps, pinned down as many corrugated sheets as I could with breeze-blocks so they couldn't fly any further, and went into the house to dry out.

Power cuts are fairly frequent for our remote household. "The electric" didn't arrive in this area till the 1960s and we are always prepared to manage without it, stocked up with candles and matches, torches and spare batteries, so the lack of electricity was no great hardship . The Rayburn stove was fairly sizzling from the draught in the chimney, and the bottled propane hummed steadily through to the gas burners, so breakfast was no trouble.

Although the radio batteries hadn't been renewed for some time, they didn't fail me; Radio Cumbria came through loud and strong. Over the next two days the BBC staff at the Carlisle studios – stranded by floodwater themselves – kept the county abreast of the storm damage, warned of impassable roads and informed those flooded-out about the refuge centres being set up. Warwick Road and much of Carlisle was flooded six feet deep; Hardwicke Circus and its underpasses became a lake, with traffic lights up to their necks in dirty water. Student canoeists paddled down Shaddongate alongside the fire services' rubber boats, rescuing people from the upper floors of their houses. The radio presenters, emergency staff and helpers deserved medals as big as dinner plates for their cheerful endurance. You couldn't blame them for making the most of the funnier stories that appeared: for instance, who could identify the goldfish that had been found swimming in the penalty area of Carlisle United's football pitch?

Gangs of Council workers armed with chainsaws spent the next month snarling their way along hundreds of country roads blocked by fallen trees. With the tonnes of timber that had fallen on our own patch in those few hours, we had enough firewood for several years.

In March, certain remarks by Councillor Jim Tootle (that's his name – honestly, I didn't make him up) hit the national news: "A local council is to debate whether to remove a huge stone from the city because it is thought to be cursed. The 'Cursing Stone' in Carlisle was made to mark the millennium, but it's being blamed for a string of bad luck that's met the city since. Fires, floods, foot and mouth disease and even a famine of goals for Carlisle United have convinced locals that the stone has to be moved or destroyed."

This hysteria conveniently ignored the fact that the curse was originally aimed at the Border Reivers, and intended to protect the farms that they were raiding. The 14 tonne stone remained in the underpass, probably through its own massive inertia. It is true that hardly any of the flooded houses were habitable again in 2005, yet the 2007 recurrence of foot and mouth didn't reach Carlisle, and the football team leapt through two divisions in two years from the Conference League to the top of Division 1.

We haven't been attacked by Border Reivers either.

FIRST FROST

Gold leaves are cast off by the tree
 in the first frost.
cold morning sunshine tears them free;
they flutter downwards helplessly
to river edges shelved with ice
where scents from earlier sacrifice,
 sharper than frost,
sting the bright air with autumn spice.
The leaves float thick down stream and shoal;
at waters-meet they sink and roll,
 deep as the frost,
into the year-end's shadowed bowl.
A few brown leaves clutch crisp and curled
where next spring's catkins, waiting furled,
will dance into a warmer world
 after the frost.

REPORT FROM "THE MESSENGER": JUDGEMENT AGAINST GRANDMOTHER

68 year old grandmother Felice Bogspawn is today beginning a 2-year suspended sentence, following a case in which she was accused of over-zealous behaviour, extreme community spirit, and disregard for political correctness.

Bogspawn, of Unity Terrace, High Dangleby, was found guilty of persistently cleaning and decorating the village's public toilet. It was alleged that over the last 40 years she had even gone to the extreme of placing pots of cut flowers beside the handbasins.

She was arrested following a tipoff by a group of youths, whom she had confronted in the street after they had been personalising the building with spray graffiti.

Testifying in court, one of the youths, who cannot be named for legal reasons, said: "She was extremely offensive. She called us little shitbags and threatened to tell our parents."

Dumbria County Council, who are currently campaigning to close the majority of public toilets, described the building in question as "a nuisance and a waste of money". "Bogspawn appears to be obsessed with it," said a spokesman, "it's not healthy."

Bogspawn was also handed an ASBO and a 200 hour community service order.

Leaving court, she said: "I look on that ASBO as an honour. I'll do my community service, whatever it is – littering in pubic parks, sticking 'Gouranga' signs on motorway bridges – whatever I'm told to do." Defiantly, she added, "But I won't promise not to go round after dark and clean it all up again."

Grandparents for Freedom, the third-age support charity whose mission statement includes "freeing grandparents from the burden of supporting the younger generation" and "enabling grandparents to express their wild side", said yesterday that it welcomed the sentence.

"Compulsive cleaning disorder is nothing to be proud of. Behaviour like this gives grandparents a bad name."

Source: Dangleby and Pullet-St-Mary Messenger, all rights reserved.

LAMB BANK

From January through to May,
the radio speaks twice a day
of ewes that have been left forlorn
and need new lambs for those stillborn;
of nibbling lips and squeaky Baas
from orphaned lambs that seek new Mas.

Some radio presenters hate
to read the lists of those who wait;
the changing ranks of lambs and ewes
less stirring than the daily news
or even, "Fisher, German Bight"
the shipping forecast every night.

A modest local service, not
a grand scheme for a public plot;
simple and humdrum local stuff,
no glory in it, just enough
to read the rote of farms and breeds,
matching the living with their needs.

THE GRUMPY OLD WOMAN AND:
BLOWING HOT AND COLD

I was loading light lambs to go to auction. It was peeing down with rain, but remembering the monstrous heat of the preceding summer it was almost a relief to feel cold. This time the lambs wouldn't have to sit panting in the heat as they travelled - though after listening to them bleating all night for their mothers I suppose there must still be a good deal of stress in the simple fact of the separation.

After the auction, I smiled to see a farmer in full waterproof kit striding through the rain back to his Land Rover, bearing a brand new hay rake. They say farmers are pessimists, but things like that make me wonder! I once met a neighbour in a narrow road and as is customary we both rolled down our vehicle windows to pass the time of day and comment on the weather.

He announced, "I've just been to buy some waterproofs ready for haytime."

Now, the animals know enough about weather to put Tomasz Schafernaker and Paul Mooney to shame. Fell ponies trek determinedly to the lee side of the mountain when snow is imminent. Or if they expect to be fed hay near the farm during a snowy spell, they will wait Cassandra-like at the fell gate although there is nothing yet falling from the sky. When the thaw is due, they take themselves off... and then the snow melts. No, I don't know how they do it, either.

At the other end of the temperature scale, Chris, a large, fit and extremely physical neighbour given to shepherding in nothing more than shorts and boots during the summer, remarked as I passed one steamy afternoon, "Reckon Ah need to tek a skin off."

But there are also more daft human sayings about weather than you can shake a stick at. Cause is confused with effect without any attempt at logic.

"Oak before ash, Only a splash; Ash before oak, In for a soak." So goes the proverb. It must be written in that order so it will rhyme, because I've seen summers with both extremes of wetness and dryness, but never seen ash trees leaf before oaks.

In early spring when the fells are still streaked with snow, it's quite common to hear Cumbrians remark, shaking knowing heads, "It won't get warmer till them snow patches go." No – the other way about – surely?

Likewise, every September the pundits who have nothing better to do than pester the local paper with repetitive letters announce that the heavy crop of hawthorn / rosehip / rowan berries must surely presage a hard winter. I can only say that I must live in a different country. Our hawthorns and rowans flowered profusely in 96 but the winter of 96/97 was not bad enough to prevent me going to work over Grayrigg Hause with a summit height of around 1300 feet. Why don't people's minds work the other way around? 95's hot summer ripened the branches, resulting in a heavy bloom of flowers in 96, the spring weather suited the pollinating insects, and the result was a tremendous crop of fruit. Effect, not cause.

Readers write to the paper to comment on the early return of the robins in their garden, again predicting a bad winter. Does anyone really think that robins all leave England in spring? What the robins would say I do not know. Ours have been known to nest in the cupped palm of our monster rhubarb; it's quite normal for them to mug you when you go innocently seeking a few late stalks for a summer pudding. Nesting robins have got better things to do than carry on their bare-branch winter activity of telling all other robins to get the hell out of it. It's just that humans overlook the little birds until leaf-fall makes them obvious again in autumn.

Let's re-run those verses:

Oak before ash,
you can put down your cash;
Ash before oak?
you're making a joke.

Not enough fruit,
blame the chilled shoot.
Hot summer's the cause
of a surfeit of haws.

No, even those don't really work.

Still, it's the animals, not the humans, who know what they are talking about. Isn't it? Do cows lying down mean the weather is going to turn to rain? My mother used to say so. Now that I know they lie down regularly to chew the cud, I guess that their intermittent lack of activity must be merely a coincidence with the renowned changeability of the British climate. Similarly it's said on the coast that the weather changes with the tide coming in or going out. I mistrust that tale for the same reason, though I know people who live there who swear that in winter if snow falls, by the time the tide has come in it will have thawed.

This "Red sky at night, shepherd's delight" business is a lot of hooey as well. Think of the number of times you've woken up to pouring rain after a fine sunset. Or a nice day has followed the "shepherd's warning" of "red sky in the morning". I would like to bet these rhymes were dreamed up by someone with a minor talent for just that - rhyme - without too much care given to the content. Does a child born on a Thursday really have far to go? (Don't we all?) If you cut your nails on Monday / Tuesday do you really grow healthy / wealthy? If you meet seven / eight / nine magpies do you really encounter

131

heaven / hell / the devil his ainsel' ? You could get into a fair old state if you really thought something might come of it.

The more of these rhymes I learn (for they are tremendously easy to pick up, simply because they both rhyme and scan, unlike much poetry today) the more I think they are a clever way of pretending to control the uncontrollable; entertainment rather than any serious attempt to pass on knowledge. You can hypnotise yourself into believing almost anything if you can remember it long enough - that's how spells work, by concentrating the mind almost without you having to try.

Farming also seems to be full of odd (often male) prophetic remarks which the novice is too diffident to question. Are they the equivalent of "If you can get close enough to put salt on its tail, you'll be able to catch it"? I was advised after ten years of shepherding that I ought always to buy Swaledale ewes which had wide-springing horns, because "that sort allers fetches twins." Needless to say, I watched the results of the scanning that year with an extra interest, but those of my ewes who had the right type of horns must not have known about the saying, because half of them had singles, and three or four were geld.

Even Paul Heiney, bless him, has been known to be tempted to mystic ovine generalisation. For instance, does the moon affect the timing of lambings? He wasn't sure but wanted his Times readers to observe for him. Are we inundated with lambs at full moon? Or, are the ewes more receptive at full moon in October and primed to produce heaps of lambs five months on from then? Well, Easter always falls on a full moon, and some years we're up to the ears in lambs that weekend, and other years I've been able to take the day off and go carriage driving – though, unlike Paul, not with John Parker.

Old wives have a lot to answer for - and I'd be willing to bet they weren't all female.

The only really useful bit of information I can recall was to pasture sheep on ground that has ragwort problems. Over the winter they will nibble any remaining ragwort seedlings down below ground level. So long as you pull the original crop of mature plants out and burn them, the sheep will keep the seedlings from regenerating the stock. I know this works because we had a field full of ragwort when we took over Daw Bank, and, after using this method, now it is clean.

Am I allowed to make up a rhyme about it?

Burn your ragwort in a heap:
Keep your pasture clean with sheep.

I just need something similar to get rid of spear thistles.

ONION MAGIC

I have a secret recipe
for growing onions bigger.
I drink two bottles of pale ale
(I think it helps MY figure).

I drink another bottle
and I loosen off my belt;
(I turn my glass and contemplate
the way the bubbles melt).

I polish off another,
then I slide out rather slow
and potter to the garden,
where I lean across the row;

I slacken off my trousers
and of braces I unsheathe;
then to improve my onions
I bend down and simply
…
breathe.

THE GRUMPY OLD WOMAN AND: TOWNIES

Graham and I live in the country. In fact he once jokingly told some lost and hungry walkers that they had "arrived at the End of the World".

It's a solitary house and we like it that way. If I want to set off the washing machine at eleven at night, nobody screams through adjoining walls. If the animals bark or whinny in greeting to us, nobody minds, because the neighbours are mostly half a mile distant and they all live with animals around them, too. And, if I go out in the dusk to fill a coal scuttle, the scarey Darth-Vader-like hisses from across the yard just mean that the resident barn owls are planning supper.

I have worked in a city, too, so it amuses me to make daily comparisons of the two different ways of thinking.

In the country, you dress for the weather, which you judge every morning by going outside and looking at the sky and feeling the air on your skin. In the city, you dress for the workplace and just hope it won't rain between the car park and the building, and you only look at the weather forecast for the weekend in case you might want to have a barbie out on the patio. I still looked wrongly dressed for the city even after a year of working there, but I see I'm not totally alone in that. Anyway, age has its compensations; I have no need to bare my midriff in winter in the interest of fashion.

In the country work is done as it is needed, and it doesn't end till it is finished. You go round the fields, seven days a week, to check the sheep and feed them, and until all are fed you keep on going, and if you feel ill you still keep on going.

In the city, you start work at a set hour – later if you can get away with it; and leave at a set hour – earlier if you can; and if you feel ill or even just want a day off, you phone in sick and don't go to work.

I knew I was lucky to have the benefits of the city by day and the peace of my home by night. I was content, therefore, to forego the night life that a city provides such as the pubs on two corners of the block, the two night clubs within five minutes' walk, the performance hall and the cinema across the centre of town. If I preferred my fifty-minute drive home, that was my choice, and if people stay in the city to enjoy it in an evening that is their choice.

It really annoys me though, when people disparage any way of life other than their own. So often that's due to ignorance. For instance, when the country is mentioned, we get an attack on hunting. Why? Hunting is only one small part of the many things that are done in the countryside and the hunting instinct exists in the city too, only there it has to express itself as other things, like theft, burglary, gambling, racism or vandalism.

In the country, where everyone knows everyone else to a greater or lesser degree, it is rude to pass someone by and not speak, because almost everyone is your neighbour and at some point they may need your help or you theirs. Even visiting strangers are usually relaxed and civil, and everyone knows who they are staying with and why. In the city, where there are just too many people for you to try to be aware of all of them, to speak to everyone you meet is not only exhausting but socially suspect. I know where I feel of greater value, and where I feel most lonely.

There was an "ac-tor" on TV last night who said he never goes to the country because "it smells and is full of sheep and cows." How does he know, if he doesn't go there? Although he is evidently someone whom the BBC thinks articulate and possibly even intelligent (two things that are not necessarily the same) his articulacy and intelligence had taken him no further than airing his own prejudice, presumably on the encouragement of the programme producer. He asked, rhetorically, what the countryside was "for". Ye gods! Where does he think his food comes from? The grain that makes his bread, the sheep that become his chops, the cattle that become his steaks and mince, the vegetables for his accompanying dishes and the cheeses and fruits for his desserts? And the wood that makes his chair and the table at which he sits, and even, dare I say, the stage on which he performs? And the sources of water for his plumbing, and electricity for his heating, and lighting for his stage? I'd like to see him creating food from concrete, tarmac, or bricks and mortar. Water into wine would be easier.

If the city is so wonderful, it's only because the rural areas provide for its basic needs. If the city is so wonderful why did house prices in rural areas skyrocket during the Covid-19 pandemic? Why did the Lake District get clogged up with visitors' cars every time lockdown was eased?

If you ate today, thank a farmer. Everything that supports life comes from the plants and the animals – from the land. And much of the refreshment that makes life worth while, instead of a drudge, comes from the natural world. For our own sake let's keep it safe, for all those reasons.

KNOWING HOW

I asked Joe, "Mend the privy door – it only needs a latch.
The hinge is fine, the boards are tight, it's just the sneck won't catch."

He nodded, and he set to work, humming a formless tune,
striped by sun and shadowy trees in a summer afternoon.

I brewed some tea. He'd finished the job before I poured it out;
so I asked how much I owed him; quick would be cheap, no doubt.

"Fifteen shilling and sixpence, ma'am," he told me with delight.
I sat down hard on the wooden seat and clutched my purse in fright.

"Fifteen shilling and sixpence, Joe! When a new latch is only three?
Threepence for latch and threepence for time makes just six pence, to me."

"Dear lady," he said, with a gentle smile, "Tha could'a bought latch thisself.
Tha'd have bought it, an' left it sitting there on the topmost pantry shelf!

"Cos it isn't the time or buying the parts that costs the fifteen bob,
It's t'experience, the knowing how, and that's t'main part o't job."

TABLES TURNED

Chris was bringing his sheep onto the fields through our yard, back sometime in July.

"Been worming them?" I enquired, as we paused to shut the gate behind them.

"Clippin'," said Chris laconically.

I felt rather silly for not noticing that the ewes wandering over the sun-baked grass were markedly naked compared to their appearance only a few hours before. After all, we used to farm; not noticing such a basic piece of stockmanship seemed evidence of lunacy. But Chris didn't say anything more on the subject and we talked of other things.

In mid December, Chris and his Dad, Willy, were up in the yard, checking and feeding the pregnant ewes. Graham and I were out also and despite the chilly weather we all gathered beside the same field-gate to pass the time of day and set the world to rights. Willy glanced round our yard and said, "Nice lot of logs there. Where'd you get them from?"

Graham gestured at the nearest corner of the midden, some ten yards away. "Felled those two trees that aren't there any more."

GRANNY'S BEEN RESURFACED

Now, Granny's eccentric, we all grant you that,
'cause over the years her hip bearing wore flat
so she clanked as she walked, and her doctor said, "Ma'am,
it is time you were lined, to prevent further harm.
For if you continue to clank as you do
your knees will drop off, and then what will you do?
You go in for surge'ry! it's ever so jolly.
Walk in on two feet and return on a trolley."

So Granny went hospital-wards, where she found
a tweed-jacketed surgeon, with X rays, came round;
then she dressed in a gown that did up at the back,
donned clean paper knickers to hide her rear crack,
and she limped somewhat consciously down to thee-att-er
where the team were all waiting, just poised to get at her.

The surgeon wore blues, and white gloves (he'd a pair)
and a neatly tied J-cloth to cover his hair.
There were people to lift her and people to spray
a cold mist on her back that would clean germs away;
then they taped a fine pipe in a handy small vein
and told her they'd give her some stuff for her pain.
The anaesthetist poked a long needle inside
of a space that her backbone would normally hide,
then although she was shivering (with cold, not with fears)
her legs both grew warm and she said, "Now, my dears,
just make sure that you close all the stitches quite tight;
I don't want my edges to fray in the night!"

When her knees had gone wobbly and legs had turned
 numb,
they knew she was painless from tiptoes to bum,

140

so they laid Granny down and they gave her a shelf
for to rest her top arm, folded over itself;
they rolled her and wedged her inside a big brace,
making quite sure she couldn't be bumped out of place.
And then while she dozed with her feet warm and glowing
the surgeon and team all scrubbed up and got going.
Just now and again as she snoozed on her side
she could hear the odd word like "this way", "open wide",
and the drilling and hammering went on without pause,
as though they were building a big chest of drawers;
the grease-monkey noises of metal repairing;
and the only things missing were paint, oil and swearing.

When all had gone quiet, her eyes opened wide,
and the surgeon came nodding and smiling with pride:
"We've relined your hip joint with cobalt and chrome;
you can stand up tomorrow and soon you'll go home."
Then they wheeled Granny out to recover her poise.
When her heart and her lungs made their usual noise,
they wheeled her away and the corridors toured,
past the sign "Orthopaedics" and back to the Ward.

Granny battled the bedpan and sometimes felt sick,
but she was determined to get well, and quick.
She got up the next day, to pilot a Zimmer,
and The Family ate all her grapes after dinner.
The third day, when Grannie was thoroughly bored
they gave her some crutches to walk down the ward.
The fourth day the surgeon said "Everything's fine!",
and he told them that Granny could leave any time.
With pills to mask pain, and some movements to learn,
and a cushion to put in the car for her stern,
like a queen on a throne she was wheeled out once more
and the porter transported her down to the door.

"They should pamper you, Granny – but pity's misplaced,"
said he; "You've just had your big-end-shells replaced.
And now that your crankshaft is no longer funny
you'll give the grandchildren a run for their money!"

ONE LEG LONGER THAN THE OTHER

Now I know you are all dedicated followers of health issues: non smokers, fat-reducers and possibly even closet vegetarians; so let me share my secret with you. Go on, let me.

Given that some hospitals are now denying surgery to patients who they consider are aggravating their own ill health, you'll know that a reduction in Body Mass Index (BMI) is something very desirable. If you have a BMI over the current "goalpost" max settings, your chances of getting NHS treatment are becoming a little slim (pardon the pun).

I have recently achieved an unexpected reduction in my BMI. Let me tell you how.

Some of it is entirely down to me; I've spent nearly a year limiting my intake of fatty or sugary foods, upping my vegetables and fruits, and taking longer walks. I'm now 17 kilos lighter, and have a BMI that is 6 points lower, than at this time last year.

However, in the past couple of weeks I've also discovered a neat trick that augments the effect. My BMI depends on which leg I stand on to be measured.

On my right leg, I'm 1 metre 61 centimetres tall. This gives me a BMI of 34.4. On my left leg, however, I'm 1 metre 62 centimetres – which gives me a BMI of 33.9. Neat, yes? Half a point shaved off just by standing on one leg.

As soon as the hospital repeats the resurfacing operation on the right hip, I'm told I'll "grow" back to the same height on both legs! When the surgical team told me that resurfacing would be my best option, they explained that because my bones are strong and thick, they have only a small inner space; this meant that a full joint replacement would have allowed me only a slender prosthesis with a small bearing-head, but for the same reason resurfacing was the perfect solution. I just smiled smugly. You see, I've told the weight-critics for years that I have heavy bones.

Ah … now I think this is where we came in; I suppose my BMI can't rely on surgery every time. Would you class that as a catch-22? Oh well. Stay off the chocolates and buttery shortbread, and try not to bite your fingernails.

NEW BALL(JOINT)S PLEASE

I needed a new battery for my car, because the old one had been on since I bought it five years before. It wasn't holding charge any more when the car stood, as it did post-op, unused for weeks on end. My husband in the meantime swapped the horsebox battery onto the car so I could get about once I was allowed to drive; but obviously, I still needed to replace the original battery. So I asked the garage to get me one.

When I called yesterday to collect, I parked and went in, where Chris, the owner/mechanic and much battered ex-rally driver, greeted me. He walked across the workshop and stood beside the wall, where I recognised a battery sitting on the floor.

He just sort of stood there and said, "There you are."

Fifteen-love.

I limped over and said, "I'm not lifting heavy things just at present."

Fifteen-all.

He said, " I'm not supposed to be lifting anything. I'm on Light Duties."

Thirty-fifteen.

I said, "And I'm signed off work completely, which is why I'm here on a weekday and not a Saturday."

Thirty-all.

I'd forgotten that next week he's due to have some body-parts overhauled in hospital, and he'd forgotten that I had been in for surgery myself only a few weeks ago.

Stand-off. Umpire?

I should have reversed the car into the bay and got close enough to lift the battery into the boot. As it was, Chris carried the battery over to my car.

Game to Mrs Millard.

Then, while I paid the bill, we shared practical and entertaining information about hospitals and joint surgeries.

Given the heavy-construction nature of orthopaedics, the garage floor was quite a suitable setting.

THE GRUMPY OLD WOMAN AND: WHEELCHAIRS A LA CLARKSON

Britain would be greater if it didn't have quite so much weather. And even better if what we got wasn't crap all the time. Outside, right this minute, visibility is down to about fifty yards, due to boring curtains of Great British rain. Not the best of conditions for road testing open topped transport. Unless you are studying how long a toupee can withstand the pull of the backdraught.

All of which makes it pleasant to recall road testing in an indoor setting. Indoor road testing? Yes indeed, and it wasn't your virtual stuff either, not an X-box in sight. This was performed last week on the faultlessly clean corridors of the Westmorland General Hospital: long, smooth, with tricky corners and busy intersections carrying traffic that may be pedestrian, may be on wheels, but is always unpredictable. So much so that although I passed a couple of my neighbours from the village they were so distracted they didn't even see me.

Well, to get down to business. The XJ-6 hospital chair. Decidedly open-topped, this set of wheels looks to have the aerodynamic qualities of John Prescott, but it's still about the best fun you'll get in any hospital.

Of course, that's not saying much. At the best of times, this is only a generous single seater. You could squeeze your fat friend from the pub into it but it doesn't stretch to carrying two. The trim is black vinyl – so retro – with aluminium accents in the foot well. There are alloy wheels and solid tyres. All eight inches of them.

There are a few options – lap belts for holding your dressing gown shut in windy conditions; paired hooks for catheter bags (discreetly hidden under the seat). If you go for the basic model without the standholder for your fluid drip, you'll need a friend to push that alongside. If you wanted a boot, forget it; bring another friend to trail the suitcase. Already we're up to four people , and that must make it the biggest single seater in the WORLD.

The controls are basic. The footbrake's only accessible from the back, so when you've been parked somewhere, it's permanent. It has a range of about half a mile, or the end of the car park. It copes robustly with any going. So long as that's smooth tiled corridors or tarmac.

Forget that silent electric panther of a thing that the one legged man uses to prowl up and down the Orthopedic ward; this straightforward, seat-of-the-pants job will leave him floundering.

And now we have to hand it over to our tame racing driver.

Some say... he has variomatic gears and is fuelled by slot-in sandwiches and drip-feed tea; that his circulatory systems contain only diesel and ethylene glycol, and that he sleeps propped in a corner of lift number two. All we know is – he's called Hospital Stig.

CUT TO TEST TRACK

It's easy-entry, so Stig will ask you to just "hop in" and go.

OFF the line ….

It's a bit underpowered uphill, but don't be deceived: with Stig at the controls, this wind-in-the-hair beauty can reach five miles an hour. Downhill, you have none of that "grab-the-rim control" of the classic wheelchair. It's pure adrenalin rush. Remember being galloped down the street on a bogie by your big brother when you were a kid? You're at the edge of what's sane.

Through Hammerhead.

Cornering looks stable, you've got good foot support, the feel's predictable with minimal understeer and the cornering's at least the equal of a supermarket trolley.

Flat to the boards through Chicago. Ooh that was – no it really wasn't fast through the tyres – you just thought it was.

Don't worry about Stig keeping within the lines – you keep your fingers within the bodyframe. You can see the scars of his previous power slides on the walls. Don't scream. Okay. TRY not to scream.

Through Gambon – massive slide there – and a-CROSS the line – oh sorry, I mean you've hit the car park.

CUT TO STUDIO – PAUSE FOR APPLAUSE

Well, I suppose it's got to go up on the lap-times board because we tested it. Hammond, you're nearer the floor than I am, would you mind sticking the time on? I mean why have a Hamster and bark yourself? Seven minutes, forty-seven seconds.

I reckon Captain Slow might go for this one, but you should definitely borrow, rather than buy it. He says the XJ-6 is built to last. I'll give him that – it is. Much, much longer than you'd like.

And that's about all for this week. We'll be back in a fortnight's time, because next week they're doing billiards or something, see you then, thanks for watching, b-bye!

TITS

In the winter hedge
still twigs gleam sharp with sunshine.
Little long-tailed birds
tumble, a breath of feathers
alive and brisk as light.

LEVERET IN THE GARDEN

Frost-bent daffodils
at sunset hang defeated.
I pick the fallen.
behind the leaves, a brown stone –
furred, flat-eared, with wild black eyes.

PERIPHERAL VISION

I suffer functions, numbers,
forms with references, letters that say
in final settlement; the claim is closed,
more forms referenced in a childish scrawl
demanding *demanding* illogically
repeated information. There's more sense
in the slight flutterings of the winter hedge
outside the office window. The pale stoat
fat-furred in the snow, I know him without
study. He has no number. Sinuous
he slips over the wall, along the verge,
back over the wall silently and gone.
The small birds, finches, robins, sit
fluffed on the brilliant branches as ice
melts under sunshine into glittering drops.
They come and go, all self responsible,
making no demands on my attention,
existing in the corner of my eye.

GOD LOVES A TRIER

His first ambition was to be a scrap man. He and my son would bring home rusty metal and pile it in our yard. Now and again they persuaded one of the local dealers to collect it, and they received a five pound note, for which I solemnly gave them change so they could divide it. When winter came, though, they tired of the muck and the effort and we were left with their last pile of scrap as a kind of mini Turner Prize.

When they were in their last year at school one of the teachers was discussing the class's future and their forthcoming exams. "You all need them, apart from Big Time Boy there, who's going to be an entrepreneur." Taking teacher at his word, Big Time Boy did not deign to sit his GCSEs.

He would have liked to be a mechanic, but to begin with neither he nor my son was old enough to drive a car so he decided they should mend bicycles and sell them. He brought a variety of corroded, chainless boneshakers to our house, and then stood by, making wrong diagnoses and suggesting impossible treatments, while my son attempted to restore them. Sometimes he tried to take a hand, but usually my son lost patience and beat him off. The pair may have actually taken some cash for their work, but probably less than they had spent and certainly not enough to cover the wear and tear on our nerves and tools. A hayrack full of bicycle frames is the legacy of this little venture.

Once he was old enough to possess a provisional licence, he began to arrive at our place on a 50cc motorcycle. Mechanical ham-handedness quickly turned his Dad's gift of a gleaming new machine into a buckled ruin. The ham-handedness was not improved by an under-age thirst for Newkie Broon and an even lower threshold for its alcoholic content. He'd wheedle a publican into selling him a bottle or two, then come wobbling over the fell road to drink and boast and shout around our yard. Usually he wobbled off home once he'd drunk up, but on the last occasion he arrived at 3 am so he settled himself in our hay-mew, and lay there finishing the bottle and smoking spliffs until he fell asleep towards dawn. His coughing and thumping around on the other side of our bedroom wall kept me awake most of the night, so I really stamped my feet at him the next morning and told him the barn was off limits because I had no ambitions to be burned in my bed.

If he were always as dreadful as he sounds, I'd have banned him entirely from the farm. The trouble is, he possesses something that gets under my guard every time: comedy. A big country house that could afford enough staff to keep an eye on his ambitions would find him a wonderful Joker. Though he isn't physically funny as so many comics can be, and certainly not witty, he is simply hysterical as an innocent abroad.

There isn't an ounce of malice in him. He'll cheerfully tackle your heavy jobs, although fags and drink have turned him into a little barrel on legs, and you do have to give him precise instructions and watch him like a hawk to save him from his own fecklessness. When he's about there is always something to laugh at and he's never in the least offended. You can tell him with stark honesty exactly why his bragging exasperates you, you can hurl insults at his grandiose plans or smack him round the head if you get mad enough, and he'll just wag his head knowingly and crow, "Aaaahh, BUT ... when I Hit The Big Time ....".

For a while after the boys left school, it was quiet, but Big Time Boy was drawn back by the magnet of our yard, our farm sheds and especially my husband's well equipped workshop. He passed his car driving test and persuaded his Dad to buy him a high-roof Transit van with a carpet steam-cleaning vacuum system installed. To advertise his business, he ordered "Big Time Cleaning" decals to put on the van panels, and cajoled my husband into helping him to apply them. The moment they

151

were perfect he was desperate to show off down the pub, so he jumped in the van and fired her up. He then hurled her backwards against our heavy goods wagon, which wiped out the near-side of "Big Time Cleaning" with a long, irreparable tear.

It was much the same with the equipment. He would "clean all my carpets and upholstery for nothing," if I would let him practise on them! To this day I can't tell you why I said yes, except for his patent desire to please. The settee was soaked for days and one of the carpets ended up looking like the aftermath of a Moth Banquet. The office escaped by the skin of its teeth, due to me standing in front of the computer with my fists on my hips. A local night club was less lucky. Big Time Boy applied heat and moisture indiscriminately to its huge main bar carpet, the two halves shrank and the long central seam came unstuck. They had told him to be careful of the join. "Aaaahhh BUT ..."

You can never be sure what vehicle he'll be driving when he arrives: in the past year it's been anything from the local courier's parcels van to a high-spec red Mazda car. How on earth -- ??? Phew – it wasn't his. A garage had trusted him – trusted HIM – to deliver it to a customer safely. *Take a photo, quick!* It never happened again.

Whenever Big Time Boy owed too much money for comfort, he would disappear for some time.

One dark, wet and windy afternoon I was mucking out the stable, when the mare flung up her head in alarm. I turned to find what had surprised her, to see a roundabout little woman (as I thought) in waterproofs, who was ducking in through the stable door. She wore rain-spotted glasses, a reflective waistcoat, and a flickering red head torch strapped round her woolly hat. It wasn't till the funny little woman spoke that I realised it was Big Time Boy, reduced once more to his earliest and cheapest form of transport: a filthy and battered mountain bike.

He's now in his thirties, and no more grown-up than he was at fifteen. Through all those years, he has been living on fantasies: going to Be A Star, Make A Million, and of course Hit The Big Time. Last week, when I was working in the office, and my husband was painting the walls of a bedroom upstairs, I was startled by a burst of yells and shouts so I rushed out thinking that my husband and his step ladder had somehow fallen out. The noise resolved itself into repeated howls of, "Are ya ready to HIT THE BIG TIME! cos BIG TIME BOY IS HERE!" provoking my husband to yell back, "NO! Stop out! Go away! Goodbye!"

The terrifying news he brings is that he's blagged his way to a driver's licence for a seven and a half tonne goods vehicle.

Ham-handedness and blind faith in his own abilities will take him to The Big Time all right. If you see a seven and a half tonner coming at you, with a short, stout, bespectacled lad at the wheel, jump, or your next stop will be the Pearly Gates.

It won't matter to Big Time Boy, though. He'll come all the way with you, nattering as you go. And St Peter will pat him on the shoulder and say, "Park your bike round the back, son. God's been hoping you'd turn up; He likes a good laugh."

THE PHILOSOPHER

Sammy is a hero, a philosopher and a teacher.

He is also a red-and-white Border Collie, though he can't claim all the lengths of a pedigree. I know, though he doesn't, that he only exists as an accident, due to a half day hiatus between his mother Molly arriving at the Collie Rescue Centre farm and his father Bob being taken to the vet's for neutering. The moment Molly arrived on the farm, they got together and a litter of five was the result.

Both Molly and Bob were non-workers, which was why they ended up at Collie Rescue. They had been sent to find new homes where no sheep demanded responsible attention. Both found, happily, in due course. Bob is now doing agility tests and taking owners for walks in between starring in Am Dram productions, while Molly is being a rural but strictly non-farming angel.

We intended Sammy to be the farm's guard dog. Shep our previous sheepdog had died, after a long and effective tenure of the role. I am not sure that I really picked Sammy out of the litter. In the goat pens where his family lived at the time, there were two red girls and himself, and I am fairly certain it was one of the girls who came forward and introduced herself to me. But we'd had girls for twelve years along with all that "taking to the vet" stuff when they were molested by the local Romeos. We wanted a boy again, so Sammy it had to be.

He loved the car ride home, sitting gravely on my husband's knee and generally behaving with decorum while I drove. Periodically he licked Graham's face and ears with great enthusiasm. For weeks before he arrived the various animals of the farm had been admonished by my husband that they would have to be careful "when my puppy dog comes." He is still emphatically Graham's dog, except when he misbehaves, when he becomes mine.

Back home on our yard Sammy attached himself to our ankles and waddled anxiously after us wherever we went. Unfortunately, because his destined role as guard dog meant he would have to spend his nights outside the house, he had to become accustomed to sleeping on his own; so we made up a bed, with straw and boxes, in the stable normally occupied by Mr T the Fell pony. We gave him water, and a meal mixed with ewe's-milk-replacer powder just like at Collie Rescue; and we went about our business. Sammy howled and cried. And then stopped. Suddenly there he was, out on the yard again, investigating the midden and delightedly waddling after us once more. We played with him. We also blocked the gap in the door with a straw bale.

When we went indoors for the evening and left him in the stable, Sammy howled and cried again. We felt like child-murderers, even though he was a big well grown pup of ten weeks old and we were pretty certain he wasn't going to fade away overnight. It was still a relief to go in early the next morning and find him bouncing with delight at seeing us again.

His first coat was rich brown with the classic sheepdog white collar, chest, muzzle, tail tip and socks. That short dense puppy coat turned into a long dense adult coat, fine and silky and remarkable for keeping itself clean in the dirtiest of weather; his long feathery white socks are almost always pristine.

He wasn't quite brave enough at first to clamber down the steps to the back door, so we have a lot of early photographs of him sitting wistfully at the top, gazing down into the kitchen. We also pounced on him in passing and carried him indoors quite a lot. This was supposed to be so he could socialise with us and learn our commands. In reality it was just such fun

155

having a pup around the place that we were quite unable to resist the temptation to play with him.

He learned very quickly that "Fetch" was a good game, and within a week of his arrival he was reliably bringing back all the toys that the family offered to throw for him. Lacking any hens to practise herding, and sternly told off for being too keen on sheep, he took to herding the family. He still does. He understands, now, that when people go away they will come back again, but nevertheless he sighs deeply when presented with the jingle of car keys, accepts very reluctantly that his group is divided, and goes to lie down somewhere and wait for our return to make the pack complete once more. This is all very well, but when we come home his insistence on trouser-browsing to find out the news from abroad can get a little wearing, especially on a wet winter day when he'd be better off snuggled down in the cart shed with the blackbirds and we'd be better off indoors with a hot coffee.

In his second summer, the brown shades in his coat bleached to foxy reds and blond highlights. In winter its density enables him to sleep out in the open, which he evidently prefers to sleeping in a building or a dog bed, though he retreats there to shelter from the rain. Whether due to the influence of ewe's-milk-replacer powder, or just being a naturally vigorous young creature, Sammy has outgrown both his Mum and Dad and become what our farming friends call "a strong dog" with seemingly boundless energy.

Both his ears, at first, flopped over. In time, one stood up like a huntaway's, but the other never managed to match it. This clownish lopsided appearance has set the character of most of Sammy's escapades. When he began to grow his adult teeth, the chewing started. Sammy has adopted many strange toys in his life so far. One of his favourites is a worn-out rubber horse feed skip that had endured some fifteen or twenty years of being snuffled, chewed, picked up and stamped on by various ponies. Having eventually developed a split down one side, it was replaced, whereupon Sammy took it over as his favourite chewing toy. Unfortunately this also developed in him a firm conviction that rubber was a good thing to chew. It led to us losing "the electrics" twice from the horsebox towbar, once from the car towbar, once from the tipper wagon, and twice from the trailer lighting board. The horsebox brake lines he only chewed once, thank God, after which I think he must have decided that brake fluid tasted really nasty and perhaps rubber was not such a good thing after all. Still, by persistence he has gradually removed both handles and all the sloping sides from the feed skip, and it is now a twelve-inch pancake that he will fetch, and throw at you, and demand that you throw, for him to fetch endlessly and throw at you again.

However, it was and is Sammy's deeply held belief that the world is a sad place. Winter is the worst time; it preys on his philosophical mind. If nothing is happening outside, he sits sighing in the rain at the top of the kitchen steps. Stopping occasionally to shiver and whine, he observes us all dimly through the frosted glass of the kitchen door and is thrown into transports of delight when we reach for our boots and bend to put them on. Occasionally, when he thinks we have all gone out, I have heard him wind up from a whine to a howl, as he used to when a puppy. Solitude is his bane; attention his only goal. He cannot believe that he and you exist in the same dimension unless he has a minimum of one foot on you, or around your leg, and to ask him to exercise self control in this is equivalent to asking him not to breathe. Yet, if you advance on him for the ultimate in attention, a good grooming, he turns into a hedgehog, rolling on his back and paddling his long white-socked paws at you to keep you at a distance. Brushing with the pin-brush (the only implement that can get through his six-inch pelt) is an activity that, he tells us, was invented by the Devil. In Spring, the fine fawn-coloured piles that I rake out of his moulting winter coat could fill several cushions.

He is a most handsome animal now, silkily feathered and in the prime of his strength; a vital young dog, sleek of muscle, deep through the heart, with tremendous speed and agility. He has a jaunty bounce to his stride as he trots round the yard flashing his white socks. Yet despite his vigour and power he is still deeply worried that his pack will vanish if he does not keep it under tense surveillance, and Graham's frequent remarks to him that he is "a hero" have a distinctly ironic flavour. True, if he were arrogant and haughty, the term would fit his appearance well, but his tendency to stick out the tip of his tongue and cock those lopsided ears would give him away. In fact, he is determined to put a brave face on his knowledge of the infinite sadness of the world. He is convinced that no human being can have, or has ever had, enough Fun, and inevitably that turns our Philosopher into Chief Clown. Because he is (of course) the only dog who knows the sad facts of life, it is his Heroic Mission to add Fun to everybody's existence.

For example: most people who have dogs, throw balls or sticks for them. Not so many families have, as we have, a dog who throws balls or sticks for us. When you go to feed in a morning, Sammy is there with a toy of some sort; he cares nothing for his breakfast and will allow the blackbirds to steal most of it while he attends to giving you the first of the day's doses of Fun. He stands up against the feed chest, plonking his big white-feathered feet on the lid until you give him a morning cuddle; then when you lift the lid and reach in for food he will be there, dropping the toy inside, licking your face with his huge tongue, then looking keenly into the depths among the sacks and scoops, waiting for you to retrieve the toy for him. Take it out and tell him to go away? it just doesn't work – he'll be right there dropping that toy in again. When on occasion you just don't have time to play, his disappointment is palpable. Put down the lid and walk away leaving the toy within, and he'll sit down and stare at the chest in disbelief, as

158

though a law of Nature had been suspended. Come in from work and cross the yard from the car, bearing a box full of groceries, and Sammy will be at, around or in front of your feet, puffing greetings through his Santa Claus playball; and as you start down the kitchen steps he will throw the ball merrily to coincide with your descent. He can't believe your curses are not friendly, and he doesn't accept your refusal to throw it back; he will sit there looking intelligently down the steps at it until you give in and throw it back up to him. You see, he KNOWS you need to do it. He only has to wait till your Fun level drops to the point at which it needs a top-up. The game ends when you throw the ball far enough that by the time he's retrieved it, you have mastered your hysterics and shut yourself indoors.

You may think that this comedy is all due to us being a load of softies: that the whole family is daft, that we humour this fool of a dog, and spoil him rotten. Not so. Let a stranger appear on the yard and Sammy will be there to witness the fact, and prove his worth in his originally intended role of guard dog. There is, however, not a shred of aggression in it. He is genuinely interested in the unusual and will take considerable pains to investigate it, and therein lies the uncertainty for newcomers. I have seen three big scaffold-building men sit doubtfully in their wagon cab, staring out at the red-blond dog who waved his tail at them and stared right back. His perfect white teeth were revealed in a cheerful grin and his sheepdog-keen amber eyes gleamed with what I knew to be a desire to share Fun. They just didn't dare to put it to the test.

He controls the yard. He's probably the only dog in the world who can do it by teaching the poor sad humans how to play. Bringing with him the immensely long rope on which he is tethered when we're away, he will bounce and sniff and dance around the stranger, uttering muffled wuffs through a mouthful of whatever toy, rock or stick he finds within reach. He almost always trips up the intruder, albeit in the friendliest

159

fashion. The Jehovah's Witnesses call him and his rope "The Reaper". If I'm indoors, it isn't Sammy's bark that warns me of visitors; no, they announce themselves, with cries of, "Gerroff, dog! Giddoot man!"

Sammy has no need to bark at strangers. He trains them instead to do what he requires. He is an excellent teacher, too; roofers, plumbers, children and postmen are usually trained in less than half an hour to throw whatever toy he presents to them. Electricians and builders, so far, have been more resistant.

Sammy's out there now, panting in the summer sunshine, watching Graham move building materials around the yard; two red haired fit animals filling the place with an atmosphere of health and vigour. Let him into the kitchen and he immediately occupies Graham's bentwood chair, sitting up very straight and quivering with pride at being allowed to fill the Pack Leader's place. Take him round the fields and he is a streak of lithe muscle, golden-red against the green grass, his white socks flying; he can gallop and leap and turn with dizzying speed and yet drop into statuesque stillness when told "Down" in the face of sheep. Give him company, let him be in on the act, and he is happy.

His one remaining ambition is to master the third dimension: the air. The red dog's deepest wish is to be a Red Arrow, to rival the swooping swallows. April to September is spent in total concentration, attempting to match the grace and speed of the birds who dive-bomb him in defence of their family's air space. It doesn't matter that in this he singularly fails. In those summer months our lovable philosopher, teacher and clown is honestly too busy to remember that the Life of Man is Sorrow.

BORN CARERS

Naomi, our grand-daughter, has had little option but to become a horsey child. With a mother and grandmother who think equine before speaking human, the odds were always strong that she'd be fluent in Horse before she could read.

Luckily, Ruby the Fell pony seems to have had much the same thought. She carries Naomi around with patient circumspection (something notably lacking when we go out carriage driving) and she is careful not to make any untoward moves that might damage the small child. Naomi is not quite three.

Ruby had a recent visit to the vet for eye treatment. Jen met me at the surgery to hand over a bottle of Ribena (a necessary sweet additive to get Ruby to eat the medication mixed into her dinner). Naomi, having accepted that she mustn't worry the mare and foal in the paddock next door, wanted to see what the vet did with Ruby, so we all stood in a darkened stable while the vet peered at Ruby's eyes with the ophthalmoscope.

Next thing we knew Naomi was hugging Ruby's leg really tightly, and kissing her elbow, which was all she could reach, "to make her feel better".

That child can be spooky - she isn't three till the end of next month and she has already decided which friends and relatives she will ask for which birthday presents (I'm down for sticker books, apparently, and her Great Granny's got to buy Iggle Piggle pyjamas - rather her than me!).

As for the rosette which Naomi accepted for being the only Fancy Dress entry at our village show, riding Ruby as The Tooth Fairy: "Please will you put the rosette up really high on my bedroom wall?"

When asked why, she explained: "So I can't reach it till I'm a big girl and I can't spoil it."

Three going on ninety-three, I'd say.

2009: NAOMI AND CHEMOTHERAPY.

19 August 2009

No time for driving today as I am going to visit my 4 yr old grand-daughter in hospital, in Newcastle (about 2 hours away from here). She had her first dose of chemotherapy against Wilms' tumour (a kidney tumour) last night so I'm not sure how she'll be. But she is a tough little mite and has been tickling the nurses and cheering everybody up. I'm taking her a glove puppet (a Squirrel called Dale), and some of Ruby's tail hair done up with a red ribbon.

Naomi was enchanted by the Giggle Doctors who came to play in her hospital room this afternoon and whose glove puppets - a Mole and a Loris - talked very cheerfully to Dale.

We hope she'll be home tomorrow night and after that everything is (relatively) routine. It will of course be a bit of an ordeal, but it's a known set of treatments with a very high chance of a good outcome. One of my colleagues at work has a brother, married and with a family, who survived Wilms' tumour as a child. When asked about his surgery scars he smiles and says, "Sharks."

21 August 2009

Naomi is home and now has 4 weeks of chemo, once a week, before her surgery. Jen and Rob have bought a big push chair to take her to places without tiring her so much with walking. (Actually I think they have future plans as well...)

Ruby and I, between the thunder showers, have clocked up 400 hours of driving today.

20 November 2009

I brought both the ponies back from an outlying field during a lull yesterday (Ruby wanted to do it backwards so she didn't have to face the rain) to spend the night indoors.

Jen, Rob and Naomi have had to evacuate their house and move in with us. They live in the centre of Cockermouth and the ground floor is flooded. They left just as the water started creeping up to the front door - probably 4ft of water in there now. The cat's still upstairs there, undoubtedly appalled and wondering when they will come back.

Seathwaite in the Borrowdale valley has had more than a foot of rain in the last day or so. Scary. I'm so glad I live on a hilltop.

FLOOD

We had already put the sofa on the dining table
and the baby's medicines in the buggy
before Pete hammered on the door, gore-texed,
hood up, heavy rucksack on his shoulder.
Get out now, he said, *my house is done.*
The water was a running skin along the street.

By the time we pulled on boots, the river
had taken the tarmac and pavement. We locked
the door, as though that was any more use
than undelivered sandbags. You carried the baby,
her nappies, our clothes. The buggy was wheels-under.
At the corner oilskinned men tensed knee deep
in a creaming current. *Take a hand each.*
Go steady. There are rocks moving in there.
*

Two days later, we left the baby with my mother
and we went back. Police had shut the torn-up street
to prevent looting. We slipped through with our keys.
Indoors the carpets floated on an inch of silt,
the kitchen stools had waltzed into the living room
and pitched like drunks into a corner to sleep.
A bowl I'd left on the worktop
sat half-empty on insurance policies
welded to passports and papers
from the filing cabinet; the fish tank, untenanted,
cloudy with river water; at the turn of the stair,
wailing on the last dry tread, the abandoned cat.

20 March 2010

Jen and Rob and Naomi are still living in the converted barn next door while their house is renovated after the flooding.

Naomi had her initial chemo, then surgery to remove the kidney and cancerous cells, then radiation therapy and a weekly chemo treatment that is only now drawing to an end. She is almost as bald as a coot, but to the astonishment of her consultant therapist she is bouncing with health - quite the opposite of most children undergoing chemo. We are attributing it to lots of fresh country air, granny's home made oatcakes at every possible excuse, and even more, lots of horsey things to do.

21 May 2010

It's almost hot, here in Cumbria!

I fed both ponies this morning, which I haven't done myself in recent weeks because Jen often gets outdoors before I do. However, today she's taken Naomi in for day surgery to remove those chemotherapy lines - last step back to normality after nine months of cancer treatment. So Mr T and Ruby had their soaked sugar-beet, soaked cubes and half scoop of mix, and a wee bite of hay to keep them happy till I came out around 10:30 am to tack up Ruby for a drive.

~~~ooo0OO0ooo~~~

There is a long, long gap here. 2010 to 2011. Once we learned that Naomi's tumour had started a new growth in her lungs, and that it was inoperable, and terminal, I didn't write many blog posts.

Jen wrote her own daily blog during this period, called *Lumps and Bumps*, in which she kept friends up to date without having to repeat it all in endless phone calls. But Naomi's long, terrible journey wasn't my story to tell.

Instead I wrote a poetry collection called *Ash Tree*.

~~~ooo0OO0ooo~~~

ASH TREE

Look there, that break. See, where the rot's exposed?
She's weak. If the next gale blows easterly
she'll be gone. Best fell her; lop off her limbs,
rip down her head and grey-ribbed trunk. Then crack
twigs into kindling, logs into billets,
chop out the rot. The rest can burn – smoke, shine,
sink, and crumble into ash – all follows
from the first clean-cut mercy of the saw.

It's different for you, child. We used knives
first, and then drugs and more knives in the hope
that love and games and laughter might survive.
We weep inside now, knowing that the rot
is swelling up to choke you. We can ask
no mercy like the saw we gave the ash.

A GOODBYE

Yesterday we said our final goodbyes to our beautiful grand-
daughter Naomi. She has been fighting cancer for the past 23
months. We thought she had beaten it several times, but it has
kept coming back, coming back. She died peacefully at home
on Friday 15th July, aged 5 years and 10 months. It was
possibly the worst day of my life.

MISSING

Requiescat Naomi
31 August 2005 – 15 July 2011

I missed you by a quarter of an hour.
I should have hurried through my morning shower,
missed eating breakfast in the sleepy sun
or read no emails, or replied to none;
denied the summery procrastination
of that prettier route to my destination.

I miss you from the house when I arrive –
everything silent that was once alive.
The nurses meet me at the stair. Their kind,
practised updating powerblasts my mind.

I miss you from that waxy, sleeplike face.
Your thin hands curl without their living grace –
no mischief – tickling doctors, climbing trees
or treating dollies for your own disease.
It's you with self subtracted. And I wail
till my throat hurts me like a swallowed nail.

I'll miss your heart, the things forever not –
the family, the life you'd yet to plot,
the cure you'll never find – the future star
that cannot now outshine the one you are.

The undertakers engaged a carriage company for Naomi. They turned out two grey Hanoverian x Hackneys, with pink plumes and russet and brass harness, pulling a perfectly beautiful little pale cream hearse.

Nothing can reduce the grief of losing a beloved child to such a cruel disease, but we could not have had a more beautiful or stylish way to send her off.

They arrived on the dot, and set off at a cracking trot, doing the 10 miles to the crematorium in 55 minutes without breaking pace, except for a 5 minute halt to let the tailback of traffic pass, and the horses have a breather.

She would have loved it ... and how she would have giggled when we came out after the service and one of the horses demonstrated a monumental ability to pee.

PINK

white horses still their clattering feet
and wait for you
in shadow street their pink-plumed heads
stand straight for you
the lady at the bus-stop signs
a cross for you
the walker with the terrier dog
sighs loss for you
the traffic at the roundabout
must queue for you
the metronome of trotting hooves
beats true for you
the wagons on the carriageway
change gears for you
the rider on the cycle-path
wipes tears for you
pink rose-bay and foxgloves paint
July for you
the sunlight on the fell pours down
goodbye for you
the smiles of all who met you weave
the pall for you
that pink box in a white hearse is
too small for you
a sailing group of pink balloons
learn flight with you
and high the wings of wheeling birds
delight with you

AFFAIR OF THE HARP

I don't usually make New Year's resolutions, but grief can feed on itself if you let it, and I had to do something to lift my spirits after the loss of Naomi. I resolved to play music regularly – every day, if at all possible.

I got out my guitar, a beautiful instrument which my husband bought for me when we were engaged. When I began to play, though, I realised painfully that although I still read music, and my fingers still remember what to do and I know many tunes, my body is arthritic and no longer wants to hold classical fretting positions. So although I still love the look of my varnished instrument and I love its sound, I found myself reluctant to play it.

It dawned on me that a harp might be the instrument to replace my guitar. I'd have all the notes laid out for me, instead of having to fret them with my left hand. I'd have two hands to play melodies. And I learned from a radio feature that I could get one in kit form.

The one I'd heard was made by Waring Harps in Connecticut, USA, with a wooden frame and nylon strings, and a soundbox made of – wait for it – strong cardboard. When I got over my surprise I realised that cardboard is not only light and portable, but inexpensive and musically resonant. I found that Backyard Music, also in CT, made a slightly larger version with 22 instead of 19 strings, so I had a very friendly e-mail discussion with the two owners of Backyard, and the next working day my 22 strings and pins, three bits of wood and cardboard soundbox were sent on their way to me.

There are drawbacks, of course, to buying from overseas. Customs not only impose VAT on the purchase price, but are apt to hang onto items for an unconscionably long time. Although the harp only took 5 days to cross the Atlantic, before that it languished with Customs in New Jersey for 9

171

days, and afterwards in England for another 6! As the wait grew longer, I would have chewed my fingers back to the elbows, if I hadn't needed them to make up the kit.

Building the harp, when I eventually got it, was fun. The prettily curved triangle of the body was easy to glue, screw and varnish, and quickly looked like a proper harp. To drive the tuning pins and bridge pins into the pre-drilled frame, I started with a rubber mallet, but I had to discard that when it began to shred! I changed it for a fairly hefty hammer, with a piece of scrap leather as a buffer. I also moved into the dining room which has a concrete floor, because in my front room each hammer-strike rebounded through the table into the floorboards and sent the harp and the table leaping back towards me.

The soundbox on a "proper" harp is normally made of wood, which is sanded and varnished to show off its beauty. The soundbox on mine, however, was boring brown cardboard. Constructing and glueing it looked tricky but really only required big rubber bands to keep things under control while the glue set. Still, even when complete, the cardboard definitely needed colour and protection. The DIY stores failed to produce the colour of paint I wanted – burgundy being so 1980s as a decorating shade – so I ended up at Halford's buying car spray paint. And primer. I had to go back next day for a second can of burgundy… the soundbox was much bigger than it looked. The spraying really had to be done in a shed because the smell was vicious.

Once the soundbox was dry, it came back into the house to be glued to the frame. The instructions said to "glue the frame and avoid the string holes," but that sounded very fiddly and, since the soundbox had a long clear slot where the strings were to pass through, it was actually easier to mark the box with pencil lines either side of the frame, and glue the box before fitting the frame over it inside the lines. Some heavy books held the two together overnight, and then it was ready to be strung.

172

Harp strings are pretty. The C strings are red, the F strings are blue or black, and the rest are uncoloured. Like a novice fisherman I struggled to tie esoteric knots in my nylon strings and like captured eels they immediately tried to untie themselves. I learned to use long nosed pliers give me grip to tighten the knot, before I pulled it inside the soundbox. Then with the string threaded loosely through the tuning pin at the top of the frame, I trimmed the excess and wound steadily with the tuning wrench, and behold! 22 strings later, I had a harp!

It took a week before the harp would stay in tune with itself. Newly fitted strings, especially on such a light frame, go flat within minutes! An old joke runs, "Everyone gets a harp, whether they go to heaven or hell. Those who go to heaven also get a tuning wrench." Another says, "Harpers spend half their time tuning strings, and the other half playing out of tune."

The digital tuner's implacable lighting display also corrected my own ear which thinks a note is in tune when it is fractionally flat. But eventually, I could play my new kit harp without snatching up the wrench to correct something. I became hypersensitive though about turning the right peg, after I went on tightening the one next to the one I thought I was tuning, and it went *Snap!*

Almost as soon as the kit harp held tune I discovered that harps are like biscuits – one is never enough. I found a very beautiful 34-string Pilgrim Clarsach (a fully levered folk harp) at a bargain price and it moved in with me almost at once. I did, however, resist buying the George III pedal harp that my daughter photographed in an antiques auction sale. It was cheap, but I think at 200 years old it would have required far more TLC than I could afford.

One sad reminder of my own age came when I sang to my digital tuner to find out whether I could pitch a middle C by ear, and was shown that I was singing the A below it. Piqued, I sang lower… and lower…I got down to the E above low C, and over the years I've dropped even further. I expect when I

173

eventually join the heavenly choir they'll put me among the tenors. Now there's something to look forward to.

For those curious about costs – in 2012 a 22 string Harp kit from Backyard Harps, CT, USA, cost $235 plus shipping (translates to GBP as approx £130). A 4 string Harp from Pilgrim Harps, Surrey, was around £2,500 in 2012.

COLD CALLERS

My landline call blocker doesn't like switchboards because they are, de facto, Number Withheld, so I had disengaged it this morning because I was expecting a call from the hospital Waiting List secretary.

Immediately I got a cold call from an unintelligible lifestyle survey man who has already called twice today, on a spoofed "local" number (well, supposedly from Blackpool, which is more local to Cumbria than wherever this call really came from).

- *Good monning Ma-am, how are you todday?*
- I'm fine, how are you?
- *I am calling from Life Style Survey.*
- Whoopee.
- *Ma-am, ve are recodding dis call for training pupposes*
- Oh goody. (Ah, bring it on. It's lunchtime and the Waiting List secretary has returned her phone number to switchboard, so I'm not missing anything.)
- *Your telephone number is: o von fife tree six tree six nine...*
- Dear me, no, you've got that all wrong...(I give him the correct number)
Long silence punctuated with an occasional Um...
- *Your telephone number is: o von fife tree six tree six nine?*
- No. (I give him the correct number again.)
Long silence...

- What number are you trying to call, dear?
He gives up trying to correct his data.
- You are Miss Christina Millud?
- No, there's nobody here called Christina Millud.
- You are family member?
- No, there's nobody here called Christina Millud.
Long silence...
(I give him my real name out of pity.)
- You are living at Dee Back, Grin Hom?
- Certainly not.
- You are living at Dee Back, Grin Hom?
- No.
Another long silence.
- You post cud is CA tin tree TA?
- Well done, have a coconut.
- Ma-am, you post cud is CA tin tree TA?
- Yes, dear.
- You are owning your house-renting-paying-morgee...?... (to
be honest I can't actually distinguish what he is rattling
off, but the list is so predictable I know what he's
asking, so I tell him.)
*- What age bracket do you fall into? tventyfive to tirtyfour,
tirtyfive to fottyfour, fottyfive to...*
- I don't.
- Ma-am, what age bracket do you fall into?
- I don't fall into anything if I can help it. Such a trial to
get out.
*- Ma-am, what age bracket do you fall into? tventyfive to
tirtyfour, tirtyfive to fottyfour, fottyfive to...*
- Christmas.
*- Ma-am, what age bracket do you fall into? tventyfive to
tirtyfour, tirtyfive to fottyfour, fottyfive to...*
At this point I move into lying mode.
- I'm a hundred and forty-seven.
He accepts this without a stagger.

- Ma-am, what newspaper do you rid?
- I don't.
- You don't rid newspaper?
- No.
- Are you smoking any cigarette?
- I don't smoke.
He's getting the idea now.
- What is your annual incom? fifteen to tventy thou--
- What the hell do you need to know that for? I'm not
going to tell you.
Long, long silence.

I'd kept him on the phone a good ten minutes by the time I
hung up.

His bloody system called me from the same number five
minutes later.

I've reconnected the call blocker. I will call the Waiting List
secretary instead of waiting for her to call me.

His bloody system has just called me AGAIN from the same
number.

I have blocked it.

A PATCHWORK OF SLEEP

I can't sleep for a whole night in a bed at the moment. The
hip complains and prods me awake. I've tried toughing it out,
but for the last couple of months I have spent the early hours,
through the dawn to 6 or 7am, in the recliner in the front
room. It's more comfortable there, and I don't keep disturbing
my husband's sleep.

I have discovered that BBC 2 broadcasts snippets of
documentaries during the night, and many versions of its
between-programmes channel "signature", and that my
favourite of those is the furry 2 that squeaks and does a

somersault. I have watched a good deal of nocturnal Olympic TV, most of it with my eyes shut - I missed Mo Farah's fall in the 10,000 metres race, but was awake for the interview after he'd won. I've also been permanently dopey during the daytime and prone to falling asleep while I work at the computer.

However, I think I've found the right balance.

Go to bed at my usual time with the usual bedtime painkillers. Expect to wake around 2am unable to find a position that doesn't hurt.

Go down to the kitchen, make a hot drink, take another dose of painkillers and set up camp in the recliner with specific cushions and a pillow, and the furry throw which I bought cheap at Poundland and seems to have an extraordinary ability to induce sleep.

Sleep till, usually, 5am.

Go back to bed and sleep till 7.30am.

On this regime I have been awake and normal (well, as normal as I ever get) for a whole two days now. Still - roll on the pre-op assessment, and a date to have the hip replaced.

VERY GRUMPY WOMAN HAS A VERY GRUMPY DAY

Arthritis is a bugger.

I'm waiting for a hip replacement, agreed in May, surgery date still unknown, but pre-op set for next Thursday. In the meantime I exist on painkillers which, on their own, put up my blood pressure and make my ankles swell, and to prevent that (and heart failure) I take high-blood-pressure medication which makes me faint if I stand up too fast. At night I sleep for an hour, wake, turn over, stifle a yelp and try to sleep for another hour, until after five hours I can't stick it any longer and go downstairs to resume the painkillers and try to sleep in an armchair.

I've snoozed through some extraordinary television in the small hours recently, but this sleeping (correction, non-sleeping) pattern does not make for a sharp and lively brain. I am irritable. Chattering noises become unbearable, whether caused by Classic FM ads at the distant end of the house or unidentified objects in the front foot-well of the Honda. A few days ago with this in mind I dug around under the front seat of the car and seized on the locking wheel-nut socket and the spare nuts which were in a rattly moulded-plastic pack and seemed to be the likely culprits. I put them on top of a box in the car shed.

I've managed despite the brain fog to keep on top of my (mostly voluntary) jobs. One of these was to re-write bits of the Fell Pony Society's Display Team script ready for 4 displays over 2 days at Lowther Show. Then, with the event in mind - and the rainy weather - I decided I'd take the car up to Harold's Tyres and have the front tyres swopped to the back and vice versa for more grip in the inevitable Lowther mud.

It didn't go well.

Mid afternoon on a Wednesday shouldn't look like a busy period on the road, should it? I was quite relaxed following Mark Broadbent's 'Fenix' articulated horsebox down from the motorway to Shap; I knew it was on its way to pitch camp at Lowther, as indeed were many of the big driving-trial competitors. I stopped off at the doctor's surgery to pick up a fresh supply of the prescribed drugs, and so I didn't see the Fenix wagon again. I did however catch up with a tail of traffic behind a tractor and loaded silage trailer, with which I chugged along between second and third gears for several miles until we all reached Bessy Gill and could overtake. At Clifton I caught up with a second slow tractor. And at Gilwilly Industrial Estate, a third.

By this time I was operating on autopilot and kept thinking I had missed my way. I hadn't, fortunately; I reached Harold's to find the place conveniently only half full. I drove into an empty bay, and reassured the helpful chap in charge of it that I hadn't "brocken" anything. I explained that I had checked all the tyre tread depths were legal, but I wanted the front tyres exchanged for the less worn back ones and vice versa.

He cast a professional glance over the Honda's alloys and asked me for the locking nut tool.

I searched my memory, discovered the picture of the locking nut socket lying in its packet in the shed, twenty-five minutes away down the motorway; swore; and departed.

On the way home the niggly rattle resumed. I was feeling savage by now. I stopped on the car park of Go Outdoors and stomped through the rain to open the passenger door, wrench out the underseat drawer and leave it in the footwell. When I drove back onto the motorway, I was moderately soothed to find the niggly rattle had disappeared. Pretty much the first good thing that had happened all afternoon.

I was going uphill somewhere around Hackthorpe when I saw a group of three HGVs ahead. I shifted into the middle lane to overtake them, but when I got level with the second wagon's tail, it began to indicate to pull out. I couldn't get out of its way into the outer lane - my mirror showed me a white Transit pickup barrelling up it far too fast and too close for me to risk moving over - but at that point the wagon began to move into mine, the driver evidently determined to keep up his revs and thinking I was just being obstinate.

The middle lane is not meant to contain a Honda CR-V and a 35-tonne artic. Not side by side at the same time. I braked. Hard. Luckily I've just had the back brakes "done" and despite the rain and the speed, they held and the car stayed in a straight line.

The wagon filled the middle lane ahead of me, the Transit whooshed on by. I had time and space a minute later to overtake safely in the third lane. But I will be replaying that gap narrowing in front of me for the rest of the evening.

And all *that,* ladies and gents, is why I've got sweet F.A. done this afternoon.

Update: I took my car to our local do-it-all garage man this morning. Chris is a former rally driver who was once badly injured as a passenger in someone else's car and so possesses more rebuilt joints than I do. He is one of the bright spots of the village. He appeared, gently sniffling, from the depths of the workshop: "I don't have a cold. I don't have hay fever. I do have a runny nose." Blowing his nose on garage cleanup paper: "I am just generally delicate."

When I proffered the locking nut socket in its packet he ignored it. "Your wheels don't have any locking nuts."

Enough said about all participants.

CARRY A BIG STICK

Free-living Fell ponies are independent of humans. Their days outside the boundaries of the farm involve their own activities, mainly involving foal-care and feeding; and on the whole life is peaceful. Walkers on the common land, on their way to who knows where, may attract the ponies' interest from time to time, but so long as the ponies are not hand-fed they don't expect food. The boss mare generally moves the group steadily away about their own business.

Not all ponies are as distant as Fells though, and the "no hand-feeding" proviso often doesn't hold good. On the Caldbeck Commons, there were Shetland type ponies, including stallions, who had been turned out for so long and so petted by visitors that they were a definite hazard. They shoved their heads into the open windows of parked cars to demand food in a most ill-mannered fashion, and if you denied them they would snap and kick.

A few years back I heard a story of horses doing serious damage to a car in a similar situation. I happened to be at a friend's house, when a nervous middle-aged lady came to knock at the door.

"I need to find out who owns the horses on that place called Sunbiggin Tarn Pasture," she said. "I have to tell my insurance company, but I can't find out who owns them."

This wasn't a very promising opening, but since she was determined to tell her story, my friend invited her in. She wouldn't sit down, she was very upset and not at all coherent, and she didn't have a clue about horses; but she was one of those people who feel they haven't told a story until they have repeated everything twice, so one way and another we got a good feel for what had really happened.

There are two cattle grids that secure the road, onto and off the Tarn Pasture. The lady, alone in a small and immaculately kept car, drove gently across the open Pasture to the cattle grid at the far end, and there she hesitated because a mixed group of horses and ponies stood completely blocking the road. She was afraid to get out and chase them, because there were a dozen of them – and from where she was sitting inside the car they all looked rather big.

The horses, in their turn, thought the car, having come to a halt, would now give them food. This is not as silly as it might sound, because that end of Tarn Pasture is a picnic place where they had been given titbits before, and horses, like elephants, never forget, especially food. So there was one timid lady inside the car, and twelve greedy horses outside.

The leading horse stepped forward and began to bite at the car. So did some of the others. The ones behind believed the ones in front were getting something good to eat, so they began biting and kicking each other. The ones in front kicked back, no doubt with added spite at having been cheated, as they saw it, of their expected treat. Soon there was a noisy melee going on round the immaculately kept little car.

181

"I was screaming by then," she said. "They knocked off the wing mirrors and they bit the door trims, and they mashed the lights – and the front wings – and the radiator grille – and the bonnet. It's going to cost me over a thousand pounds to get the damage put right!"

My friend and I clucked and made sympathetic noises. "And were you all right? Did you manage to chase them off in the end?"

"No, somebody, a farmer, came along from the other direction. He chased them off for me so I could drive over the cattle grid and get away. Oh I was in a state. And my car!" She trembled over the memory; but then perhaps she noticed us looking at the evidently undamaged vehicle out in the street. "I've had to borrow that one from the garage, mine just isn't fit to drive." She stiffened suddenly and went onto the offensive. "So I need to find out whose horses they are, don't I? My insurance company says it has to deal with the owners to get my costs paid for."

My friend shook his head. "Well, they're not my horses," he said; "you see the landowner just lets t' Paster off for the summer. It goes to the highest bidder through the Auction, so it's not always the same person each year."

"Mr So-and-So said they would be yours," she insisted.

"No," he said perfectly calmly. "He's mistaken. I don't use Tarn Paster, I never have done. I have rights on Tebay Fell, do you see? So I wouldn't need Tarn Paster. I'm very sorry to hear of all that damage, but I don't know whose horses they would be."

I think she was about to launch into the tale a fourth time, as though that would convince him of her urgent need for information, but he managed gently to edge her to the door. Eventually she got into her courtesy car, still gritting her teeth over her terrible ordeal, and drove away. My friend paused behind the closed door for a moment, then he dropped into his armchair and he began to laugh. We both did, we couldn't help it. The picture of a car being eaten by a greedy posse of horses was just too silly to resist.

At last he wiped his face with his hand and said, "I suppose somebody eventually will tell her whose horses they are, but I wasn't going to. Well, let that be a lesson to her. If you're going into horse country – don't feed the natives, and carry a big stick."

SMALL WORLD

Appleby Horse Fair is upon us once again. The "gypsies" are variously tagged by the locals as "gyppos", "potters", "pikeys", "tinkers" or "Irish travellers", but we actually see little of any of them over here at Greenholme. I take the precaution of padlocking the carriages to something solid, and cover the ponies with fly rugs to look as though they suffer from "sweet-itch" which makes them unsellable; but the less desirable elements of the Fair have not troubled us.

This year I needed a few photographs to include in this book, and in particular I wanted a photo of a gipsy camp and a living van, so on my way home on Wednesday I wandered through some out-of-the-way villages, looking for people who were camped on roadsides awaiting the opening of The Hill on Thursday morning. I saw a lot of police in fluorescent jackets, and traffic advisory notices warning motorised traffic to be careful of horse-drawn vehicles (excellent!), but I saw no travellers until I reached Appleby itself. There I found huge numbers of No Parking cones, and posts and wire along most of the verges, but few travelling parties as yet, so I drove on through the town and past the still-closed Hill without achieving my goal.

On the way out I took the turning towards a friend's farm and was amused to see that every other field was full of cobs and trotters, obviously earning him a little money for their grazing. However, it wasn't until I had passed his farm and taken the turning for home that I finally saw a small camp on the roadside, and the highly distinctive pale green-canvassed roof and cream-painted shafts of a genuine living van. There was enough space for me to park my car out of the way, so I grabbed my camera and climbed out.

I had passed previous groups of men with horses nearer to Appleby. Although I had waved in a friendly fashion I hadn't felt brave enough, as a solo woman, to stop and accost them for photographs. But here I could see women and children in the party, probably two families or groups of friends, sitting on semicircles of folding chairs and enjoying tea and sunshine on the grass. It looked very like a weekend gathering of competitors at a driving trial, apart from the fact that the motorised vehicles were all three-ton pickups or seven-ton drop-side wagons, and the trailer caravans were bigger and newer than those on the carriage-driving circuit. I strolled back along the verge to scrape acquaintance.

"Morning, nice day, isn't it? Nice living van there … would you mind if I took some photographs?"

No, of course they didn't mind – the van wasn't theirs! They laughed and I laughed with them and asked who did own it, and they directed me to the next trailer caravan. I spoke to a young woman there with her daughter, and they told me it was fine for me to take photographs. So I took a couple of photos of the living van, clean and trim in its burgundy paint, its patterned interior mirrors cheerfully reflecting the light. There was a four wheeled flat dray alongside so I photographed that too. Then I walked up the verge, passing the trailer caravan and the wood fire with its black iron pots, tripods and hooks, to the shade of the trees where the horses were standing in deep grass, quietly watching the day go by. The black and white gelding considered me carefully, then moved up to sniff my proffered knuckles. He was a powerful little cob, standing about 14 hands with a lot of bone and a decent amount of feather. He took several deep breaths, then pulled up his top lip to hold and analyse my scent. I must have smelt satisfactory, because he then let me stroke his muzzle. I didn't disturb him further though, as tethered animals can't get away, and the half-circle of their tether has to be their rest space as well as their feeding area, so it's not fair to invade it. I walked back to the brown and white mare, who was another strong sort of about 15 hands, in really hard, fit condition. Like the gelding, she was tethered to a tree by a neck-strap and chain, which was sensibly covered for the first ten feet by plastic hose-pipe so it could neither rub nor kink around an unwary hoof. Both horses looked like good kind animals who knew tethering as part of their job. I spoke to the mare, who flicked an ear at me in acknowledgement, but her attention seemed to be on something several fields away so I admired and moved on.

As I passed by the trailer caravan, a rough coated terrier tethered to a wooden kennel yapped at me briefly. The older lady of the family looked up from tending the fire to see what he was reacting to. I smiled and she called a greeting, I replied with a complimentary remark about the two cobs, and we were off! Within five minutes we were sitting in folding chairs by the fire and talking "horses and driving" nineteen-to-the-dozen. She told me about their trip over the Pennines from the North-East along the Middleton-in-Teesdale road, and we discussed its quietness in terms of traffic and the steepness of its banks and drags. She described how the horses had tackled them with the living van and the dray, and how her husband had had to give them rest stops after cresting each of the steeper hills. "He got a bit wild, said he wouldn't come by that road again, it was cruel on the horses."

Would I like a cup of tea? I accepted, though I'm normally a coffee drinker. She hung the black kettle over the mended fire and very soon it was steaming merrily.

"I don't like cooking in the trailer [caravan]," she said. "I like my open fire, and to be outside in the sunshine." They didn't normally camp this far out from Appleby, she said, but it was good to be away from the main bustle of the Fair, where some of the menfolk were too prone to drink themselves silly and then "make a noise late at night and disturb everybody" or go driving their horses in the dark, "which isn't fair on them." However, her husband didn't drink, so although she didn't know quite where he was right now, she wasn't worried about him. It was easier to tether the horses here, too, with the trees for shade.

"There's a lot of lads come over for the Fair and they think because they have a coloured horse and they drive it here they know it all, but they don't. They know nothing. They don't know how to treat them, not like us, when we've been born and bred to it. The tradition isn't there, or else they don't care about it any more."

Two PG Tips teabags went into the Harrods china mugs, and we sat and sipped and chatted.

The disadvantage of the quiet roadside was that there wasn't a handy water supply and they'd had to go to the village pub to fill up. She said, "I like to stop where there are lavatories really, but it's all right with the trailer." Their rubbish was in two plastic sacks which they would take to the skip on Fair Hill once the main site was open.

I mentioned that I had been taking photographs for a book and she at once went into the trailer to bring out a big shiny hardback in which she showed me photographs of her family. If I'd had a tape recorder running I could have catalogued all her brothers and sisters and their spouses and offspring right then and there, but as it was I nodded and smiled and made the wordless noises of agreement that keep conversations going.

We discovered an acquaintance in common, Walter Lloyd, a very well spoken and well educated man who by then was in his eighties. "When we met him he was cooking a hedgehog and he asked if I would like a bit. I said, No, I would NOT!" Later that weekend, she complained of "a bit of an upset stomach, oh I was badly" and so Walter had taken a pan and gone picking leaves out of the hedgerows for her. "Grass and weeds and all sorts, and he brewed it up and poured it into a pot, as black as that kettle, I wouldn't have drunk out of it. He said, 'Drink that and by the time it's all gone you'll be better.' Well I didn't like to offend him so I took the pot off him, but when he wasn't looking I poured it all away. I went to the doctor instead. I wasn't going to drink that, I didn't know what was in it. Would you have drunk it?"

I have a garden full of medicinal plants and a head full of botanical trivia, so I admitted that if the brew had been made by Walter, I might have asked for details, but so long as I knew the plants I would have drunk it. We both laughed, but she shook her head: "Well I wasn't going to risk it!"

As I stood up to take leave, I mentioned that a family from her area was coming to stay with us for Fair Week, but that the husband wouldn't bring a horse to the Fair, saying he'd be worried someone let it loose for a lark, or even stole it. He would be going home each night to tend his stock.

"Oh yes? Who's that then?" I gave the surname and she said at once, "Oh, that'll be Joe and Violet. They live a couple of miles from us. When you see them, tell them you've met Michelle."

The horse world is indeed a small one.

THE ROAD TO APPLEBY FAIR

A fictionalised tale built up from real incidents.

Pied and skewbalds, roans and greys, horses bay or brown or dun,
four white legs, a star or blaze; they drowse on verges in the sun.
Flicking tails at teasing flies, the summer grass long eaten bare,
tether chains and patient eyes, beside the road to Appleby Fair.

Traffic stares, in passing, at old vardoes with new canvas tops,
shirts and towels draped to dry on shafts parked up on wooden
      props;
but others camp in trailer homes where four-wheel-drives replace the
      mare;
caravans here flash with chrome, beside the road to Appleby Fair.

Dark-haired girls with sidelong eyes will sell you shiny brass as gold.
Canny women will advise with fortunes patched from what you've
      told;
peddlers drag out coloured clothes and wheedle you to buy their
      ware.
Rough-haired lurchers pant and doze, beside the road to Appleby
      Fair.

Plunging into Eden's pools, fat cob or swiftest equine prince
bow equally to wise or fools who wash and scrub and soap and rinse.

Trotting bareback up the hill, with dung-dust rising in the air,
"Mind yer backs, giddout the way!" along the road to Appleby Fair.

Brass and nickel buckles clink on harness dumped astride a fence.
Tattooed men sit out and drink till alcohol has drowned their sense.
Road-horse bets are won and lost; "we'll dodge police, I'll race you
      there!"
Caution to the wind is tossed, along the road to Appleby Fair.

Trotting in a lightweight frame to flash a quick mare at her best;
opposites in crowded lanes can slam the shafts in neck or breast.
Crashing steel on tarmac roads, horse-eyes are wild and nostrils flare
at racing speeds with yelling loads, along the road to Appleby Fair.

After racing, "Cool her off" means washing her in Eden's pools;
"Ride and swim her." But the 'drop' is hidden, steep and waits for
    fools.
Tied to a sulky, head pulled down, no heaving struggle brings her air.
The mare drowns on the halter rope; no road home from Appleby
    Fair.

Visitors can hardly tell which men are Romani in truth.
No mark of skin, no gipsy spell, can split the *rai* from *gorgio* youth.
The elders with their horsey lore despise the town boys' lack of care,
and spit, descriptively, before they turn away at Appleby Fair.

THE "FELL PONY" NAME

There is very scant evidence of British ponies in the 12
centuries between the end of Roman rule and the era of
Elizabeth I. Every positive statement that can be made about
them has a "but" attached to it.

Harness fittings and small pony-size 3.5" to 4" bits have
survived from the Roman period and there are some sculptures
which portray horses in Britain as small, eg the Roman
tombstone to Flavinus in Hexham Abbey (on display at Tullie
House Museum, Carlisle, in 2014), *but* we don't have evidence
of a local Cumbrian type, much less a breed.

The Bayeux Tapestry shows a pack pony smaller than the
cavalry horses who seem to be about 14 hands, *but* it is way too
far south in its origins to be a reference for Northern England.

Paintings throughout history show horses in the service of
monarchs and generals, *but* no-one commissioned paintings of
the working ponies in the inhospitable North.

We may guess that they were around—*but* who's going to write about a scruffy pickup truck when there are Ferraris or Rolls Royces to admire?

Literature

Eventually, when printed material becomes more common, evidence of local ponies appears as it does today, in literature and in trivia such as advertisements. The term "Galloway" comes into use in Shakespeare's time (1597) referring to a small horse in common use. Daniel Defoe in the early 1700s describes Scotland as having "the best breed of strong low horses in Britain, if not in Europe … from whence we call all small truss-strong riding horses Galloways."

Small ads

The most specific references to local Cumbrian horses are notices in newspapers seeking information about "missing" saddle horses. "DARK BAY GALLOWAY, Eleven Hands and a Half high…. the Mane and Tail rather inclined to black, and had two or three white Saddle Marks… Reward for information leading to retrieval."

The word "pony"

A plausible explanation is frequently trotted out that the word "pony" traces to the Celtic horse goddess Epona. Sadly that doesn't really hold water because her name had disappeared from common English usage by the 6th century AD—a thousand years before the earliest known date for "powny" which is a diary entry in 1659: "Diary 18 June, I caused to bring home the powny…" and 1675 W. Cunningham's Diary, 24 May, "Sent to Glasgow for a gang of shoo's to Cuninghamheid's pownie." Both are cited by the Oxford English Dictionary which adds that "pony" comes from Scottish, apparently from French *poulenet* "little foal", and that the Irish *pónaí* and Scottish Gaelic *pònaidh* are derived from the English word *pony* and not the other way around.

In 1710 Defoe describes characters riding on "Bastard Turks, half-bred Barbs, and Union Ponies, a Kind of Horses foaled upon the Borders, and occasionally owning either Country". "Union Ponies" might suggest he is thinking of Scottish Galloways or predecessors of the English Fell. Defoe had been sent to Edinburgh in 1706 to worm his way into the confidence of the Scottish Parliament and help secure the Union of England and Scotland, so he may simply be poking fun at himself and at recent political history. In any case, later in the pamphlet he remarks, "it is not my business as a Historian, to be over sollicitous about the Truth of Facts" (unusual honesty on the part of a secret agent and a journalist). Perhaps it's safest to assume he has his tongue firmly in his cheek, and just to note his use of the word "ponies."

Small ads again

Spelt "poney" the word appears in 1838 in local advertisements in the Westmorland Gazette where it is linked to the terms "Scotch horse" or "Galloway" but not yet to "Fell". Through the 19th Century the horses of Cumberland and Westmorland were still referred to as Fell-Galloways, and I have heard old farmers even as recently as 2021 using the term "Gallower" about Fell ponies.

Agricultural horses, cobs, Hackneys, Galloways and "fell ponies"

Local shows - mostly held in September after the hay crop had been cleared from the fields - divided classes for horses and ponies into various types: Agricultural horses (ie, Clydesdales and their crosses and others suitable to pull farm equipment); cobs; Hackneys; and ponies. These "ponies" were not defined as any breed but usually the classes specified height limits such as "under 14 hands" or "under 13½ hands".

191

The earliest use of the term "fell pony" (without a capital F) that I've found so far is from the Kendal newspaper, the *Westmorland Gazette*, October 1853, reporting on the horse sale at Dent where trade in "fell ponies" had been better than in previous years (so the term was in use before 1853).The lack of a capital F, as opposed to the G of Galloway or H of Hackney, suggests that the term "fell pony" was not a breed name yet: it was being used for "a pony suitable to live at the fell" or "pony that has been living at the fell", in the same way that modern sheep breeds like Swaledales, Roughs and Herdwicks could be grouped under the one term "fell sheep". The Penrith newspaper, the Cumberland and Westmorland Herald, 6th September, 1885 reported that at Dufton show "the entry of fell ponies was good and the competition keen". This version of the term "fell pony" as any fell-going pony is supported by a slightly later report in the Penrith Observer of 25th October, 1887 which, having stated that "the Judges for Shorthorns, Cobs, Ponies and Whitefaced Sheep were Mr. W. Ellwood, Skelling and Mr. Bousfield, Langwathby," reported under Special Prizes for Ponies the following result: "Fell-gone pony, with foal at foot - 1, Messrs. Dargue; 2. Mr. Hutchinson." *(With thanks to Dorothy Ewin of Dufton.)*

The Polo and Riding Pony Society

In 1893 the Polo Pony Society became the Polo and Riding Pony Society and began to register native pony types suitable for breeding light horses for sport and recreation. It registered the ponies by the areas in which they were located, and stipulated that they must be at least three-quarters "native" bred. This is when the names of areas such as Wales and the Scottish Highlands began to be linked to pony registrations, and the idea of a local breed with recorded ancestry emerged in place of a local "type".

Agricultural Show reports

The Cumberland and Westmorland Herald reports from agricultural shows at first described classes as scheduled for Ponies not over 13½ hands, Cobs over 13½ hands and under 14½ hands, and Hackneys over 14½ hands. Orton (1860s), Hesket-New-Market (1894) and Shap (1895) were other shows that offered classes specifically for "Fell ponies."

In 1898 the Polo and Riding Pony Society Stud Book registered the first 2 stallions and 6 mares in its Fell section, and the Fell Pony Society, formally created in 1922, celebrated 100 years in 2022.

But we still call them 'osses, even now.

HOW TO MAKE A SMALL FORTUNE
FROM WRITING

Let me spin you a yarn about my day. Today, for instance.

I rose at 7 am, and fed our animals. Just before 8 am, I hoisted a rucksack-cum-shopping-trolley of books into the car and set off on a 40 mile journey to a "pop up book shop" as part of a brand-new local Literary Festival. Nota bene - the experienced indie author will always choose to transport books on wheels rather than directly by hand. Thus, I was instantly able to identify same, and distinguish them from the unpractised bag-and-box brigade, when we converged at 9am on the library which was our destination.

After a short round of greetings to those whom I knew in the PUBS (this does not mean the Rose and Crown. It is an acronym for Pop Up Book Shop) I left my stout plastic butcher's-tray of books in what I trusted were capable hands, and drove home again to get a few things done. Recycling was high on the list: for instance, plastic bags, and dog-food tins.

Just after 2:30 pm I set off with another load of recycling and the empty shopping trolley. The library at 3:45 pm was pleasingly full of people behind and around the book tables, but it was pretty clear from their behaviour that they were writers, not buyers. Still, I had a very interesting conversation with a fellow historical novelist sitting in the "Ask the Author Anything" area, who was kind enough to say she didn't consider this "work" and also told me that the stall-holding writers had laughed a lot while reading my *Dragon Bait*. I was relieved to find that the laughter was because they thought it was funny, rather than peculiar.

Dragon Bait was my star of that day – it made one sale to a member of the public, and one to a fellow writer. I bought a collection of short stories written by a chap who teaches SS

194

writing as a specialism at the University, and I intend to study them to learn about modern SS style. I also bought a historical novel by the lady in the AAA area, and very nearly doubled my day's takings when she offered me change from my £20 in the form of.... wait for it... a £20 note and a couple of £1 coins. Being honest (or stupid) I suggested she reconsidered this. I really should have offered, instead, a copy of *Dragon Bait*, which she had said she intended to buy - but there we are, I too can be a bit slow after an earlier-than-usual start.

When I was re-packing I couldn't locate some of the books I had taken to the PUBS (stop it now!). The slim poetry pamphlet, it seemed, had too closely resembled the kids' activity books - they were printed by the same firm - and the two activity books had not been displayed individually because they were the same thickness. The three items all spent the day in the same stack, and registered no sales at all. Moral - if taking several books which are similar, pack them in widely separated batches so that even those who are unfamiliar with your stuff will realise they are not all the same thing.

The accounts for today look like this:

> Car mileage: 160 miles (40 miles there and back, morning and afternoon)
> Parking fees: £1 x 2 (very reasonable and handy for the venue)
> Donation per sale to the PUBS (stop sniggering at the back please): £1 per book, ie £2
> Costs: £4 outgoings, car fuel discounted as part of recycling run... which is frankly bloody optimistic)
> Book Sale: £6 x 2
> Income: £12
> Net income: £8 (see remark on Costs)
> Purchases: errrrm... *coughs*

See, this is why writers are rubbish at business. Having "made" a few quid at the expense of 4 hours of driving, I blew it all and more by buying 2 books that cost (together) more than

I had actually taken, which in any case I can't dignify by the term "profit" (see remark on Costs!)

All in all, a very typical writer's "sales" day. Lots of batting around, lots of jawing, a bit of networking, a bit of positive feedback, and one or two lessons learned.

Oh, and how to make a small fortune from writing?

Start with a large one.

NEW SONGS TO OLD TUNES (1)

There's a perfectly good tune whose words have become non-PC through no fault of their own.

The Six Fell Packs
(original version)

Now I'll give you a toast, lads, to all the fell packs,
To masters, to huntsmen and whips of aw maks,
You can have your athletics and games of all sorts,
But this hunting is surely the greatest of sports.
Tally Ho! Tally Ho! Tally Ho!
Hark For'ard good hounds, Tally Ho!

Look at all the other hunting songs we Cumbrians have, that are just being wasted... well what does a writer do? She writes some new words. And if Maddy Prior can sing about the Uppies and Downies at Workington, then I can sing about an agricultural show. So this one goes to the tune of "The Six Fell Packs."

Crosby Ravensworth Show

The heather is bright on the top of the Scar.
The family packs in the seats of the car.
There's Granddad and Grannie, the kids and the hound
and we're all on the road, Crosby-Ravensworth-bound.
Let it rain, let it shine, let it blow -
we're going to Ravensworth Show.

Now Granddad and Grannie they go every year
to catch up with crack and to share some good cheer;
they've got to the age where they're thin in the thatch
and where most of their talk is hatch, match and dispatch.
Let it rain, let it shine, let it blow -
we're all at the Ravensworth Show.

The Industry tent is where mother is bound
which leaves me out here with the kids and the hound.
I'd bet on the ferrets, which pipe they would run -
but they sleep in their burrow to hide from the sun!
Let it rain, let it shine, let it blow -
we're all at the Ravensworth Show.

The ponies are trotting to show at their best,
where beauty and manners are part of the test;
the cattle lie dozing, the sheep stand in pens,
there's a tent for the rabbits, the ducks and the hens.
Let it rain, let it shine, let it blow -
we're all at the Ravensworth Show.

We sit on the benches to eat an ice cream
or hot dogs that give off a savoury steam
with onions and ketchup. The hound licks his lips
so we give him the crusts and the last of the chips.
Let it rain, let it shine, let it blow -
we're all at the Ravensworth Show.

The big bouncy castle is where the kids play;
they take off their shoes and go bounding away;
the dog wants to join them and leaps like a clown,
but Granddad and Grannie just want a sit-down.
Let it rain, let it shine, let it blow -
we're tired at the Ravensworth Show.

The sunshine has fled and it's going to shower;
if you don't like the weather just wait half an hour.
It was fun in the sun through the sideshows to roam,
but now we're wet through so I think we'll go home.
Let it rain, let it shine, let it blow -
we've been to the Ravensworth Show.

NEW SONGS TO OLD TUNES (2)

This one goes to the tune of "Keilder Hunt."

The Lunesbridge Rail Disaster

The night is cold in Tebay Gorge, the wind is keening sore
in the February darkness of the year two thousand-four.
The railway lads are set to work between mid-night and morn,
from Saturday the fourteenth to the Sunday's frozen dawn.
Gone away, gone away,
out of Scout Green down to Tebay, gone away.

The scrappers' gang is working on the trackside at Scout Green
unloading sixteen tons of steel with a heavy crane machine.
And down at Lunesbridge level there's a cutting gang and all
who work by floodlight through the night with the generator's
    growl.

A shift of steel, a broken brake, a clang that shakes the tracks;
the flat-bed truck has pushed aside its feeble wooden blocks.
With sixteen tons of rusty rail she runs from where she parked
and down the one in seventy-five goes rumbling through the
    dark.

Get out your phone and call them up and warn the
    Lunesbridge crew -
Tell Tindall, Buckley, Burgess, *Jump and go, she's bound for you.*
She's cleared the cut at Scotchman's Bridge, the bank above Low
    Scales,
Low Greenholme's airy viaduct and Loups Fell's trembling rails.

All sixteen tons down seventy-five is killing weight indeed;
that minute while you try to call ramps up the wagon's speed.
The cutters of the Lunesbridge gang they fall without a cry;
she throws five men from out her path and sends four more to
    die.

In vain the phones are ringing now; an answer cannot come,
for Waters', Buckley's, Burgess', Tindall's time on earth is done.
No monument can bring them back, no killer's years in jail.
Remember, when you pass Lune's Bridge, the men who mend
    the rail.
Gone away, gone away,
out of Scout Green down to Tebay, gone away.

INSULTS A LA CARTE

I see via Murderati that there is a "Shakespearean Insult Kit" comprising words the Bard employed. I rather enjoy Bardic vitriol. I once rehearsed in King Lear as Goneril and was joyously enabled to scream "milk-liver'd man!" at my husband on stage.

As a theatre director Ngaio Marsh must have taught many young actors to handle Will's bad language. She has fun with some of her playwright characters in various novels, particularly Dr Rutherford who scorns someone by pronouncing, "Get you gone, you dwarf - you minimus of hind'ring knot-grass made, you bead, you acorn."

Myself, I'd be tempted to add the good old Midlands word "orts" that has been out of use now for three generations. Shakespeare used it in the phrase "abjects, orts and imitations" - things thrown aside as of no use, waste, or bad copies. The phrase has been misinterpreted as "objects, arts and imitations" but I know the word "orts" existed because my grandad used to say when you left food on your plate, "eat it up, I don't want your orts." It would combine well with some of our Cumbrian insults, I think. "Thou's nobbut an ort. Waste of a good skin."

Mind you in Cumbria we have a great many place-names and hill names that could be used as insults. Zoe Sharp suggested "Eeh, you great Wet Sleddle." To that I'd like to add, "E's nobbut a Subberthwaite," and "Thou's a Great Cockup."

More on names another time. I have to go now, I'm feeling a bit Witherslack.

ON THE VERGE

When I went shopping in the middle of the week, instead of flitting up the M6 from Greenholme to Shap I took the scenic route. And, luckily, I had the little Fuji camera in my handbag, because the grass verges beside the motorway bridges were a gleaming tapestry of purple and gold. Cohorts that were positively Assyrian.

If you've ever thought that "anything that isn't growing in a tub or a garden bed, and anything other than clipped grass in the lawn, is a weed" then you should have another look at the wonders of Britain's grassland.

I parked the car and I swear I didn't walk more than 100 yards from it but I found over 3 dozen flowering plants:

Yellow ones

Yellow pea
Bird's foot trefoil
Yellow rattle
Cat's ear
Meadow buttercup
Creeping buttercup
Tormentil
Crosswort
John Go-To-Bed-At-Noon   (and he does)

Green to yellow

Lady's mantle

Yellow to pink

Water avens - several showing a little aberration that it
throws occasionally, double flowers

Pink
Ragged robin
Red clover
White clover
Eyebright
Cow parsley
Pignut
Daisy
Ox-eye daisy
Yarrow
Mouse-ear chickweed (the smaller one)
Not to mention the rowan and the hawthorn bushes.

Purple
Marsh orchid (and magnificent big fat hybrid spikes of them)
Wood cranesbill
Bush vetch

Blue
Germander speedwell

Brownish and rusty
Ribwort plantain
Sorrel dock

And that's just the things that were flowering. July will bring us the lavender-and-white common spotted orchids and the foamy cream of meadowsweet; thistles of the creeping, musk, marsh, spear and melancholy species; and the bristly brown-and-purple shaving brushes of knapweed.

Green is also a colour
Don't forget the flowering grasses - they are nearly up into your face!

Grasses

Timothy
Cocksfoot
Sweet vernal
Crested dogstail
Yorkshire fog
False brome
Red fescue

A little way along the verge from my house I also find the small Quaking grass, with its pendulous flowers trembling on stems like thin wire.

Even a thistle or a nettle has a use: sheep, cattle and horses eat the flowers of thistles (sometimes more), and the nettle has a history varying from cloth and rope to soup and beer, as well as being an ingredient in spring "dock pudding" and, of course, a feasting place for butterfly caterpillars.

One of the few benefits of Council budget cuts is that they don't send men round quite so often with mowing machines. Look at the glory they have left for us.

A BOTANICAL RANT

It's Summer solstice, and the local grass verges are looking amazing. I am lucky in that I live in Cumbria in the middle of nowhere and that the County Council doesn't get round to mowing our verges till the autumn. Also that the nearest large village is surrounded by what the CC designates "special verges" of high botanical importance.

All this experience makes me sceptical on social media about people who post photographs of big urban areas which are sowing "wild flowers" in "meadows" (quotation marks for irony). These are sown with seed mixes containing arable annuals, including non-natives such as the California Poppy and French Spinach (Red Orache). The result may be pretty but by definition these are not meadows, which are permanent grassland not arable fields. It is gardening – admirable in the right place, well carried out, eye-catching, but not, as some claim, restoring any degraded habitat. Yes, it's more colourful and a bit more diverse than super-mown grass verges, and it saves the councils some expense, which is a fair enough reason to do it, but outside of urban settings it's inappropriate.

I fear for the natural British flora at the hands of well intentioned but uninformed gardeners.

As I mentioned above, I'm in a rural area. So step out of the farm gate with me, onto the lane which is an ancient drove road, in its heyday a route for cattle and goods being walked into the industrial towns. It's mown once a year now by the Council, in September or October. I don't suppose it ever held as much floral or insect life in the old days as it does now – travelling hooves and teeth will have seen to that. But there were meadows and moorland either side of it and when the hooves and teeth disappeared from the road, the plants came back.

Our verges now are astonishingly diverse.

Walk 200 yards each way with me. Although I have come to prefer the scientific binomials for plants, I'll give you their common English names, which to a writer are as much of a joy as the flowers themselves.

Northwards:
1. Grasses: Rye grass
2. Rough meadow grass
3. Wavy hair grass
4. Quaking grass
5. Sweet vernal grass
6. Yorkshire fog
7. False Oat
8. False brome
9. Cocksfoot
10. Ferns: Male Fern
11. Lady Fern
12. Shrubs: Northern Downy Rose
13. Sherard's Downy Rose
14. Summer snowflake (an escape from my garden, not planted)
15. Geranium macrorrhizum (foreign; an escape from my garden, not planted)
16. Giant Bellflower (native but an escape from my garden, not planted)
17. Wood cranesbill
18. Meadow cranesbill
19. Herb Robert
20. Nipplewort
21. Meadow vetchling
22. Bush vetch
23. Birds-foot trefoil
24. White clover
25. Red clover
26. Feverfew
27. Cinquefoil
28. Silverweed
29. Meadow buttercup
30. Bulbous buttercup
31. Common chickweed
32. Mouse-ear chickweed
33. Common sallow
34. Eyebright
35. Great willowherb
36. Lady's mantle
37. Water avens
38. Mouse-ear hawkweed
39. Rough hawkbit
40. Marsh thistle

41. Spear thistle
42. 3 different species of dandelions
43. Common daisy
44. Ox-eye daisy
45. Germander speedwell
46. Field speedwell
47. Meadowsweet
48. Betony
49. Self-heal
50. Hedge woundwort

51. Harebell
52. Crosswort
53. Common sorrel
54. Cow parsley
55. Black Knapweed
56. Garlic Mustard
57. Hedge bedstraw
58. Lady's bedstraw
59. Foxglove
60. Yarrow
61. Welsh Poppy
62. Ribwort plantain

Southwards
1. Grasses: Rye grass
2. Rough meadow grass
3. Wavy hair grass
4. Sweet vernal grass
5. Yorkshire fog
6. False Oat
7. Cocksfoot
8. Ferns: Male Fern
9. Lady Fern
10. Common Polypody
11. Shrubs: Common sallow
12. Bay willow
13. Blackthorn
14. Wild plum (Prunus domestica)
15. Hawthorn

16. Bird cherry
17. Ash
18. Hazel
19. Northern Downy Rose
20. Sherard's Downy Rose
21. Wood cranesbill
22. Meadow cranesbill
23. Herb Robert
24. Shining cranesbill
25. Meadow vetchling
26. Bush vetch
27. Tufted vetch
28. Birds-foot trefoil
29. White clover
30. Red clover
31. Cinquefoil

32. Silverweed
33. Meadow buttercup
34. Celandine
35. Common chickweed
36. Mouse-ear chickweed
37. Broad-leaved willowherb
38. Lady's mantle
39. Water avens
40. Wood avens
41. Rough hawkbit
42. Marsh thistle
43. 3 different species of dandelions
44. Ox-eye daisy
45. Goat's-beard
46. Germander speedwell
47. Field speedwell
48. Meadowsweet
49. Betony
50. Self-heal
51. Hedge woundwort
52. Crosswort
53. Common sorrel
54. Cow parsley
55. Pignut
56. Raspberry
57. Wild strawberry
58. Barren strawberry
59. Common Dog-violet
60. Blinks
61. Brooklime
62. Black Knapweed
63. Melancholy thistle
64. Garlic Mustard
65. Lady's Smock
66. Wood forgetmenot
67. Changing forgetmenot
68. Cleavers
69. Hedge bedstraw
70. Lady's bedstraw
71. Hogweed
72. Foxglove
73. Yarrow
74. Red Campion
75. Welsh Poppy
76. Ribwort plantain

There are also the odd nettles and common docks, but not many because everything else keeps them in check.

These lists are from memory alone…And that's without going half a mile up the road where the verges are graced by Northern Marsh Orchid and Common Spotted Orchid and a myriad of their hybrids, plus Bilberry, Lemon-Scented Fern and Hard Fern. All on the roadside. If I went out with a clipboard throughout the year and noted everything I saw either side of our house I could easily list up to 100 species of plant in a quarter-mile of road.

Lots of plant diversity brings lots of insect diversity, and plentiful insects bring diverse bird and animal life.

Many other verges could be as diverse as ours if they were not mown to within an inch of their life by lawn-obsessives – and if they were also spared the attentions of the sow-a-meadow apostles.

Yes, OK, sow native annuals, *if* all you have got is a degraded grass verge, but not non-native plants, because our fauna doesn't have a use for them.

And leave the good verges alone please.

SPRING CLEANING

2008

We didn't "do" Christmas in 2008; that was partly on account of the snow, but more because our grand-daughter, aged five, spent the whole holiday period in hospital. Somehow, jollifications didn't seem in order, and the usual tidying up didn't happen either. I've been ignoring it now for months. Not putting it off, simply refusing to acknowledge that my house needs re-organizing.

Suddenly, this morning, I feel compelled to pack unwanted clothes into a bag for recycling. Also, I hear a diesel engine start up outside. I look through the window, and there's my husband, driving the front-loader which is pushing his very very vintage Nuffield tractor down the yard. Panic! Then I notice that only two wheels out of its four are still capable of rolling. No danger of a runaway there, then.

He gets down every now and again to adjust the steering so the Nuffield turns towards the workshop doors.

My God, he has finally decided it's time for some restoration! I had better get him up into the bathroom NOW. Otherwise, though Spring may have provoked us both into re-organizing and restoring, it could be summer before he gets the shower mended.

MAD AS A BOX OF FROGS

2011

"Good morning," said my husband as I came into the kitchen. "And say good morning to your friend there."

Sleepily, I looked round for the cat. "Where?"

"There, in the corner." He pointed to the nook between the washing machine and the plinth under the kitchen cupboard. A brownish, motionless lump.

My first thought was, "How did the cat manage to crap in such a small space?" and my second was, "It's got legs. And claws. And eyes! IT'S A FROG."

"Oh my goodness. How did that get in?"

He shrugged and went on making his mug of tea.

Outside on the windowsill, the cat paddled with alternate paws at the pane. "Let me in! It's raining! I'm hungry!"

"I'd better put the frog out, or she'll eat it."

Thinking that the frog was likely to jump if I put a hand on it, I chose an old glass off the shelf in which to trap it.

"Wet the glass," suggested my husband.

So I did. I held it behind the frog, and put a finger in front of its nose. It didn't move, so I pushed it gently. It was cold, heavy, and damp. It turned and leapt into the glass, then became immobile again.

With one hand over the top of the glass, I unlocked the back door. The cat rushed in and I went out. I tipped the frog onto the grass. It sat so still and unblinking, I wondered if it had died of shock, but no, its throat pulsed with its breathing, so I left it there in the rain-swept garden. And came back indoors and fed the cat.

Of course, the question was, how can a frog get into a locked kitchen? The clue was there in the washed-out glass: traces of coal dust. Froggie must have been in the coal bunker; been scooped up by my husband's shovel, then poured with the wet coke into the hod.

I'd stoked the fire from that hod last night before I let out the cat and went to bed. I don't know how many lives a frog has, but she used up two of them today.

A HISTORICAL RUN-DOWN ON HORSES

First published on English Historical Fiction Authors *in January 2014.*

I was going to start this blog post with a quick trot through the history of the horse since the Bronze Age—skipping through Roman, Anglo Saxon and medieval history with a click of the tongue and a crack of the whip. But, as I've done a good deal of that already and it's called The Fell Pony and Countryside Museums, I won't. For which you should be jolly grateful, otherwise this post would have been even longer.

However, I had better clear up a few technical terms here which I'll be using throughout:

> Horse or stallion – an entire adult male with all his breeding equipment intact, a bit touchy and difficult to handle if there is a nice mare nearby.
> Mare – an adult female.
> Gelding – a male horse of age over 1 year, who has been castrated to stop him breeding, and make him easier to handle.
> Colt – young horse under the age of 4 years (in England, also, usually this refers to a male).
> Filly – young mare under the age of 4 years.
> Foal – young horse under 1 year of age.
> Hand – a term of immense age, the width of a man's hand, standardised as 4 inches. Horses are measured for height at the withers, the bony part of the spine just above the shoulder; when a horse puts its head down to graze, the wither is the highest point of its body. A horse of 12 hands high measures 48 inches / 4 feet /

122 centimetres from ground to wither; one that is 13.2 hands high measures 54 inches / 4 foot 6 inches / 137.2 cms; 15 hands high is 60 inches / 5 feet / 152.4 cms. And so on.

Time span

The horse has been around people for an awfully long time —since circa 5,500 years ago, when they were domesticated in the steppes of central Asia. Since then the horse has developed an almost symbiotic relationship with humans and, like the dog, cat, sheep and cow, has become a highly successful domestic species.

From the time of the Botai Culture of *Kazakhstan*, up to the advent of steam locomotion in Britain in the 1830s, the horse's job has been to supply power and/or speed.

Quality over quantity

Just as with cars in modern times, the more power and speed you want, the more you have to pay for it. This means that the most powerful people have the fastest and most powerful horses while the poor old foot soldier and farmer has to make do with what he can get—or else, do without. Historically, though, the speed and power requirement doesn't imply that the rich own very tall horses. Tall horses are a very modern development.

"... in the Iron Age, horses (or more accurately ponies) averaged 12.1 hh in height and resembled the modern Exmoor breed in terms of overall build. Roman horses show two distinct types; the first similar to the Iron Age ponies but taller (13.3 hh), the second taller still (14-15 hh) and more heavily built (much like a modern cob). During the Saxon period there appears to be a change back to predominantly smaller (13.2 hh) but quite robust ponies. In the Medieval period the average

213

horse appears very similar to Saxon ones, although a few relatively large individuals begin to appear."

The horse found accompanying the Anglo-Saxon Lakenheath burial (~570 AD) was about 14 hands high although the man is estimated to have been six feet tall.

Most British "horses", through many centuries, would be classed as ponies by modern standards. It was a world where the horse population probably looked like the current British native pony breeds.

Kinds of horses

There were no distinct horse "breeds" until the late 18th century; no pedigree societies and no stud books except the memories of the men who handled horses as part of their employment.

Horses were classified by the work they were suitable for. They were sumpters (pack horses); rouncies or cobs or nags who trotted along carrying tradespeople (including the young squire struggling with his master's war stallion). Small horses did the work of all the industries, bore messages, carried people on pilgrimages and transported packs of goods many hundreds of miles from farm to consumer. A few horses drew farm carts harnessed side by side in pairs or "at length" nose to tail but, given the often poor state of the roads until the toll system was introduced, probably far more were employed carrying packs and people on their backs. Pack horses from Kendal walked to London and back within a month, taking wool, cheeses and other produce southwards and bringing back all the dainties of civilised life from the capital to the rural communities.

Powerful and warlike men of course required war-horses. These stallions were led by mounted squires to keep them fresh for a knight's use, hence the term destrier, from dextrarius, the

214

"horse at the right hand". A war horse, even for an armoured man, was nowhere near as tall as the modern Shire or Clydesdale draught horse; most likely he stood around 15 to 15 and a half hands at the shoulder and was a square-trotting powerful cob like the "Powys Horse" of South Wales, or the modern Welsh Section D cob (before it began to shoot skyward in modern times).

Hobelars (mounted local militia, used for skirmishing in times of war) rode hobbies of 13 to 14 hands high. Hobbies were quick and sturdy, like Fell ponies, Connemaras, and the taller types of the New Forest ponies. There is some discussion about whether they trotted, as all British breeds now do, or whether they paced or ambled; those "lateral" gaits where the legs on each side move together were easier for a lady to "sit" safely (sideways) and more comfortable for anyone travelling long distances.

Gentlefolk, both men and women, rode palfreys or pads that paced or ambled; the old term was paraveredus from which palfrey comes, as does the Regency word prad. My Lady might be seated on a palfrey on a pillion pad behind her older brother or husband, perched completely sideways; if she rode alone, she would have both her feet on a *planchette* (footboard), and her palfrey perhaps led by a servant—both positions that didn't encourage independence. The side-saddle, enabling ladies to control their own mounts without needing a servant, developed from the mid-16th century onward.

Under Henry VIII the owners of certain sizes of property had to keep a given number of mares over 13 hands, for breeding—which strongly suggests that English horses in many cases were under that height. Henry's much cited edict required autumn drives to round up the stock, within 15 days of Michaelmas, and any "unlikely tits" or "unprofitable beastes" were then to be killed off. A tit is a small or young horse, a term dating from the 1500s or earlier, that developed, as many

215

words do: 1726, "*Tit*, a little Horse, and some call a Horse of a middling Size a double Tit." Dent suggests it is from Icelandic, teitr, meaning "fresh". The word "tit" persisted till at least the 1890s, with various meanings including a girl, a young man, or a junior or weaker party of any kind, as well as its remaining modern meanings of a bird or a female breast.

Henry VIII's laws seem to have been widely disregarded, however, as in 1580 Elizabeth I had to proclaim that to ensure the "breed and encrease of horses", in future the penalties for non-compliance would actually be applied, and not winked at as in previous times.

In the late 1500s the term Galloway appeared in print (the earliest surviving reference being in a letter from a Scottish bishop) and its meaning quickly developed from a small Scottish horse to any short, stout, quick, general-purpose animal—replacing the old "hobby horse" who is only remembered now as a child's wooden toy or a phrase dismissing obsessive enthusiasm. Even as late as this such animals were still known as horses; the word pony or "poney" for a smaller equine didn't appear until the mid 17th century, probably from French "poulenet". In any case, you didn't really need the word *pony* when you had the word *tit*!

Certainly in the 17th C the Galloways could either trot or pace/rack – the "little Scotch horses" were tireless, but variously described, sometimes as "trottynge geldynges" and sometimes as "easy pacers".

It isn't until the 17th century that pedigrees begin to be found, primarily for what developed into the Thoroughbred racehorse. Horsey children are told about the three foundation stallions—the Darley Arabian, the Byerley Turk and the Godolphin Arabian—but the original Thoroughbred coursers or "running horses" were bred out of native British mares, using these Oriental stallions as sires. Many of the racehorses

216

competing under the patronage of Charles II would have been only 13.2 hands high—a very long way short of modern racehorses who are generally closer to 16 hands than 15. Every proud racehorse still carries the mitochondrial DNA of those little British and Irish mares.

There were also local types of ponies and horses, such as the north-country Chapman horses which were stout, short-legged pack horses which travelling pedlars or "chapmen" used; these were said to be the foundation of the tall Cleveland Bay and in turn the Thoroughbred-cross Yorkshire coach horses, which were in demand for fast coach travel because of their strength and the ease of matching them for colour.

Horses vs. Oxen in farming

Until the mid 18th century, heavy ploughing was more often the job of oxen (bullocks) than of horses. Rob Johnson, who has worked bullocks in Australia, tells me:

Bullocks are stoic, and willing to please. A bullock team works on what it can graze, while a horse team needs supplements like oats. Ploughing deeply in heavy clay would be easier with bullocks' slow, steady, cloven hooves, and bullocks tend to work concertedly together, better than horses. The early wooden ploughs would have been fairly rudimentary as well. As the variables improved, like the ploughs requiring less draught power, feed for horses being more freely available and harnesses becoming better, then the quality of the farm horses was improved, and they became better all round animals. They probably still wouldn't match bullocks for the heavy going, but they were more versatile.

There were even ox-teams working in England up till the end of the 19th century. Another point in favour of working farms with oxen was that when they were no longer useful they

217

could be eaten, whereas in England for millennia there has been a taboo on eating horses.

Feeding

Horses belonging to land-owning families seem to have been generally well looked-after. They were so useful that they couldn't be neglected! Stabled horses, then as now, needed to be fed corn (oats or occasionally barley) to fuel them for hard work, and in the absence of their natural food, grass (or green meat as it has sometimes been called) they must have generous quantities of hay to keep their digestive systems working; plus large amounts of water, between 5 and 8 gallons a day. Not to mention straw for bedding!

Letters to Margaret Paston written in 1471 tell us that her son, who had been detained away from his Norfolk home for some time, wished to make sure that his horses were well fed, healthy and available for him to use when he returned:

... I have now enough hay of my own, and as for oats, Dollys will purvey (buy/provide) for him, or I will pay whoever does so. And I beseech you that he have every week three bushels of oats, and every day a penny worth of bread [probably horse-bread, made of beans]. And if Boton is not at Norwich and Syme keeps him, I shall pay him well for his labour. Also that Philip Loveday should put the other horse out to grass there as he and I agreed....

Colours

The Fenlands of East Anglia were drained by Dutch engineers in the 17th century and these engineers are said to have brought Friesian trotters with them. These in turn influenced the Norfolk trotter, and the Old English Black (later the Shire)—and the word "black" brings me to the colours we might have seen among the horses of historic times.

Many of the horses described after the battle of Flodden in 1513 were grey; out of 252 horses, 95 were grey. It was easily the most frequent colour of all, and "grey" did not include the ones the accounting clerk recorded as "white". These horses belonged to the ordinary Dales farmer-soldiers who were being "demobbed" after Henry VIII's Scottish campaign.

The hair colours in another account, from the monthly horse sales at Appleby in Westmorland (1623 to 1646) ranged through a drab rainbow from black, black bay, black brown, brown bay, red bay (with a "white main"), bay, mouse brown, lead-coloured, roaned, and piebald (black-and-white, coloured, pinto) to grey (not "white" although a grey horse as it ages will look white).

It's interesting that, in searching these Civil War period accounts, I haven't yet turned up an example of the term "chestnut." The Oxford English Dictionary cites it being used as a term for a horse colour in 1636 and Shakespeare used it as a hair colour for people in 1600 in *As You Like It*, so it was in use in Southern England some 50 years before these sales were being recorded. But the alternative term "sorrel" is not in those Appleby accounts either. I wonder what the red bay horse with the white mane looked like.

Over the centuries, increasing control of horse-breeding, through gelding colts, allowed less-skilled people to handle horses safely. It also exerted a selection process over which animals got to pass on their qualities to subsequent generations. Some areas even spayed filly foals: I learned from a university vet that spaying mares had become so commonplace in France that it had to be banned by Ordinance in 1717—and being a good academic he even gave me the reference for it, which being a twit I have now lost.

Since the improvement of farming equipment and harness, and the beginnings of selective breeding, draught horse breeds

219

such as the Shire, Clydesdale and Suffolk had been used to plough and harvest, as well as to draw heavy waggons in the arable counties of the east of Britain. But the poorer the owner was, the rougher the horse, vanner, cob or pony he would own, down to the local milk lady who might well be serving her produce out of churns strapped either side of a donkey.

Once the railway age began in the 1830s the need for relays of well-bred horses to draw mail coaches declined somewhat, but they were still heavily used by private individuals who could afford to race, ride, hunt, or drive. With the advent of the internal combustion engine in the 1890s the horse began to escape his task of providing practical day-to-day power and speed, and to be wanted mainly for the leisure uses we see today.

Here's a little thought for you to go away with: picture a farm horse coming home from ploughing. Of course the ploughman has jumped up on its back to save his tired legs after stomping along, mile after mile after mile, in a day of single furrow ploughing. You might not realise, though, that he's riding sideways like a medieval lady, rather than astride. Plough horses are built for power and their backs are groin-achingly wide. I am reliably informed from the Other Side of the Bed that without a saddle (or even with) there are certain aspects of male physique that discourage men from riding astride. So spare an admiring thought for the warriors of ancient times who spent so much time on horseback and still came home from war to father a family!

NEVER LET THE TRUTH GET IN THE WAY OF A GOOD STORY

I regularly see and groan at the "Roman chariots -> two horses' asses -> 4 foot 8 and a half inches -> wheel ruts -> railway gauge -> USA tunnel width -> space shuttle boosters width" story. (You can apparently find it on more than 2,000 web sites now so I'm not going to give it oxygen by quoting it in full here.) It's currently doing the rounds again on social media.

The origin of the "chariot" story seems to have been in *Popular Mechanics*, May 1905, in which there was a simple account that George Stephenson had measured the ruts going into a fort on Hadrian's Wall and decided on his wheel gauge by that.

It seems to have escaped all the subsequent speculators that possibly Stephenson simply decided on 5 foot width for his wheels from his experience with the quarrying and mining wagonways; then by subtracting the width of the wheels either side, 2 inches x 2, he arrived at a 4 foot 8 track gauge, with half an inch extra for tolerance of the flanges on curves.

But Roman chariots made a much more romantic tale. The next version of the story, which I think was post-WW2 and certainly American, in effect asserted that chariot widths in Roman times had been the basis for *all* subsequent horse-drawn vehicles. It concluded: "So, the next time you are handed a specification and wonder what horse's ass came up with it, you may be exactly right." The final bit about the solid booster rockets for the Space Shuttle was embroidered onto the tale much later by another unknown joker.

All of which has prompted me to go out with a tape measure and Actually Measure "a Horse's Ass".

Both our ponies are 13.3hh tall, which makes them a little taller than Yer Actual Roman Horse. Ruby is 23 inches wide at the hips, and Eric is 21 inches wide at the hips.

While I'm out here with the tape measure, let's look at my carriage. The swingletree (drawbar, whippletree etc) on the carriage that fits my ponies, driving single, is 25 inches long. Excuse me working in feet and inches, but the joke is American and the original story pre-dates UK metric.

To harness my two ponies side by side and hitch them to a pairs carriage you would need a splinterbar (drawbar) that measured 25 + 25 + 4 inches (nominal separation space between swingletree ends) = 54 inches or 4 foot 6. That would be the biggest splinterbar width needed to accommodate two Actual Roman Horses.

However, those measurements turn out to be pretty much irrelevant, and here's why.

For a start there wasn't a uniform "Roman carriage width" (Julius Caesar *didn't* issue a law about it, though there was a law about no wagons being allowed in Roman cities in daytime). There also wasn't a uniform horse-drawn vehicle width in Victorian Britain, which is when the railways were proliferating.

Actual examples (modern measurements approximated from metric):

Lady Georgiana Curzon in the 1890s drove a pony tandem – that's two ponies of much the size of mine, one in front of the other, to a single-pony carriage – and that carriage, though probably narrower between the shafts than mine, had an astonishing axle width of 6 feet.

The most standardised vehicle immediately before the arrival of the railways in the UK was the Victorian Post Office Mail coach drawn by four horses, and even then the measurements could vary. Official measurements of the time, obtainable from the Post Office Museum's records, describe the outer track width of a typical Mail coach as 5 ft 1½ inches.

For modern competition vehicles, Horse Team outer track width must be a minimum of 5 ft 2 inches (very close to that of the Mail coach), and Pony Single width 4 ft 6 inches. My single-pony carriage, which is 2 foot 6 inches wide between the shafts, still has a 4 foot 6 track width.

Do you see it yet? There was a *wide range* of widths for horsedrawn road traffic, and the number of horses involved in drawing a carriage doesn't seem to have a great deal of influence. There are obviously going to be occasions when the width of the splinterbar *might* be the same as the track width, but tit doesn't have to be. For instance, if my single-pony carriage was only 2 foot 6 wide at ground level, which is all it would be if you apply the logic of the chariot story, it would be very unstable. That might have been the width, though, of hand carts needing to go through doorways, with no horse, pony, donkey or ox involved.

Finally, you could easily have a carriage whose overall width is greater or smaller than the wheels at ground level. The tunnel width in the Shuttle story depends more on carriage width than wheel track. However, railways and rolling stock are not my concern as a carriage driver and equine history enthusiast, and I'm not going to delve into the development of standard *vs* broad *vs* narrow gauges across the world. Wikipedia is your friend there.

My points about the "Roman horse's asses" defining any railway standard gauge are these:

- not all vehicles were pulled by two horses side by side – they might be drawn by one, or three, or four

- the width of the horses is not necessarily the same as the carriage width, nor the track width on the road

- traffic ruts are unreliable references because a horse-drawn carriage on the road doesn't travel in a precisely straight line, any more than a bicycle does, so ruts over time always end up wider than the carriages that made them

- carriage track widths on the road actually varied enormously

Therefore the attempt in the story to infer that the width of the space shuttle booster rockets was "based on" the width of two "Roman horse's asses", even via "ruts" at Pompeii, is just that, a story, embroidered over recent years into a very, very longwinded joke.

None of these humorists ever drove two horses, either.

PS the best debunking I have seen: Skeptoid

https://skeptoid.com/episodes/4818?
fbclid=IwAR2Z_TIMO3dJ2X3fQLwFlMi5LrKCeX6p-
ldrOPB3LO9sK7oGNGp6t9q-vPE

A COB IS A COB IS A COB

I've been trying to explain on a carriage driving list in America that the word "cob" in Britain covers a multitude of animals. So, I thought I'd stick up a blog post about it.

It depends where you are and what you are doing, whether you hear all the varied uses of the word "cob".

As a general term it means a stocky, powerful, active *type* of horse "suitable for an elderly gentleman to enjoy a day's hunting" - ie, not too high off the ground, broad, loads of stamina, weight carrying and comfortable and above all well mannered. Breeding is not an issue - they can be part TB, part Shire or Clyde, part pony. They are shown trimmed out, no feather on the heels, mane often roached and tails pulled and cut fairly short (a nod to their hunting purposes). Not a breed as such. Often called a "show cob." Power, stamina and good manners make a cob a good driving animal for a country turnout.

"Coloured cob" means a broken-coloured / pinto / piebald / skewbald horse and usually one with a lot of mane, tail and feather. They are heavy-boned, often with a Fell or Dales pony close up in the ancestry but also Clydesdale further back. These are the type that came over from Ireland in the 50s and 60s and became popular with the tinker/potter men and are now famed as "gypsy horses" (before that, a gipsy horse was usually a Clydesdale cross, black or brown with white socks!) They have a couple of registries for *type* and are rapidly becoming a pedigreed breed in their own right though I can't say whether their stud book is a closed one - I suspect not, since I know people who sometimes breed small coloured cobs from registered Fell ponies. They are shown in full mane/tail/feather as a "traditional" cob but occasionally trimmed out and shown as a "show cob". There are also "coloured" horses that are NOT necessarily cobs and these are referred to as "non-traditional" coloureds - they are shown trimmed.

Traditionals make good driving horses for trade and exercise/leisure/pleasure classes, and of course the bigger sorts can pull a "van" of any of the gipsy varieties. Non-traditionals have famously been included in coaching teams and competitive (HDTA/FEI) tandems.

Confused yet?

"Welsh cob" and "Welsh pony of cob type" are the stocky, active horses and ponies from Wales with historic pedigrees recorded by the Welsh Pony and Cob Society. They are a breed, although "Welsh pony of cob type, Section C" is for cobs under 13.2 hands and "Welsh cob, Section D" is for cobs over 13.2, and it depends on their height rather than their breeding which section they are registered in. "On the basis of height certified by a Veterinary Surgeon, the Society may sanction:

> 4.1 A transfer from Section A to Section B of stock which has grown over 12 hands.
> 4.2 A transfer from Section C to Section D of stock which has grown over 13 hands 2 inches.
> 4.3 A transfer from Section D to Section C of stock, seven years old or over, which does not exceed 13 hands 2 inches."

Often these are referred to a Section D or Section C cobs, with "Welsh" assumed from the word Section. (One of my gripes is that the Sec D cob in particular often doesn't look cobby any more but like a plump Arabian. And an Arabian is NOT a cob by any stretch of the imagination.) Welsh cobs vary from "hot" to "placid" as driving horses - can be very good, can also be very bad, and while they move spectacularly when seen from the side they often dish or plait at either front or back or both despite the requirement for "true" straight movement which is still mentioned in the Welsh breed standard.

Therefore!!! when you hear people in England talking about "a cob" they may mean one of several things. If you ask them to be more specific they should define what they mean by saying "show cob", "coloured cob" (traditional or non-traditional) or "Welsh Cob" (plus its section, C or D).

Here endeth the lecture.

DRIVING LESSONS

Ooh you couldn't make it up… I have just had a phone call from a youngish man wanting driving lessons, and he said he'd found our phone number through Google. I teach carriage driving, and he said he was a beginner, so I got out the diary to make an appointment for him, and I listened.

It wasn't till he asked for 2 consecutive days of lessons because he "wanted to drive to Oxford next week" in the Renault he had just bought, that I thought I'd better break it gently to him that I do not teach people to drive a car.

I didn't mention the fact that he was going to have to get a licence by passing both his theory and practical car-driving tests. I thought it might be too much for him to take in all at once.

WHY I WROTE *COACHMAN*

A neighbour of ours mentioned more than once that her family's fortune had been made by her great-grandfather, who had been a coach proprietor in Victorian London. He was William James Chaplin (no relation to Charlie Chaplin the silent-film actor). In 1994 our neighbour asked me to transcribe a letter, written by Chaplin, which a bookseller had bought at auction and brought to show her. Neither of them could read his writing, but I could.

As a result I wrote an article for "Carriage Driving" magazine about Chaplin's career. I knew I still wanted to do more with it, though, and it simply had to be a novel – the themes were too big for anything else.

Some of the phrases Chaplin used in that letter appear in his conversations in COACHMAN. Our neighbour also gave me a copy of the family tree, and permission to write the novel about her ancestor.

The idea, though, sat in my head for 18 years! It took all that length of time for the internet resources to appear, like Project Gutenberg and the Internet Archive, where I could read the full text of coaching books that were long out of print and hideously expensive to buy second-hand. The MS itself took about five months, but I kept going back and rewriting, developing the storylines, then putting it away and coming back and rewriting yet again. It's been the messiest thing I've ever written, because I had to do a lot of U turns – into the history, then back to the characters. I did a lot of "killing my darlings" as the story itself straightened out in my head and much of my research became unnecessary, so I probably have half a novel in the "spike" folder on my computer; journeys that my main character made, and people he met, both before and after this story is told.

There are many historical novels set during that age when the horse was the fastest thing on the road, and there are a few written about the dawn of the railway age, such as Malcolm MacDonald's "World From Rough Stones" sequence, but there's nothing fictional – so far as I know, anyway – about what happened to the men who had been the Knights of the Road and whose work suddenly vanished. So I thought it was time to redress the balance. Of course, that single thread as the main theme of the book wasn't enough; I had to make up characters and relationships that would be interesting, too. I had to tell a story about people whose lives would touch Chaplin's, so I could show what might have happened to the drivers, stablemen and horses when railways took the heart out of coaching. I invented an ambitious young coachman who would travel to London with his bride to take up a new job with Chaplin.

I've been involved in carriage driving since 1985, and when I'm interested in a subject I read widely round it so I have shelves full of books about the coaching age, plus lots of material in digital format. My own great-grandfather was a coachman. However, he drove in domestic service, rather than on a commercial route; also he was born 50 years after Chaplin's time, so I can make no claims about the two ever having met. Still, his existence in my family tree gave me a name to hang my story on: George Davenport. His wife, my great-grandmother, really was called Lucy Hennessy, though she didn't live in Carlisle and my relatives will no doubt be relieved to hear that I have completely invented her unpleasant mother and their unsavoury history.

William Chaplin had a patriarchal number of children, including twin girls, Marianne and Sarah. I've omitted any mention of her twin sister for the sake of simplicity. Sarah was the only one of Chaplin's children who died unmarried (not counting Rosa who died aged 8 and Horace who died in infancy). Nothing is known of Sarah Chaplin other than her dates of birth and death. That meant I could safely invent whatever reasons I liked to account for her unmarried status. She may have been an invalid, or that Victorian euphemism, "a confirmed spinster", we don't know; my view of her – privileged, bright and frustrated – sprang from her father's dedication and an observation by a former coachman, who remarked that Chaplin's business was founded on "systematic application ... in which the female members of the family were called to assist." As the story developed I realised that as a successful businessman's daughter Sarah could have designs on George that had nothing to do with his driving.

Many of the drivers mentioned in COACHMAN were real people in the golden age of coaching: the brilliantly skilful Ward brothers, for instance, and deaf George Eade. I've invented the less attractive ones like Anderson. Some of the real coachmen, such as Cross, wrote autobiographies during their twilight years for the benefit of Coaching Revivalists in later Victorian times. Their works were rich sources for this novel.

We think now of 1838 as the year of Queen Victoria's Coronation, marking the opening of the Victorian age. It was fun to set my characters against the colourful backdrop of the Coronation year, but the book is by no means a fluffy fantasy of a past era. Novels that use historical settings simply to write about heaving bosoms, tight breeches and randy behaviour really annoy me as they are so often inaccurate on the history, habits and behaviour of the time in which they pretend to be set. Just call them costume porn and be done with it.

The main energy in my story was the huge change that began in transport, and hence in industry, due to the opening of the railways. It's that upheaval which is the catalyst for many of my book's central events. However, as I wove-in threads about about abusive family relationships, and about same-sex relationships which were still punishable by hanging at that time, and about the religious belief that sustains Lucy (a known factor in the emotional survival of some modern victims of child abuse), COACHMAN opened up into a story about marriage and friendships in difficult times.

RESEARCHING THE HISTORY OF
THE ROYAL MAIL

I learnt a lot about the British postal service when I was writing COACHMAN.

One obvious reason for this was that my hero George Davenport aspired to drive a Royal Mail coach. Mails were well designed and well maintained, they were supplied with good quality horses and above all they were required to be fast. Other individual coaching routes perhaps exceeded the Post Office's average speed: a commercial stage coach, the Shrewsbury "Wonder," was timetabled to cover the 153 miles between that city and London in 15¾ hours including meal breaks and changes of horses. Its arrival in St Albans was so punctual that people regulated their watches and clocks by it, and in its latter years its average speed was said to have gone up to 15mph. That exceeded the fastest of the Royal Mail routes, Liverpool to Preston, which was 10.5 mph, and it more than doubled one of Royal Mail's slowest, the Kent route between Canterbury and Deal, which at times only managed 6 mph; but the sheer scale of the network that carried His (or later, Her) Majesty's Mail across the British Isles has to be admired. A letter posted in London at Monday teatime could be in Glasgow early on Wednesday afternoon.

The Royal Mail was assisted by laws such as the automatic right of way of the Mail coach on the road, its exemption from stopping to pay toll at toll gates, and the outlawing of letter carriage by any other commercial means. The Mails were not just the best-organised and quickest method of transporting letters and parcels across the country: they were a Royal monopoly. While the Mail coachman was employed by the proprietor who supplied the horses, and was not directly responsible for the Mail, the guard was a Royal employee whose duty was to protect and carry the mails forward even when blizzards and floods might stop the coach itself - and these men carried out their duty so conscientiously that some of them died doing it. George, my coachman, was lucky not to encounter such conditions in his brief spell in this work.

The annual procession of Mail coaches took place in May each year up to 1838, as shown in the drawing on the cover of COACHMAN. The 27 London Mails assembled in Lincoln's Inn Fields. The "bang-up" (excellent) teams were provided by the coaching proprietors or lent by wealthy London "whips" (drivers) and they trotted with great style and pride through the streets of London to the West End of the city. They stopped to salute first the Postmaster General in St James's Square, and then the reigning monarch in St James's Palace, before going on a circuit through Hyde Park and coming back into the city via Regent Street and Trafalgar Square. I decided that if George wasn't at that time a Mail coachman, for my purposes he would be far better as a spectator, with an overview of what was going on and the ability to interact with people, which of course he could not have done if I'd put him as a driver on a coach; and anyway he wouldn't have been senior enough to merit such a place.

In their daily work the Mail coaches all left London at the same hour each evening, 8pm, which enabled them to cover the busiest part of their routes overnight when the roads were quiet. This meant that the London inns which horsed the Mails were jam-packed with horses and staff up to 7.30pm, which was when the coaches went round the block to be loaded at the General Post Office in St Martins le Grand.

The Mail coaches were a popular sight, hence George's admiration of them while they were loading at the Swan with Two Necks. (The name of the inn, by the way, is a corruption of "Swan with two NICKS". The beaks of swans on the Thames are marked with notches to indicate ownership, and two "nicks", one either side, denote the Vintners' Company who were, of course, innkeepers.)

Mails that originated in provincial cities, however, set off at all sorts of times, depending on the distances they had to cover. The Mail from Carlisle to Newcastle, for instance, left Carlisle at 7am in company with the Scottish coaches for Edinburgh, Glasgow and Port Patrick, and reached its destination around 1pm.

Another aspect of my story that had to be researched was postage itself, because George had left Lucy behind in Carlisle when she was ill, which meant he had to keep in touch by letter. In order to put these little snapshots of their lives into the right places, I needed to know how long it would take to send and receive responses. Alan Bates' *Directory of Stage Coach Services 1836* was invaluable as my starting point, and I began to feel rather like a trainspotter as I flicked forward and back through the pages of Mail coach timetables.

I also needed to know how much Lucy would have to pay for her letter from Carlisle to London. In 1838 letter postage was still priced by distance and by number of sheets of paper. I was able to calculate that one sheet cost 11 pence to travel that distance. In an era when the coach guard was paid ten shillings and sixpence for a week's work, it's clear that sending a letter over a long distance was not something that every person could have done, which we now expect almost as a right.

233

My grandmother had a little collection of family letters which had been written at that period of time, so even as a child I was aware that there had been an age in which you had three alternatives when you ran out of space on a single sheet: you cut your letter short, added another page (and paid a higher price), or you "crossed" the lines. Crossing meant writing on the same sheet a second or even a third time, with the direction of the 2nd or 3rd set of lines being at 90 or 45 degrees from the first set. The Penny Post that was then being planned must have promised a great improvement to the puzzles produced under this system.

My grandmother also had a seal ring and several sticks of sealing wax. I never discovered how old they were but I do remember that the wax was bright red, hard and brittle. At the time I was rewriting COACHMAN I discovered an antiques web site with Victorian seals for sale and I'm afraid seal-lust overcame me. With the excuse that it was my birthday I splashed out and bought myself one. When it arrived I couldn't believe how tiny it was. Its handle is delicately turned mother of pearl, with pierced silver mountings to hold an amethyst stone that forms the seal, with a black-letter M carved into its flat surface. I felt it must once have graced a lady's desk, and now here it was on mine.

Well, I had to have a go with it, didn't I? I bought some sticks of sealing wax: two red and one gold, both of which would have been used in Victorian times. I suppose a lady might have preferred the gold, or rose or some other colour, to the red.

That's when I discovered that modern sealing wax is softer and more flexible than the old wax I remember, which may of course have hardened with age. The sticks I bought have a wick in the middle but even when the wick is lit the wax is not very easy to use. There's a distinct edge of danger in lighting a stick of wax in the midst of your correspondence, and a great deal of dexterity is needed in handling the naked flame and dripping

234

wax. You have to get the blob to fall in the correct place on your document, juggle the seal and the flame (and with luck, blow it out) before you set the seal (right way round) onto the blob at the exact moment when it's beginning to set but has not yet hardened.

It was difficult to get the M the right way up when I was working by ceiling-mounted electric light, but curiously, I found when I did it by the light of a candle on the desk it was much easier, simply because the light was closer to the level of the paper.

Sealing a folded piece of paper to create a postable, private letter is tricky, but I have photos to prove I did it. Complete with blobs that went astray in the process!

I'm still finding stray examples of "test" seals I made, little red discs with an M stamped on them, hiding in my desk tray. I'm too taken with them to throw them away.

Bates, A (compiler), 1969, Directory of Stage Coach Services 1836

Beaufort, Duke of, 1890, Driving.

Cross, Thomas, Autobiography of a Stage Coachman.

Dixon, H.H., 1895, Saddle and Sirloin.

Harper, Charles G., Stage Coach and Mail in Days of Yore

Harris, Stanley, 1885, The Coaching Age.

Mountfield, The Coaching Age

British Postal Museum and Archive

Vintners' Hall - Swan upping

COLLOQUIALISMS IN HISTORICAL FICTION

Since writing COACHMAN I've had a few discussions on the topic of fictional dialogue - as in, *were the words I put in my characters' mouths actually current in the year 1838?*

Well, yes they were.

Weren't "mate" and "kid" too modern for a Victorian coachman to use?

Well, no, they weren't.

Rest assured folks - when writing of characters in a past era, the dear old Oxford English Dictionary Online is an ever-open tab in my browser. It has a fantastic Historical Thesaurus which details when words appeared in print with quotations from the earliest examples of how they were used. (And the OED online is free to access if you have a library membership card. Just type in its number to sign in.)

Words I've looked up for earliest usage have included these: (dates follow if you want to check your guesses!)

> mate - my friend
> kid - child
> customer - client
> sandwich - bread & filling
> chit-chat - idle talk
> slipshod - careless workmanship
> fusty - ancient and old-fashioned
> upright - righteous
> cash - ready money
> brat - two meanings, child, rough apron
> cocky - my friend
> daft - foolish
> dasher - elegantly dressed and attractive person
> gob - mouth
> snotty-nosed - contemptible

I've had queries from readers about the contemporary use of *mate* and *kid* in particular, which is why they are the first on that list.

One word I encountered in a mid-Victorian carriage driving book, *An Old Coachman's Chatter* (1890), was the term *muff*. You probably are familiar with its use for a hand-warmer, often of fur, and hence also a coarser slang meaning. My grandmother left me a fox-fur muff, complete with head, whose jaws were sprung so you could put a scarf or a pair of gloves into its grip. However, in *An Old Coachman's Chatter*, "muff" seems to have been a term of contempt - a stupid, inept, clumsy person; a *klutz*; and "muffish" described something badly done, not stylishly. It was so emphatically used in Edward Corbett's advice about how NOT to drive that I just had to check to see whether it was something I could use in 1838!

So here are the dates:

mate - 1380 "man" and 1500 a term of friendly address
kid - 1690
customer - 1480
sandwich - 1762
chit-chat - 1710
slipshod - 1818
fusty – 1492 and1609
upright -1530
cash - 1596
brat
- child - 1557;
- rough apron - 1691
cocky -1693
daft - 1450
dasher - 1807
gob - 1568
snotty-nosed - 1682

Oh, and muff - 1819.
Happy word hunting.

WAITING FOR THE FILM CREW

2007: In honour of "The Dales Diary"

Hello there. You're early. Not at all, you haven't disturbed me; I was already up and about. I don't sleep a lot. Even in summer, I'm up before dawn. Life is too short to spend flat out with your eyes shut. Up and at 'em is my motto. It's going to be a fine day, don't you think? Not bad for winter; no wind, no rain, just a touch of invigorating frost. I think the sun will soon shine in through the window.

Breakfast is served just after dawn at this time of year, so we haven't long to wait. I'll walk about a bit if you don't mind; hunger makes you impatient, I don't know if you've noticed. I know they can hear me, so don't worry, they won't be long. The floor vibrates a little, and I think it must be audible in their quarters, so there's no need to shout for room service.

They're pretty good to me here; they know my likes and dislikes, and quite often they'll produce something really tasty. You know how being sharp-set makes all food taste just wonderful.

Oh, yes, I'm afraid I'm always on a diet. I'm sure you know the feeling; it's all too easy for the tum and bum to start expanding when you don't work out in the winter. They do a nice line here in fruit, fibre and cereals, and even though I've always eaten a wide range of vegetable foods they've introduced me to a lot of new things. Some are quite exotic, like melon, and sweet potatoes. Even after Christmas is over, it's fun seeing what might appear next on the menu.

No, I don't have any eating disorders. My only trouble is that if it's there I eat it; so I suppose it's for my own good that sometimes, when I've eaten one portion I just have to wait for the next. Ah well. I see nobody's been to feed those sheep yet;

239

they'll be hungry too, poor things, and they're worse off, being out there in the frost. On the other hand, the sun is up now and at least they're getting some warmth after the chilly night. The grass will be thawing too, what there is of it anyway.

The sun'll be round to my window soon. I'll enjoy that. I sunbathe as often as I can, don't you? The sun does you good; it makes vitamin D and keeps you healthy. You know, while there's always plenty of grub here and it's the best quality, they're a bit slow bringing it this morning, aren't they? I'll look out of the window, if you'll excuse me; no, there's still no-one coming.

What to do to pass the time? How about a drink? Yes, I think so. I admit, I'm quite a big drinker; one has to keep a lovely body hydrated, and being so active, I use a lot of water. I'll have a good deep drink right now to stave off the hunger pangs. Ooh, that's cold on the stomach; it fairly makes your lips curl when there's a touch of frost about, doesn't it? I'll have to walk round a bit more to settle it and warm myself up again.

Do you like the way I fling my hair over my shoulder as I stalk about? Wish they'd give me a mirror in here. I'm sure this great black mane of mine is tangled. It's so long and thick, I really need help to comb it out. What – you think it suits me like this? How kind. You should take a photograph of it. Men do admire it a great deal, even though it often hides my face. Notice my mobile, teasing mouth; and my very long, dark eyelashes too.

I've been told that my eyes are admirably expressive. They are a lovely brown, aren't they? Wide set, large and clear. No, I don't need kohl; this black-pencilled outline is quite natural. You can be quite sure, darling, that I'd use it if I needed to! I make the very best use of assets like these. I can do things nobody else would dare. Trespass, greed or theft – trust me, I've done it – but one bat of my eyelashes, one seductive turn of the head and I am forgiven.

240

I may be allowed outside today, you know. That would be good. I'll take another turn, if you wouldn't mind stepping back out of my space. I don't want to tread on your toes. It's cosy in here really; I ought not to fret at confinement. The weather in a Cumbrian winter can be appalling so even if they let me out I'd probably be desperate to come back in! The bed's changed regularly and everything's tidied twice a day. People pop in for a natter and I'm always glad to see them, whether I'm working or not.

Next door they're doing a barn conversion so there's lots of activity. I like to feel I'm part of things. When I'm out there I always offer them my help. I am curious about their tools, though I'm not so good at using them; but then building is hardly my real purpose in life! It just helps to pass the time until the new season opens. I get plenty of work then to keep my mind engaged.

Are you taping this? You sly dog. Still, it shows a professional attitude on your part. I've been 'done' before, you know; local papers and Radio 4. Dylan Winter - do you know him? - he quite fell in love with me. You can always tell by that note in their voice when they say my name. I hope the builders get the yard cleared of rubble before Luke and the film crew come next month.

What else can we talk about to keep my mind off food? Well, I could tell you about the offspring, I suppose: I have two, one of each gender, what they call a pigeon pair. Yes, I admit, they do have different fathers; lovely fellows both of them. Both of them quite famous in their own right, too, though I didn't realise it at the time. Was it Love at First Sight? Oh yes indeed!

Both of the youngsters take after my own colouring, and pretty nice-looking they are, if I do say it myself. They're grown up now and very fit and lively. They're both working, and quite independent. They send me news from time to time through the staff here. I had cards from them at Christmas.

241

What's that? Lonely, me? Not at all. Let me explain. When I first arrived, I had a companion, in the next room over there. He was all over me at first, as though he couldn't believe his luck; went quite off his feed, poor boy. I'm afraid I ignored him while I found my feet and learned the systems here. Was that hard of me? Uncaring? I don't know. If you don't look after yourself, who is to do it for you? Anyway, it didn't take more than a day or two for his ardour to cool.

After that he turned out rather domineering; been here years and thought the place was his own, I daresay – good looks can cause a good deal of jealousy, can't they? He moved away just over a year ago and I hear he's doing OK, but really I don't miss him. There's nothing quite like being the only girl around, you know. When you're on your own, you get all the attention; the press calls and the photographers – yes, OK, you took that hint quite beautifully. Shall I pose in this shaft of sunlight by the window? How's that? Warm breath curling into steam; so atmospheric. Darling, you WILL Photoshop me if they don't come out quite perfect, won't you?

AH! Look. Here's the dinner lady now. She's a bit late – I think I mentioned that normally breakfast is shortly after dawn – but what can you expect? You can't get the staff these days. My word, I AM hungry. What is breakfast going to be today? Come on woman, tip it out and let me at it. Ah, lovely oats again, embellished with apple peelings and carrot sticks. And a nice generous slab of that sweet smelling hay.

Excuse me turning my back on you, but I just have to eat.

You could help by filling up my water-bucket, by the way, while she goes for the wheelbarrow.

Oh. Are you leaving already? Well, thanks. So nice to have met you. I'll look forward to reading your piece.

PONY BOOKS RULE!

2011

I was looking for something else (as I usually am) when I ran across the Jane Badger Books web site here: http://www.janebadgerbooks.co.uk/ It's full of reviews of all the books you read as a kid and you wish your mother hadn't thrown away. I am delighted to find that one of mine features there - Against the Odds - in a well-written review. It even provides a glossary of all the Welsh phrases I sweated over with my Teach Yourself book. Jane's page originally observed: "The book itself is an excellent read: Sue Millard has alas written no more pony books ... She writes a very good blog." My thanks for the blogging praise, but I was sad about the phrase "no more pony books," because although I had in fact got 3 horsey fictions tucked away waiting for homes (agents? publishers?), I couldn't find anyone with the balls that J A Allen had when they tried to revive the genre in the 1990s. When they were eventually taken over, their junior "pony book" fiction was one of the first bits of their stable to be discarded. I had to go indie, and Jane's site now lists all my equine titles.

Is there a prejudice among mainstream publishers against horsey backgrounds? Perhaps some inverted snobbery? But "pony books" today don't have to be about posh kids, however privileged the settings of some of the mid-20th C novels may have been. They were in any case rarely about haves vs. have-nots, or rural vs. urban. They're about valuing and caring for other living beings, even if the beings don't happen to be human. Actually living with horses and ponies demands a down to earth attitude to shovelling shit, a self-deprecatory sense of humour and an awareness of the need to make choices. Do I buy that new electronic device, or a load of hay? Do I go to that party, or sit up with the foaling mare? Even, do I sell the pony to someone with more money because I can't afford to keep her properly? Responsibility, hard work, dedication, thinking about another living being rather than about oneself…

There are times when I wonder how many more gritty, single-parent inner-city stories our schoolchildren can actually take – and it seems the choice is either those, or swoony pre-chick lit, or kid-wizard-saves-the-world epics. Perhaps we could achieve a little more light and shade in junior fiction by reviving the "pony book" genre.

ERIC: BRETHERDALE, WITH COMPANY

Our neighbour Margaret came up to the yard today to have a drive with me and Eric-the-Dales (Nipna Tudor Prince). The Lad was full of hay and feeling mellow so he didn't mind at all that I made him walk round the yard a couple of times to get the balance right on the carriage for two people. I do this quite often anyway if I have been adjusting harness or carriage, so often in fact there are some days when, if I set off straight out of the yard, he is puzzled and sends me messages that say, This is Not Normal.

With the balance of the carriage nicely set for me and Margaret, we walked quietly down to Dolly Bridge, where we waited on the wide bit of road for an oncoming van and trailer to pass. Eric went off again in trot, and wheeled cheerfully up the Bretherdale road (which he thinks is an easier option than going over Pikestoll as we did earlier in the week...not today, boy!).

At the cattle grid gate - which is next to the Millennium sheepfold (Megan's Fold, built by Andy Goldsworthy and Steve Allen) - Margaret opened the gate for us, and Eric behaved nicely while she got down and back up.

He trotted manfully up Nichol Hill, despite not feeling safe because there were NO WALLS, only the road over the open allotment. He's been up here before, but that was way back in August when he had another pony to follow, and since then he'd forgotten that there are patches of new tarmac, and odd bits of fallen wall and boulders on the roadside, which he had to dance round suspiciously.

At the very awkward cattle grid gate near Bretherdale Hall he had to wait for a pickup to drive across, but he only flinched a bit at the rumble of the wheels on the hollow metal bars.

When we went on he was listening for other horses (so perhaps remembering the Fell ponies who had been up in the fields in August) and when we drove down to the level of the river meadows he had to stop and assess the view and update his mental database before he would go on. I didn't make a fuss about that, and once he had satisfied his curiosity we went on at a good trot. Over a couple of becks, by bridges that have replaced the original "waths" or fords that you can still see when the water isn't too high; and through the next gate at Midwathstead ("the farm by the middle ford").

We had an option there to turn right over North Side and do a full circuit back to Greenholme via four other gates, but it's a real hard pull to climb up from the dale onto the top. I felt Eric wasn't yet fit enough to pull two of us up there, so we carried on along the beckside as far as the gate to Bretherdale Head. We stopped there for five minutes to let Eric have a breather. I also fished out my phone and started the tracker app that I'd forgotten before we set off!

Once turned around, Eric set sail for home and forgot all about the fallen walls and roadside boulders. Back at Midwath he flinched a bit when three beagles bounded across a paddock barking at us, but the owner called them back and nothing came of it. He walked and trotted home without any arguments; paused at the "awkward" gate to enjoy the view across to Orton Scar and the Pennines; walked carefully back down Nichol Hill (yes, it always seems steeper going down) and managed not to break into trot.

I decided to take Margaret back to her house (rather than ungraciously decanting her at our place and expecting her to walk home) so Eric pouted a bit at not being allowed to turn into our yard. He also hoped he could just turn around a hundred yards further on, but we didn't let him. But when I had delivered Margaret to her house, and we finally did arrive home and I unharnessed and threw a fleecy rug over him, he was VERY pleased to get his bowl of feed – and delighted, once out of the rug, to plaster himself with mud while Ruby ate his haynet.

ERIC AND THE QUICK-RELEASE – 1 – 19 MARCH 2023

35.8 kph.

That's how fast Eric can gallop when a trace quick-release lets go and the metal dee on the trace -endstarts hitting him.

We were coming home from Beckside on the Scout Green road. I wasn't really worried until we reached the top of Whiteham at full pelt and started going downhill... It took a very long couple of minutes of releasing contact and taking it up more gently before I got the "neck unstiffening" and Eric began to listen to me saying, "Steaaaa-deeee…" By which time we'd travelled almost a mile.

He did kick a couple of times, but I think that was excusable with that chunk of metal on the trace-end smacking him round the hocks and belly.

Anyhow… we kept the dirty side down. We didn't meet any traffic. We walked to a safe gateway where I tied him to a good solid gate to refasten the trace. Mind you, he then managed to put his head under the halter rope to have a scratch and almost dragged off his bridle, but I always have the head collar on under the bridle, and the throatlash through the head collar, so I was able to retrieve that too. Thanks to using a full neck collar, which sat steadily in place even though only drawing with one trace, and having well-curved shafts that sat firmly in the tugs without risk of slipping out, and having trace carriers that limited the amount of lashing the free trace could do, we survived.

Eric was very sweaty when we walked home, but I left him to calm down in the stable with a haynet, with Ruby nattering hormonally at him over the partition, before I turned them both out.

He's unscathed, and so is the carriage, and so are all the other parts of the harness. I shall however be revising my use of quick releases...

Just as well we had waited until all the steam-train photographers had gone away before we went out to drive. I gather that we have had a car rally through here as well but we missed that too.

Tomorrow I think we need a session of him standing on the yard in full harness with the traces hanging down, and me standing well aside with a long piece of string tied to the trace ends and making them swing against his legs until he doesn't feel like kicking them...

For those who don't do metric, 35.8 kph is 22.2 mph.

UPDATE 2 – 20 MARCH

Eric's sound this morning, with no obvious damage from the steel dee smacking him yesterday or from his irritated kicks at it. I know from the noise his kicks made that they had hit "something" but I've no idea what. The carriage is unmarked. (He's unshod. Discussion with farrier who's due next week, re possibly shoeing if needed.)

I have put harness on Eric and left long traces with Dee ends hanging from likely and unlikely places, with me swinging them via baler twine to hit his legs and belly. He didn't react at all (I have video to prove it) - as you'd expect of a pony who was trained to harness by someone who knew what he was doing.

The snap shackles are sound but would benefit from new compression springs inside. Looking at prices, that would cost under £5. I would need to dismantle the shackles and measure what diameter and length I need. But I'm just not sure I trust them any more.

Next trip out with Eric (with ordinary Dee end traces) will be to repeat our journey, traversing the "bolt route" several times at slow then at faster paces to practise control. Possibly not today though as I am surprisingly stiff in the shoulders...!

Our son has arrived with a Mother's Day card. Eric is in the yard, sprinting round Ruby and doing sliding stops, and son is tutting about the skid marks in the earth. But as I pointed out, Eric is a young(ish) high energy pony. I'd rather he burned off his high spirits outdoors and without the carriage!

Later

Eric and I ventured out this morning along the route we took on Saturday. (I fitted a kicking strap, as well as using different traces *without* quick-releases.)

We had a couple of brief trots on the outward journey but when he realised where we were headed he began to worry. He wasn't his usual relaxed-but-keen self. He required several data-collecting stops and two dung stops (he usually only needs one).

We walked over the moorland and down the steep bank at Beckside, and turned round at the bottom, at the farm lane where we'd set off to spring the bank on Saturday. He collected himself to do the same again - and I made him walk up it. I walked him up to the top of the brow, and then turned him around and walked him back down, and walked him back up it again. He kept collecting himself and trying to break into trot but I kept talking him down, because what he was doing wasn't just the cheerful half-hop that asks, Can We Go Now. It was a bit too nervy for my liking, and all I wanted of him today was to listen, listen, listen, and not make unilateral decisions about our speed. I had to consciously keep my hand light on him unless he was being silly.

We walked all the way home. Still with the dirty side down.

UPDATE 3 - 26 MARCH

We've had a week of high winds and torrential rain (equinoctial gales I suppose) so Ruby and Eric have spent a lot of time indoors, and in the brief spaces between stormy periods I have allowed Eric to let off steam outside, but not added a carriage to complicate his energy. He comes and looms over me when I'm filling haynets or mucking out, so clearly he hasn't fallen out with me. I did spot him trying to pick out a wood-dust pellet from among his bedding this morning, presumably on the basis that it might be something edible he had overlooked from his feed bowl. I worry sometimes... but we'll have used up all the pellets shortly and sawdust doesn't seem to attract his attention that way.

Today the sun was shining, so after he and Ruby had eaten most of their morning hay I dragged a currycomb over his mucky bits and set him up to drive. I even put on my body protector which I find difficult because it doesn't really fit either under my coats or over them. And although it's (probably) the right size I am not the right shape, so even when it's fitted snugly at my waist it rises to my chin when I sit down. But I thought, it's there, and maybe it'll be like carrying an umbrella - if available, will not be needed. So I hauled it on over my wind "shell" jacket and put my high vis waistcoat over the top.

Eric, meanwhile, was quietly tucking in to a second haynet outside the stable, and not in the least bothered by being harnessed and put to, or being interrupted halfway through when a Fell pony breeder dropped by to ask technical questions about a proposed addition to the paperwork for foals.

We set off on our drive with the usual mild discussion about when it's appropriate to walk on (which Eric thinks is when he's hitched and doesn't have a human at his head, and I think is

251

not until all humans are aboard the carriage). He stood and waited, however, and we waited a bit more once I had mounted. We walked round the yard before going out onto the road and down into Greenholme. At the T junction we carried on into the village to let a car behind us turn to take the road up the hill, instead of us going up in front of it.

Eric was still doing quite a bit of "looking" at his surroundings and he thought, when we turned round, that going home fast would be a fine idea, but I gently disabused him of that, and off we went at a trot up the hill towards the railway bridge. The plan for the drive was to trot *only* on the way out, and not at all on the way back. And all changes of pace were to be my decision, rather than his.

It was a busy morning traffic-wise, with lots of electric cars passing to and from the charge-points on the motorway services, but Eric wasn't really bothered by them and they all behaved respectfully towards us. He trotted over the two big motorway bridges without too much fuss about the crash-barriers (I still haven't worked out why he thinks they are horse-eaters; possibly they bounce back the sound of his own trotting feet).

It was cold though, with ice in the wind, and after another half mile I was quite glad to halt him and let him watch two rug-wearing horses in a field who thought the Pony With Wheels was vastly entertaining and were prepared to show their amusement by kicking up their heels if it came close. As Eric had had three equines doing that last Saturday as an overture to his home-going runaway, I didn't push my luck today. I let him watch them from a safe distance, then turned him homeward and began my careful "walk, and keep walking" return journey.

His ears were pricked, paying attention forward. He kept flicking the left ear towards me when I spoke to him, so I knew he was listening to me behind - I repeat myself a lot when I'm driving, commenting on how he's doing, telling him the scary things are not scary, praising him when he's doing what I want, keeping my speech patterns regular and my tone light and encouraging.

On Saturday when the trace came off, both his ears had been back in fright and irritation. On Monday when we re-traced our route there had been too many both-ears-back moments to do much trotting, so seeing both ears working independently again today was a really good sign. He did try to scuttle into trot a few times homeward, especially when there was a brief hail shower!

Over the motorway bridges, walking, walking. He did a bit of tongue flapping which let me know he wasn't entirely relaxed, but the brain was working all right. I talked to him and kept my hands soft, and he listened to my voice and never challenged the bit. We did at times have a very stroppy fast walk, but we were doing the gait I wanted without argument, so I didn't worry about that (and anyway, it was bloody cold and I wanted to go home, too!) The further we went at walk, the more his neck and back relaxed.

Ruby welcomed him home with a big whinny. She's in love with him at the moment - 28 years old at the end of next month and *still* coming into season - but Eric has forgotten what to do with mares, so he was more bothered about making sure she didn't get the chance to lick out his after-work feed bowl than anything else.

Then he found a nice black patch of semi-dry mud to plaster himself with. Oh well. At least I know he scrubs up all right once he's dry.

UPDATE 4 – 2 APRIL

April has arrived and with it a warm, dry, sunny day. Ian from the farm up the road brought us a trailer load of hay this morning, and after that I scraped the mud off Eric and took him for a schooling drive. Plan as before, trotting only on the way out and only when I asked, lots of changes of pace between halt and walk and trot and down again; walking on the way home.

We went round the yard a couple of times, walking and halting, before we went out onto the road. I turned him downhill towards Bretherdale, walking and halting, keeping to walk at the uphill slopes where he was (generously) offering to trot; then I asked for short stretches of trot in places where he wasn't anticipating it, and turned round at points where we haven't done it before, like the bridge over the little beck on the Bretherdale road.

Coming back to the T junction at Low Greenholme where Eric might reasonably have expected to turn left for home, I turned him right and made him trot up Pikestoll, which is a steep pull; then before he got out of breath I paused at a gateway and turned him for home again, back to walk, again very tempting to get pushed into trot by the downhill gradient, but I asked him to stay in walk, and he did. A neighbour in his car waited for us on the bridge over Bretherdale Beck, but I didn't hurry Eric, just kept him walking. Ears forward and quiet, and although the head was up, it came down as he moved into a relaxed and active walk going up the hill back to the yard gate.

Annnd... keep walking! Past the gate!

Past a farm 'gator (which he thought might have food in the back!) and down to Greenholme where two visitors from Gloucestershire wanted to take our photo and to talk about

254

their neighbour who has a Fell pony and goes driving. Were we going far? I said no, we were just schooling. Eric waited with quiet feet (although his wiggly neck is always a challenge for keeping the reins off the shaft ends). I turned him round to face home, and we had another little chat with the visitors before I set him off to walk up the hill again. Two cars were waiting behind us but I didn't hustle Eric. I made him stand on the layby in front of the house for the cars to pass, before turning into the yard.

Up the slope, turn. down the slope, practise halting and then backing up the slope - hard work!

I thought I'd take him out onto the road again so we headed down to the front gate, but he made one wrong sideways step as we approached, and that move brought my left wheel up against the corner of the house. Ahh... just as well he had just been practising that "halt, and back up a slope!" Because we had to do it in earnest. He did, and that got us off the stonework . Round the yard again, back to the gateway, out and down the road as though starting all over for Bretherdale.

I asked him for a couple more trots going outward along the level, and he was cheerful and listening to me, walk, trot, walk, so we turned at Low Greenholme farm gate and set off to walk home. Over the bridge, and walking up the slope, staying in walk, keeping in walk despite him offering to trot.

Halfway up, as everything had gone well, I did ask him to trot the last 100 yards. This is the first trot he's done *going homeward* since the exciting mile over the fell 2 weeks ago. He did trot when I told him to - but there was still a little anxious "shall I bolt" feel to it, with flickering ears, which had been absent on the outward stretches.

He came down to walk when I steadied him, without any argument, but that fifty yards of trot made it clear that we're still going to have to work on the gear changes and not do much fast work homeward for a while.

PS I have found the ideal framework for filling haynets - the upended body of a shopping trolley left with us some years ago as a wreck (don't ask!) by one of David's schoolmates. I shall have to get photos.

UPDATE 5 – 4 APRIL

After an "interesting" morning when I and my 4WD were needed to help pull a broken-down car off the road, I took Eric out after lunch. He was feeling very mellow. Although he offered to hop into trot a couple of times, he took it in good part when I reminded him it's my job to decide when to change gear, and not his. We climbed part-way up Pikestoll, but didn't go all the way up because the Fell mares were relatively close to the fence line. I don't think the stallion will be with them, as they won't foal till next month at the earliest, but I couldn't tell from the view of their distant backs; and although Eric was fine with excited ponies in the autumn, that was autumn and this is spring and post-runaway, and I still don't want to take a risk with either sex until I'm sure he is really taking notice of me and not of any stray ideas inside his head. I want to keep everything as smooth and non-distracting as possible.

We went up the Bretherdale road and back, and Eric maintained his power walk without breaking pace. Squeaks and rattles and gravel noises attracted his attention but he listened to my voice and kept walking. We did walks and halts and a little bit of trotting; also I'm trying to let the reins flap on his rump for short stretches while asking him to maintain the walk, which is quite a test of his nerves as he thinks a flap should mean "go faster". We came home quietly, passed the front gate, turned on the layby and drove round the yard, halting, sidepassing, halting, backing, before I took him out of the shafts and gave him his haynet and a little feed.

He was really listening today, so although it was a relatively short and boring drive, it was a success, and that'll do me.

UPDATE 6 – 9 APRIL

The weather has begun to cool from the warm sunshine we've had for the past few days, and the wind is getting up, so I decided to go out this afternoon with Eric as I probably shan't drive tomorrow if the weather is as wild as forecast. My husband went out to enjoy a Vintage vehicle fair this morning so, although I had cleaned the ponies and done all my stable jobs, I waited until he came home before going out. Also, I noticed a few dirt-bike riders buzzing about, so at least the wait meant they had left the area before we drove. No point in doing a schooling run with any excuses for distraction!

I set Eric off towards Roundthwaite, which is 2 miles away on the other side of Pikestoll, the big hill to the south. He only tried to skip into trot a couple of times without being asked, and when I did set him off with his nose towards the hill, he stayed firm in the correct gait. I looked up towards the Dyke when we reached the fence that ends Horse Pasture but couldn't see any of the Fell mares, so I kept him going. He managed not to shy at any grit-heaps or the piece of wall that is being repaired and looks odd.

As we reached the top, though, I realised that the stallion was standing in the corner of the field at the Dyke lane-end, on "sentry duty". I brought Eric down to a polite walk and kept him going, well over to our side of the road so as not to provoke any excitement in either of them! And we didn't have any fuss.

We haven't driven down to Roundthwaite since last back-end, so a couple of hundred yards further on where we could see the view across the Lune valley to the Howgill fells, Eric had to stop and "update his database". While he was doing that, a white delivery van came up from the Roundthwaite side. There is only room to pass at passing-places, and the nearest was behind me at, of course, Dyke road-end. So I turned and walked Eric back towards the stallion, again sticking to the far side of the road and signalling very firmly to the van what we were doing. Eric, bless his heart, did exactly what he was told, and after the van had gone by, he turned as requested and we made for Roundthwaite once more, walking briskly down the steep slope. He was a little perturbed by the rushing water in the little beck that runs under the road and the bigger one that runs beside it, but he listened to me and didn't break into trot. I halted him and let him stand on one of the passing places before turning him homeward, again at a walk. He saw the hill ahead and was itching to break into trot. CAN WE GO, CAN WE GO! I checked him gently twice, and made him walk until we had cleared two of the awkward bends, and he listened. Then I asked for trot, and away he went, head up, ears forward, calm but vigorous and keeping his pace quick but regular. I had to push him just a little as we were nearing the top, because one of our neighbours was behind us in his pickup; I put Eric onto a passing place and let him stand while the pickup went past. Again, no flinching or arguments.

The stallion was still doing sentry at the Dyke, but he wasn't feeling anything but curious about Eric. He did follow us down the fence line, but at a walk, without prancing or snorting, and Eric just kept going. (If anyone thinks I am being unnecessarily cautious about a stallion with his herd on the other side of a stone wall - long ago our daughter's pony came home without her after a different stallion jumped a wall, charged him, and knocked her off, then jumped back into his field to his mares. Later in the year that horse did the same to someone else riding by, and broke her arm.) However, today everything went calmly, and the only twitch from Eric came when he ran a wheel over some fallen twigs and they all snapped loudly.

We walked until we reached the river meadows between Low Greenholme farm and ours. I practised shallow serpentines (this is fun when you drive English style because if you can do it one-handed without it feeling clumsy, it means your equine is really, really listening - and Eric was.) So when we got to the foot of Daw Bank I set him off in trot and did the shallow serpentine exercise again at the faster pace. This is: homeward; uphill; fast - all the things that were part of his meltdown when the quick release gave way. He did the exercise perfectly without any signs of unease. So of course he got lots of verbal praise, and when we reached the farm gate (in walk) I didn't make him walk past, but turned him in as soon as we were in the right position.

Took him up the yard, unhitched, took all his gear off and gave him a small feed (with Ruby nattering at him from the stable). He was dark grey with sweat, but completely calm - and of course when I let him loose he dug a nice hole in the dampest part of the yard and turned himself black with a splendiferous bout of rolling.

It's taken until today for us both to feel calm about trotting vigorously homeward. That hasn't been with going out every day - as you can see from the Update numbers, it's been taking time out, doing a quiet drive maybe twice a week and keeping the tasks small and unchallenging, allowing the calmness to percolate for a few days before doing another. Spaced Practice rather than Massed Practice. It's working.

UPDATE 7 – 14 APRIL

Eric and I have been out again today. I cleaned him up mid-morning and he was very chilled about everything, including me getting into the carriage; instead of trampling back and forth he stood like a good'un. We admired the scenery for several minutes before I asked him to walk away with the carriage. This may or may not have been due to the distraction of the Polo mint I offered him before I climbed in…

We set off into Greenholme, walking smartly, until he caught sight of some of the children in the village, 200 yards away, playing on skateboards. He couldn't work that out at all, so we spent a minute or two at halt, while Eric had a Jolly Good Stare. When he didn't move on to my command, or a touch on his shoulder, I got him out of his trance with a soft flip of the whip on his side, but I think it touched him lower than he liked, because there was a definite startle in how he set off. A small warning sign for me to be careful and accurate.

A neighbour pulled into a gateway to let us by; another with with a quad bike and trailer waited to let us out of the road end. All good, and thanked with a smile and a wave.

We trotted up the hill out of the village, and over the railway bridge; I let him keep going. It was all steady, cheerful working trot, over the motorway bridges without too much sideways peeping at the crash barriers, and no worries at all about the HGVs and cars zooming along underneath. I let him bowl along on an easy rein, then turned him in at Claire Pearson's farm (where we get our hay from). There was no-one about, not even a horse visible from the yard, so I let Eric stand there and catch his breath, then did an about-turn and went homeward.

I kept him in walk for most of the trip back. Cars overtaking were very polite so he had no excuses to startle, and although he wanted, and tried, to trot several times, he listened. He wasn't as settled, though, as he had been on the outward journey. Still, because he was listening I eventually asked him to trot over the last of the motorway bridges. The peace quickly disappeared - he broke into canter as soon as he could!

However, he was still under my control. I brought him back down to trot by a combination of rein and voice, then to walk; and let him settle again before I asked once more for trot. He had another go to burst into canter, but came back down almost as soon as I took up the rein.

I thought the best choice from there onward was to continue to walk, and check any unscheduled impulses every time from Eric trying "let's go up a gear", just as we've been doing for the last month. Outward, this startled feeling has gone away, but it's still there and shows on the homeward journey. He's not being naughty; he really thinks, after that gallop homeward a month ago, that that's what he is expected to do. He doesn't actually like it any more than I do. We need time and miles to reassure him that his splendid trot is all we need.

When we got home, Graham was filling the water for the sheep, with a hosepipe over the wall from the yard and across the road. It didn't block our path into the yard, but I made Eric stand on the layby and watch Graham and wait for a while, even though he was keen to go in and get the gear off and have his feed.

When I did drive into the yard, he waited patiently for me to take the carriage and the harness off, then ate his feed. I let Ruby out to join him and they had a plunge about the yard together. Finally he rolled, as usual, turning himself black on one side; they are now in the paddock imperilling any blades of grass that have come up in the last few days.

I was quite glad I had done two things - kept the kicking-strap on the harness, and put my wedding-ring on my key fob so it didn't interfere with my rein handling. The kicking-strap wasn't needed, but it was *there* in case the canter had escalated;

and my rein handling was definitely easier, when I needed firm hands, with the ring *not* on my finger. And Eric's "this is when I have to bolt" attempt was only half the speed of the one a month ago. (Yes I did have my Ride Tracker app running on the phone.)

UPDATE 8 – 17 APRIL

Things are slowly getting back to normal. I made today a very local schooling outing, using roads because we don't take the carriage into the fields among new lambs.

Eric's haynet usage has to be monitored. Either he shakes the net and flings it about so much that it goes over the partition into Ruby's box, or she reaches over and pulls it. Graham has put up two vertical baffle boards to try to prevent it happening, but I regularly find the net on the side that Eric can't reach, and if he's "hangry" when I want to drive him, that doesn't make for good training! So both last night and this morning he had his haynet rescued / topped up.

One of our neighbours had called in to collect a diesel-powered gardening tool of some sort, and he and Graham were making attempts to start it in the shed while I was harnessing up. I did ask them to stop while I put to, just until Eric and I had left the yard!

I gave Eric a few feed-nuts while I got into the carriage, and again, it seemed to keep his mind off rushing away too soon. We stood and contemplated for a minute or two before moving off. All very civilised.

We walked down the hill and across the river. He's doing well with ignoring roadside grit heaps, and patches in the tarmac, although he always looks with great interest at the gateway into the hayfield where he can see the ewes and lambs, and once on the level I set him off in trot and kept him going, turning up the sharp rise into the Bretherdale road. His head was up, his ears were forward and he was enjoying himself. I brought him down to walk twice and set him off again in trot, and before we reached the cattle grid I halted him and turned for home in walk. Up and down the gears, from halt to walk, walk to trot, and down again. The ears were forward and cheerful. Back along the river meadow, into trot homeward; his ears began to show worry, but he listened and came back down to walk, then we trotted again up the brow and past our yard gate, over towards Greenholme. Walked and turned at the wide gateway before we reached the village; walked back up the brow. Although he fancied trotting, I kept him in walk until he was listening, asked for trot, brought him down, walked past our gate again and returned down the hill to the river, where we went back into trot.

I let him bowl along on a nice light contact and pushed him straight forward past the Bretherdale junction so he hit Pikestoll at "full welly" in trot without any cantering. I let him go up the hill as far as the first gateway, turned him there, and walked down homeward to the river meadow. He was calm, head in a lowered, easy working position, ears forward, so I trotted him to the bridge, brought him down to walk, trotted him up the hill. The ears did go back a couple of times indicating tenseness, as though he was waiting to be smacked by the trace again, but today every time we trotted homeward *he stayed in trot*. I don't mind how fast he goes so long as the gait is the one I have asked for!

He'd done enough by then to show me he was "in hand" so at the gateway I brought him to walk and turned him into the yard.

Husband and neighbour were still gossiping but at least the machinery had made it into the boot of the car!

As I was unharnessing Eric I said to Graham, "His brain's coming back to normal."

He said, "And when you've only got a little brain, it takes a while!"

True. Our escapade a month ago had seriously fried it - just in that one area of "putting in serious effort uphill and homeward". But it's definitely becoming un-fried now.

I went into the stable to bring Ruby out to join Eric grazing the yard, and found she had eaten his haynet. Minx.

UPDATE 9 - 21 APRIL

This month has been sunny and dry but yesterday and today have been very windy, Force 4 to 6, coming from the north-east and feeling very cold. I thought the briskness of the wind was itself a challenge for driving: not just because it's hard for Eric to hear me over the noise of the air whooshing through the trees, but because wild weather is upsetting for horses and ponies; they worry about things moving that are normally static.

So I thought a short drive up Pikestoll would be enough yesterday, after lunch when the day was likely to be warmest.

I had returned the Bennington swingletree to its original designed position, just in case some of Eric's startles were being prompted by the suspended swingletree swaying sideways and slapping the traces about and reminding him of the quick release failure (I don't *think* they were, but...) it was worth trying the original configuration in which the swingletree is simply pivoted on a central bracket and not suspended. I also put the shafts a little deeper into the sockets to see if I could stop the plastic covering squeaking when we go downhill!

Eric was full of hay and relaxed and he wasn't too dirty for once - his winter coat is still shedding and as I groomed him, the wind blew it - and the dirt - generously all over me. The

264

wind was quite strong and it was flowing from the north over the stable roof and curling back over us as if from the south.

Once harnessed he kept wanting to turn his quarters to the wind, ie at 90 degrees to the wall; he wasn't really being naughty, just a bit of a princess, but it took several attempts to return him to position parallel to the wall so I could pull the carriage to him on the level. We're on a strong slope on top of a bank, so level places are rare. I gently replaced him each time and insisted he stayed in place, so it's all good discipline. He moves about very willingly just to a touch and a word.

I walked him around the yard (up and down hill) to make sure I'd got the traces and breeching correctly adjusted for the different swingletree position and the slightly shorter shaft length. Everything looked fine, so we went out onto the road. Eric was a bit twitchy with the wind, and I didn't ask him to trot until he had settled down to walk, then we went up the hill at a real good pace. The pine trees up Pikestoll were roaring like surf, and I was pleased that Eric took no notice of them. On the way back down, though, he was flummoxed by the shadows being in All The Wrong Places because usually we go up there before noon.

I was very tempted to let him trot on the way home, but the point of today was calmness despite the boisterous weather, so I didn't. We walked. We walked past the yard. We walked into and around the yard. We waited for ages before I got down and took him out of the carriage. It was a very, very boring drive, and Eric put up with it, so I expect the boringness to continue when the weather settles down and we go a bit further afield once more.

UPDATE 10 – 23 APRIL

St George's Day, Shakespeare's birthday and the day when the government is testing an innovative National Emergency Alert via our mobile phones. (3pm.) Not that I think I want to be alerted; we'll probably know about bad weather, fire or floods before any government body knows enough to inform us. (and would the rest be things it would be futile to try to do much about?)

So I took That Eric out this morning. I had already turned off Alerts on my personal mobile, as I don't want distractions while driving him, but I've left them on the "house mobile" so when I am home in the afternoon I can hear what the alert sound would be.

Eric munched on a haynet while I scraped the dry mud off him. On Ruby, who is bay, the remnants of grey paddock-dust and coat-waterproofing would show up; but Eric comes up surprisingly clean once I have scraped his "base layer" off and got a brush onto the hair underneath. I am beginning to think a grey horse is not such a bad thing after all. As I have rubber-matted the stable and Eric complies tidily stallion-fashion with the minimal sawdust-area for his liquid and solid waste, he doesn't lie down now in anything that's going to stain him. The weather is warming up and most of his winter coat has shed, so I might even give him a bath and a tail-shampoo sometime soon. (Ruby is still shedding mightily.)

There was no wind today so our putting-to was uneventful. We each had a Polo mint and watched the world go by before starting off in the carriage. I set Eric off into trot when we got out of our "narrows" where the lane goes by the veg garden, but when he was in sight of Greenholme he had to stop and update the sat nav, and check whether the skateboarding children were in the village. They weren't, so after a minute or so we went on, and trotted through the village. This doesn't take long as there are only a handful of houses; it's more of a hamlet really, and there are only a score of houses in the whole postal area.

We trotted up the brow onto the bit of open common called Whiteham, with Eric going strongly and cheerfully. Of course once we reached the top he had to pause to do the sat nav update, check the distant traffic going north up the motorway, listen for potential Scary Things on farms half a mile distant, etc. He spotted two long-distance cyclists approaching, and stood rooted while they toiled up the slope towards us. He didn't mind them passing us, but he wasn't going to move for them! So I made a small joke to them, and they toiled onward, and Eric came out of his planted mode and walked on.

A little further on I turned him and we walked homeward. He does a very powerful walk when he's facing home, and every now and again it breaks pattern and goes towards trot, but this is part of the stretch of road where we had the "Rapid Unscheduled Disassembly of Equipment" last month so I kept him calm, contained his enthusiasm and talked him back into walk, praising him when he stayed where I wanted him. Back through Greenholme, up the brow towards home. He thought about bursting into trot up the hill but I kept him walking, which was just as well because a small car appeared round the blind corner and we'd have had to shift back down anyway. Walked past the yard gate (with a wobble or two because he wanted to go in) and on towards the Bretherdale road, and when we reached the bridge Eric had to stop and update the sat nav once again! However, we trotted the level section, and negotiated the right hand turn in trot to go up Bretherdale. He was fairly motoring by then, ears up, doing a good 11 mph. And then, click, back went the ears, up went the speed. So I took a gentle hold and talked him back down into a more moderate pace, after which he came back to walk on the word. We turned and walked, walked, walked, all the way back; down to the junction and along the stretch over the meadow; and I

267

didn't let him trot until we were starting the steep pull up Daw Bank. Halfway up, the ears went back again and the speed went up again, so I took another gentle hold and talked him down from the fast trot to the moderate one, and we walked into the yard to unharness. Must check his feet; being still unshod, possibly he's a bit footsore and when he hits motoring mode he feels it.

He was sweaty when we got in, and itchy and wanting to be out of the carriage and the harness, so the job took longer than it should do because he was fidgeting. The keeper on the bellyband came unstitched as I pulled the end of the strap loose (but no worries, I've been meaning to replace the keepers on that for a while). I long reined him down to his tying place rather than have him rubbing his itchy head on me if I'd led him. He was glad to get his bridle off and rub his face on the haynet.

He got his little feed as a reward, and I let Ruby out of the stable to join him. He had his usual Big Filthy Roll, and they are both out in the paddock now keeping the grass under tight control.

I've replaced the keepers on the bellyband; it has only had 2 for several years and it now has 4 again. The original keepers were a neat fit, but the double-layered biothane of the backband doesn't bend too well and is a devil to get into the keepers in cold weather, so I've made the new ones a bit slacker. Win all round. The house phone gave the "Alert" on time too. For what that's worth.

UPDATE 11 – 28 APRIL

A mild morning after a cold night. Eric and Ruby are in the stable and relatively clean; they have had breakfast and full haynets.

Eric is keen to be out and is standing at the door, tossing his head and flinging his mane about, making terrifyingly impatient snatches at the air with his teeth when I approach, then clacking his jaws like a hobby-horse, sticking his tongue out sideways and ducking away in apology. He is however happy to have his headcollar put on and to be tied outside the tack room and cleaned. I rake my fingers through his immense mane, taking out several handfuls of loose long hair from the middle of his crest where it was beginning to cling together like felt after the winter. His tail, for once, is also clean, but his body coat is still shedding so there is quite a fur-ball to clear up once I have groomed him. I feel some scabby bits of winter-accumulated grease in his feather so I make a start at picking some of that out too. I bet he wishes it wasn't spring, as then I wouldn't be spring-cleaning him.

He still has enough foot for me to drive him on the roads, but I'm worried he may become footsore once we really get going, so the blacksmith is coming (whenever he can fit us in) for a discussion about whether to fit steel shoes. In Ruby's twilight years our road wear and her hoof growth have been about equal so no need for protection, but even Eric's rock-crushing Dales paws won't stand up to three or four drives a week of 5 miles or more, on top of the abrasion of him tearing up and down our mostly tarmac yard. I do have one pair of Easyboots that fit his front feet, but they take me 10 minutes to put on (and off) and my knackered/replaced hips and knees complain for the rest of the day, so I'm afraid it's metal shoes for us if we are to do justice to Eric's energies!

I harness him to the Bennington, remembering to locate the kicking-strap within the loops of the breeching strap, and I mount the carriage. We stand and do a slow count to to 60, then walk round the yard a couple of times to allow a car to go by on the lane before we set off. Eric is all bustle, to begin with, but again he needs to pause and update the sat nav when the village comes in sight. Graham delivered two half ton bags of well rotted manure down there yesterday, so Eric is highly suspicious of those and I make a point of walking him past them a few times before we trot up the hill past Bridge End.

The light is subdued and there is no bright sunshine to cast the fence-shadows that made Eric wary last time we crossed the railway. He trots along chirpily, past the motorway services, over both motorway bridges, and forgets that he doesn't like the crash barriers there.

He's a big, white, flouncy object, and between that, and the flashing bike lights, and my high-vis waistcoat and the rear carriage sign which both say "PASS WIDE PLEASE", the cars that overtake us, do so very carefully. The only startle that Eric does, is occasioned when the overtaking traffic turned out to be TWO cars rather than the ONE that he expected.

We meet a neighbour coming homeward in her car and Eric is happy to stand while we pass the time of day. She asks if her event horses have been silly about Eric going by, but they weren't and I say they weren't, thank you. Then it's off in trot again.

We are well attuned to each other today. I am driving him English-style (AKA coaching hand or Achenbach; as I always do, of course). I find today that I can adjust his position on the road solely by the weight of the rein, as I move my left hand across towards my right or left hip. Lots of verbal praise for him. Most of the time I don't even need my whip-hand to assist. This is a real pleasure driving horse.

We proceed to the four road-ends guide post and I steady him for a turn left towards Scout Green. I don't actually plan to go as far as Scout Green, but the turn is neatly done (still one-handed) and Eric gets yet more praise for his compliance. We pop onto the grass verge to let an oncoming car go by, after which I turn him and walk back to the guide post to I let him have a breather. He's sweating freely but keen to keep going; he waits to be told to set off again.

It's uphill homeward from the guide post so I ask him to trot. Again, he's happy to go. I let him bowl along with the lightest of contacts, aware that this "fast and homeward" trot is quite a test of our mutual nerve, but reasoning that if he's going to "go" then having almost three miles of nearly-straight, wide road is probably a good place to let him. But he doesn't. He's hypnotised by his own trotting rhythm, and although he's aware of the big event horses watching him again as we go past their field, he doesn't break stride. Back past the services entrances, over the two motorway bridges, over Scotchman's Bridge and down the hill, still in trot. I steady him for the last section, which is a short steep drop to Bridge End, and I walk him to turn up our road and home. He wants to trot up the brow so I give him the word and away he goes. No startles, just the occasional flick of the ears to check what I am saying to him. This is a very good drive. I bring him down to walk to turn into the yard, and send him up to the tying place where I unhitch him. This time he has done enough not to fidget while I unyoke!

I unharness him, feed him, put the carriage away, and turn on the hose to fill the drinking-water barrel outside the stable; then I sponge his face, and use the hose to give him a wash - his first of the year - resulting in a very handsome and CLEAN dappled grey. And of course, when I turn him loose, he coats himself with the darkest mud he can find and pretends he is a black-silver dapple.

Oh well. Ruby is pleased to see him anyway!

UPDATE 12 – 1 MAY

We're waiting for the farrier to call in and check whether Eric needs to be traditionally shod with steel, or whether he can get away with boots every third or fourth drive. I personally think his front feet are coping really well, but I need an expert's eye for his hind feet, which (like every driving horse I have had) do most of the work and wear more quickly, especially the outside heels. I've assured the farrier that if on inspection we decide not to shoe Eric I'll pay him the fee he asks for trimming.

We drove for 50 minutes or so this morning: 3 miles of on-road schooling, over some of the ground where Eric had his Big Fright at the start of April, with me concentrating on not allowing him to pre-empt me as to changes of pace – whether that's going up or down the gears. He thought of doing the sat nav update twice soon after setting off, once as we came over the brow and again into view of Greenholme, but he took my brisk "Walk On!" in good part both times and carried on. I kept him in walk through the village onto the Scout Green road, and let him trot once we were going uphill onto Whiteham. He was keen but attentive. I turned him left into the road for Ewelock Bank, where he powered up to 12mph going up the hill, and came back down easily before we reached the cattle grid. I notice that this road is going to be resurfaced in the coming week, from the junction onward, so the shoes/boots will be necessary for a while if we go up there while there are fresh, sharp chippings underfoot.

We walked back from the cattle grid, and trotted along the Scout Green road over the fell. This is close to where Eric had had the Big Fright, so he demanded a poo stop, but otherwise he listened to me, and walked down the steep bank to Beckside without fussing.

He's often a bit distracted by the noise of Bretherdale Beck, and by other tiny becks running into it under the road, so I kept him in walk to give him time to pay attention, and on the way back made him halt precisely over one of the culverts instead of twitching and trying to break into trot. That puzzled him, but he said, "Oh, OK, if you insist!" We passed Beckside, and walked up the brow where the trace had popped off six weeks ago. He offered to trot there, but I kept him in walk and he bustled along nicely, only trying to break into trot once more as we reached the top of the hill. Again I said, "No." Then he heard a distant quad bike working where our neighbours were penning sheep down in the river meadow, but he kept walking. He paid attention when I asked him to move over and walk on the grass verge, and to wait at Yew Tree for a tractor that was shifting fertiliser equipment and needed to shunt across the road and back into the yard. He rather wanted to go in and investigate; its farmyard seems to remind him of somewhere else.

We went through Greenholme at walk and up the brow past Brown Bank, where I asked him to trot. He decided to chance going up to canter, but came back when I steadied him, so he did his 12mph power trot all the way through the narrows to our gateway where, shock horror, I made him keep trotting straight on instead of turning in. Big dithering as if on skates! He went on, and picked up his gait again, down the hill to Bretherdale Beck, and along the river level to Low Greenholme. We drew rein in the farm gateway to let a car come out of the Bretherdale road-end, then turned and walked homeward, only going up into trot when we reached the bank. Again he chanced moving up to canter, but he listened when I checked him, and trotted nicely up to the gateway where we wheeled and went in.

I unhitched him at the top of our yard and yet again he managed to wallop me in the face with his nose when I wasn't expecting it. I wish I knew why he does that, so I could (a) avoid it and (b) persuade him not to do it.

I unharnessed and fed him and put him back into the stable, which surprised him a little, but as the farrier was due, I didn't want him to go out in the paddock and get his feet filthy.

Later: We've had the foot inspection. Although Eric's hind feet look quite short, he's definitely not been lame today, so we have decided not to apply shoes to his "rock crushers". I am not competing, so I'm not fixed to a training schedule, and if Eric's hooves wear too much I can just take a week off or fit hoof boots, while his feet grow a little. I have some size 3 Wide Easyboot Gloves that fit his fronts; I just need to source a pair of 2 Wide that fit his hind feet. What a shame I gave away the size 2s that were Ruby's front boots eight years ago...

PS the farrier didn't want a fee.

HORSE SENSE

2011

I am getting bored with Natural Horsemanship, Thinking Riding, Horse Whispering and all the other commercial titles that are being sold to us to manage horses in the 21st century.

Look at it this way. Horses are large, herbivorous quadrupeds who like to live in herds, and are domesticated by man. Cows are also large, herbivorous quadrupeds, ditto ditto, but do we see gurus setting up seven-step programmes to sell secret tips for Cow Whispering? Hm? Why not?

The difference, as I see it, lies in the human perception of the two species. In the English-speaking world, we do not eat horse meat. We ennoble the horse. We publish anthropomorphic stories – books, films, cartoons – in which horses can not only talk, but detail their biographies and contribute to human business. Nobody makes films titled *Black Mooey; National Big-Ears; Cowbiscuit,* or *My Friend Filthytail;* nobody advertises tuition in Natural Cowmanship or Thinking Milking (I make an exception for the noble Dr Temple Grandin here).

Almost all of us humans ignore the fact that horses just don't work the way people do, and there's a further difficulty for the horses in the "me-and-my-horse-are-family" approach which draws in people who may not have had any experience of handling large herbivorous animals. We keep horses and ponies now to a very large extent as pets, rather than as working animals, and we are also very prone to try to do things with them which will reflect upon ourselves and our abilities.

Horses are thus becoming an extension of the human personality, a delusion which I doubt they share. When a horse doesn't respond to human behaviour in the way we expect, we seek ways to solve the "problem" with our possession by

275

changing its bitting, saddlery, shoeing, or feeding, by sending it to a trainer, or by adopting a fashionable training technique. Only very occasionally do we think of changing our own attitude!

A well known bit-maker once said something like, "Of twenty bits I make, nineteen are for men's heads and one for the horse's." I think this could well be said of all the alternatives to traditional horse management that are being sold to the horse-owning public.

Now before you rush to your keyboard and rattle out, "But you can't want me to treat my horse the way they treat cows! People eat cows! Darling Dobbin is too precious to be sold to a French butcher!" – let's not be extreme. I am not in favour of sending ANY animal thousands of miles, alive, in a crowded wagon without water, feed or rest, I'm all for improving the lot of the third-world horse, and I'm not advocating or condoning cruelty, or decrying kindness.

I do, however, think that even the best methods, new or old, will not turn a horse into a dog or a cat or a substitute human, and for many "pet" horses the application of a little experience, common sense and observation would in fact be kinder and cheaper than So-and-So's latest salesmanship.

ARE ALL HORSES FRIGHTENED OF EVERYTHING?

A friend asked me this recently when I had been recounting some nerve-wracking moments in the progress of Eric-the-Dales. The question brought me up short, because I've been a horse inside my head for 7 decades now and I sometimes need reminding that other human beings do not share my odd perspective on life.

Horses and ponies are hard-wired to mistrust anything that appears predatory. Because of that, new things, or things that seem to stare at them or make noises they can't identify as "safe", will trigger a "High Alert" response and readiness to run away at great speed. There's an increase in heart rate and breathing, even if they don't make a visible move away from the perceived threat. If you're riding or if you're a perceptive driver you can feel the potential swerve or scoot away in the horse's body before they make that move. When I used to drive Mr T who was very afraid of motorcycles, I could hear his heart pounding from 3 metres behind him in the carriage, if he heard a bike engine. A rider can reassure a horse physically with their own body, or a driver can "talk him down", to bring a horse out of the High Alert and back into "routine" mode.

In trusted surroundings, and with other equines as company, horses and ponies are very peaceable, and their slow heart rate (30 to 40 beats per minute) and slow respiration (8 to 15 to the minute) tend to make many humans feel calm too. "The outside of a horse is good for the inside of a (hu)man." Anxious people with rapid heartbeats, shallow breathing patterns and tense movements are soothed when they are close to quiet horses. Hence a trend the advertisement of "healing horses" therapies for people. While I have no doubt it works for the human patients, I'm not sure how commercial "healing horses" feel about being compelled to remain in the presence of not-entirely-sound people whose standard physical and mental condition is High Alert.

Some breeds are much more reactive and likely to hit High Alert than others (eg Arabians or Thoroughbreds more reactive than Dales or Fells). I know that's a generalisation, and there may well be examples of confident Arabs and TBs and hysterical native ponies. But because of the equine hard-wiring, and whatever the breed, when horses have to work alone it puts them in a scary situation. They have no herd mates to rely on for warnings or reassurances, so they will take longer to be confident in new surroundings. Deprived of the signs of confidence from companions, they automatically rely on High Alert to keep themselves safe. A horse who has been well treated by humans will eventually rely on his rider or driver to be his reassuring herd mate, but in completely new surroundings it can take a while for that bond to become second nature and damp down the natural default of High Alert.

Horse people say it takes one year for a pony to settle into a new home, and two years to make a seasoned driving pony out of a green or newly trained one. Eric has been with me now for just 12 months, so perhaps we are about halfway to being a proper partnership. He is bold and even excessively friendly at home, and calm when he's hacking out with neighbours' horses, but now Ruby is retired so he has to work a lot of the time on his own. It has taken him a longer time than I expected, to feel settled when out driving solo.

He was very chilled-out today while I was harnessing up and putting-to, and he wasn't inclined to peep at the grit heaps or the motorway crash barriers. Passing cars didn't bother him, except that he was surprised by the rustle of my coat when I waved thank-you to some of them. But it was a very quiet morning and the air was damp so tiny sounds carried strongly, like the faint tinkling of a chain against a gate, and water

278

trickling in roadside gullies which he "put an ear on" as he passed in case he needed to flee. I couldn't hear them until a couple of metres later when the carriage came level with them. Big ambient noises like cars and the motorway, he took very little notice of. I think the only noise we haven't yet driven through is a low-flying jet, and I'm not in a hurry for that because I know he doesn't like them when he's in the field. It was good to feel, though, that he was confident and grown-up today, and no longer a Little Boy Lost.

BRAVO, 2012

I've used the word "bravo" a lot over the past two weeks. Not physically, in the "standing to applaud the operatic diva" way, but internally, while I've been watching TV as the various members of Team GB (as we must call them) did their utmost to win Olympic medals.

Yesterday I watched Valegro ridden by Charlotte Dujardin in a beautiful, soft, rhythmic, forward dressage to music in a manicured arena. Today, by contrast, when I came to drive my Fell mare Ruby, the haymaking tractors were whizzing to and fro on the roads, which gave me a really good excuse to school her among the sheep in the field. Most of this 'summer' (hollow laugh) it's been too wet to use it for Proper Schooling, but the ground was sound enough today, and Ruby does enjoy being out there on the grass. Her purpose in life, she tells me, is to reclaim it from That Damned Flock.

So we worked quietly away, with me asking her to slow down when turning, and remember to use her stiff hind leg equally with the other, instead of hurtling round every right handed corner like a motorbike with her head pointing left.

Lots of little exercises, bends, circles and walk pirouettes - all interspersed with bursts of what she enjoys best, storming along the edge of the wood in extended trot!

When she got things right I told her, "Good girl," because, not being Italian, she doesn't understand, "Bravo."

In the middle of it I felt a little tickle in the brain that said, "Hang on, 'bravo' has another meaning as well, doesn't it?"

So, after the schooling, I came indoors and looked it up in the Oxford English Dictionary, which I often have open in my browser. As you do. (What do you mean, you don't? Doesn't every writer in England know that online access to the full OED is free if you've got a library card? And doesn't every historical novelist use its Historical Thesaurus to check what phrases and words were available to characters in their chosen period?)

While the Dictionary describes the interjection "Bravo!" as a shout of praise, "Well done!" the Historical Thesaurus also defines a noun "bravo" thus: "A daring villain, a hired soldier or assassin; 'a man who murders for hire' (Johnson); a reckless desperado." The dates of recorded usage stretch from 1597 to 1876.

OED quotes Ben Jonson using "bravo" in this way in "The Silent Woman," so I hunted down the full text of the play, and browsing through that I found another interesting snippet:

> *Epicene: And have you those excellent Receits, Madam, to keep your selves from bearing of Children?*
> *Haughty: O yes.*
> *Morose: How should we maintain our Youth and Beauty else? Many Births of a Woman make her Old...*

Contraception being described on stage as "excellent" back in 1616? Wow!

I think I may have a new novel brewing. It has a title. And a hero and heroine.

Well, it's a start. Bravo.

LOST IN TRANSLATION

A beaut - the Jehovah's Witnesses called yesterday. We stood in the kitchen and talked about tomato plants and washing up.

On our wall-chart they observed that we had written the following note:

2 A 3 Ch 1 Pet 6:30.

– so being, as you will know, Biblically well-informed, they said, "But 1 Peter only has 4 chapters."

Graham and I translated it back to them in chorus: "2 adults, 3 children, 1 pet, arriving 6:30 this evening."

We see what we expect to see…

CUEING UP

Mancunian author David W Robinson once remarked joyfully that the BBC's subtitles "aren't perfect, but every time the commentator mentions Gabriel Agbonlahor, the subs translate it as 'Gabriel upon the whore'."

One mustn't forget, of course, the utter filth that is perpetrated for weeks on end by the BBC's snooker commentators. I had already cobbled together this little effort: (First published by Lighten up Online, December 2010.)

he's going for a colour
got a bit of a kick
after that double kiss
it's a touching ball

waggles lead to
a good wrist cock
and follow through
oh that was a snatch

it's very tight
on the bottom cushion
he's trying one leg on the bed
should play a deep screw

he can't quite keep that foot on the floor
he'll need the extension
and after all that
he'll have to go for a long rest

EUPHEMISMS

Knickers, smallclothes, underwear,
things that cover bits down there;
hipsters, Y fronts, passion killers,
big-pants, smalls and crotchless thrillers,
boxers, underpants and panties,
directoires as worn by aunties,
lon-jer-ray and thongs and things,
inexpressibles and strings;
slimmers, hi-legs, trunks and naughties,
tangas, briefs and lacy shorties –
all must fall when nature calls
and we are screened by modest walls:
bathrooms, washrooms, smallest rooms,
loos in cupboards full of brooms,
lavatories, netties, johns,
toilets with sitdownupons;
privies, closets, single-bowlers,
one- and two- and family-holers.
Plastic potty, thing of wonder,
used to be a plain gazunder,
jerry, china pot or po,
brimful with night's overflow.
Pay a visit, wash your hands,
spend a penny (man just stands)
to plant a sweet pea down the drain,
point Percy at the porcelain,
or sit in state upon the throne
whereon the Pope must go alone
to do his reigning over China,
painted by a fine designer.
Shake hands with your oldest friend.
It's bound to come out in the end.

AN ABSENCE OF DRAGONS

After six months of rain, cloud, wind and mud that even an Englishwoman couldn't call Summer, we have our third day in a row of sparkling October sun. Blissful, that's what it is. I've opened the windows and changed the bed-linen, and the washed sheets are actually drying outdoors on the line and not drooping round the house.

The wet, miserable summer has meant I've done far more writing than normal. I like working from home, though of course it encourages bad habits. One of them is that I eat breakfast at the computer while I catch up on social media. I do this mainly to postpone reading the e-mails that have come in overnight.

I've polished three books this year, though – copy edited, proofed, typeset, be-Kindled, covers designed and uploaded to print on demand, and ten of each delivered here last week as potential giveaways and samples. I've built myself another web site and got my tax return in early. I've registered for an American Employee Identification Number and filled in forms to stop Uncle Sam withholding 30% from my earnings over there.

On Friday I enveloped sales brochures, trade terms and promotional blurbs for bookshops and broadcasters. On Saturday I posted them. I've even got around to brushing up the crumbs of breakfast cereal from under the desk.

It's a curious sensation, to have nothing driving me to write. The crystalline beauty of autumn crocuses and colchicums isn't urging me to poetry. My ambitious young coachman isn't fighting off women, my grumpy old bat isn't cuffing her grandson for misbehaving, my princess isn't flying a mission across country on a dragon. I feel like a mother whose children have been miraculously swept away to their grandparents. The house in my head is empty.

I suppose this is what's called peace.

I know it won't last. The advertising will kick in and people will start asking for interviews and talks, and books (with any luck) will start selling. I think I want to try NANOWRIMO. I've only got three weeks to get a plot sorted out, but whether I do or not, I will certainly gather up some long-shelved project in November and start re-building it.

Only not today. Today I'm going to submit to peace. I'm learning a Welsh tune for the harp, a lost battle remembered in a lament a thousand years old. My head needs to hold nothing more.

ALSO BY SUE MILLARD

From www.jackdawebooks.co.uk

AGAINST THE ODDS

Leaving home to work in a racing stable, Sian finds that the long hours and hard work are more than she bargained for. The only compensation is her responsibility for her favourite filly, Double Jump.

Sian is badly treated by her boyfriend, the trainer's arrogant son, Justin. When Double Jump's owner moves the filly to another yard, Sian follows so she can escape him.

At the new yard she meets stable jockey Madoc Owen, who is battling to make a National Hunt winner out of Cymru, a bored flat-race stallion. Sian and Madoc may have a future together but there will be more than steeplechase fences in their way – Justin will see to that.

GENRE: Fiction, romance, sporting, equestrian
First Published by J A Allen, 1995. ISBN 978-0-851316301 (now Remaindered - only available direct from author.) .
2nd Edition 2018, ISBN: 978-1-720047285 (paperback).
Kindle edition
https://www.amazon.co.uk/dp/B00BGBIGNU

SCRATCH

Sequel to Against the Odds

From www.jackdawebooks.co.uk

A Woman. A Family. A Farm.

Sian and Madoc have borrowed heavily to buy a neglected farm, Stone Side, in the beautiful countryside of east Cumbria. They are land-rich now but short of cash and indebted not only to the bank but to members of their family.

Racehorses and Fell Ponies

In this sequel to Against the Odds Madoc has reluctantly had to give up his ambition to breed thoroughbreds, and instead runs the sheep farm and pre-trains young horses for National Hunt racing. Sian is a fierce mother of their three teenage children, Robbie, Cerys and Jack. In what free time she has, she buys and trains Fell ponies.

Someone is Out to Destroy Them

When Madoc's brother calls-in a big loan, the tensions begin to mount… and on the wild fellside, for someone the stakes are as high as murder.

GENRE: Fiction, family saga / thriller, sporting, equestrian
ISBN: 978-0-957361294 (paperback)
Kindle edition
https://www.amazon.co.uk/dp/B07J6PWCS5

HOOFPRINTS IN EDEN

From www.jackdawebooks.co.uk

Winner of the Saint and Company Prize at the Lake District Book of the Year Awards, 20 June 2006. Based on a 2-year-long series of interviews with established breeders, this book explores the Fell pony breed and its traditions at the start of the new millennium.

Read about the Fell pony's Cumbrian background, the events of a typical year, its life on the fell, its traditional keeping and its links with hill farming, its characteristics and the work it can do.

Fully illustrated. Includes a dictionary of Cumbrian farming expressions.

GENRE: Non-fiction, equestrian, history, farm & working animals
Second edition, paperback, Jackdaw E Books.
ISBN 978-1-731565969 (paperback)
Kindle edition
https://www.amazon.co.uk/dp/B07KPLQ9RG

A CENTURY OF FELLS

From www.jackdawebooks.co.uk

Produced for the Centenary of the Fell Pony Society in 2022, A Century of Fells follows Hoofprints in Eden. It celebrates the 100th year of the FPS, with sequenced photographs of many families of ponies recorded in the Stud Book through the years. It also prompts consideration of how the breed may develop in the next century.

> GENRE: Non-fiction, equestrian, history, farm & working animals
> ISBN 978-1-913-106171 (hardback), ISBN 978-1-913-106164 (paperback)
> Both from www.jackdawebooks.co.uk/century.htm

PONIES WITH WHEELS

From www.jackdawebooks.co.uk

In 40 years of carriage driving I've had a lot of fun with Fell and Dales ponies - Mr T "The Yes Man", Eric "The Comedian", Sonny "The Stroppy Teenager" and his mother Ruby "The Magnificent".

This selection of my chatty posts from my blog, the RED list driving forum and social media, amounts to a novel in length. I've decided to retain their conversational tone, rather than tidying everything up. It's more entertaining that way.

> ISBN 978-1-913-106225 (paperback)
> Kindle edition:
> https://www.amazon.co.uk/dp/B0BGCVXVMY

ONE FELL SWOOP

From www.jackdawebooks.co.uk

This is where it all started, with humour, history and horses.

Norman Thelwell was Sue's hero (they both hailed from the Wirral) so when Sue moved to Cumbria and bought a Fell pony this "fellwell" book was the inevitable result.

A series of affectionate cartoons, poking gentle fun at the Fell breed and its history.

> GENRE: Cartoon humour, farm & working animals.
> ISBN 978-0-9573612-7-0 (paperback)
> Kindle edition,
> https://www.amazon.co.uk/dp/B008ZBPB14

THE FORTHRIGHT SAGA

From www.jackdawebooks.co.uk

Nothing ever happens in a small country town ... does it?

Nora Forthright and her grandson Wayne stumble through the fictional Cumbrian towns of Dangleby and Pullet St Mary, putting things right entirely by accident.

> GENRE: Comedy thriller / cosy crime.
> ISBN: 978-0-9573612-3-2 (paperback)
> Kindle Edition,
> https://www.amazon.co.uk/dp/B0099RQNLU

FOR CHILDREN

DRAGON BAIT

From www.jackdawebooks.co.uk

Princess Andra volunteers to act as bait for the dragon ravaging her father's lands, on condition that she is released from an arrangement to marry a foreign prince.

Unfortunately the Knight Rescuer who turns up is not the trusty old retainer she expects, but an unknown conservationist who wants the dragon, not the lady. After that very little goes according to plan.

GENRE: Comic fantasy (age 9-12).
ISBN : 978-1-913106-15-7 (paperback)
Kindle edition:
https://www.amazon.co.uk/dp/B008K8SDWG

STRING OF HORSES

From www.jackdawebooks.co.uk

Fourteen-year-old Claire Armstrong's Mum and Dad run a country pub in the Lake District. Pony trekking is part of its attractions, and Claire's love of the ponies teaches her a great deal about herself. But it's the humans in the pub who cause her the most heartache.

A coming-of-age novel set in the 1970s.
ISBN : 9781913106119 (paperback)
Kindle edition
https://www.amazon.co.uk/dp/191310611X

www.ingramcontent.com/pod-product-compliance
Lightning Source LLC
Chambersburg PA
CBHW051943090426
42741CB00008B/1250